Revelation

BOOKS IN THE BIBLE STUDY COMMENTARY SERIES

BIBLE STUDY COMMENTARY

Revelation

ALAN F. JOHNSON

ZONDERVAN PUBLISHING HOUSE
OF THE ZONDERVAN CORPORATION
GRAND RAPIDS, MICHIGAN 49506

REVELATION: BIBLE STUDY COMMENTARY
Copyright © 1983 by The Zondervan Corporation
Grand Rapids, Michigan

Library of Congress Cataloging in Publication Data

Johnson, Alan F.
  Revelation: Bible study commentary.

  Bibliography: p.
    1. Bible. N.T. Revelation—Commentaries.   I. Title.
BS2825.3.J63 1983   228'.07   83-6647
ISBN 0-310-45173-6

Edited by Ed van der Maas

Printed in the United States of America

83 84 85 86 87 88 / 10 9 8 7 6 5 4 3 2 1

*To Rea—who taught me
how to communicate
the truth to people
where they live*

Contents

Introduction

The Book of Revelation fascinates and also perplexes the modern reader, to whom it is the most obscure and controversial book in the Bible. Yet those who study it with care agree that it is a unique source of Christian teaching and a book of timeless relevance. Indeed, it may well be that, with the exception of the Gospels, the Apocalypse contains the most profound and moving teaching on Christian doctrine and discipleship found anywhere in Holy Scripture.

Neither the fanaticism of some who have fixed their attention on prophecy rather than on Christ, nor the diversity of interpretive viewpoints should discourage us from pursuing Christian truth in this marvelous book.

A. General Literary Character and Historical Background

The Book of Revelation differs from the other New Testament writings, not in doctrine but in literary genre and subject matter. It is a book of prophecy (1:3; 22:7, 18–19) that contains both warning and consolation—announcements of future judgment and blessing—communicated by means of symbols and visions.

Why did the Lord use a method that seemingly makes His message so obscure? The answer is twofold. First, the language and imagery were not as strange to first-century readers as they are to many of us today. Faced with the apocalyptic style of the book, the modern reader who knows little about biblical literature and its parallels is like a person who, though unfamiliar with stocks and bonds, tries to understand the Dow-Jones reports. Therefore, familiarity with the prophetic books of the Old Testament (especially Dan. and Ezek.) and with other nonbiblical literature current in the first century[1] will help the reader grasp the message of the Apocalypse. (See the commentary for references to this literature.)

---

[1]Especially the apocalyptic type pseudepigraphical literature (e.g., the Book of Enoch, the Sybilline Oracles, and the Apocalypse of Baruch), the Dead Sea Scrolls, and the Targums (Aramaic and Greek paraphrases of the Old Testament).

Second, the subject matter, with its glimpses into the future and even into heaven itself, required the kind of language John used. Only through symbolism and imagery can we gain some understanding of the things the Lord unveiled through the writer John. Moreover, while the symbolic and visionary mode of presentation creates ambiguity and frustration for many of us, it actually lends to the description of unseen realities a poignancy and clarity unattainable by any other method. For example, "evil" is an abstract term, but a woman "drunk with the blood of the saints" graphically sets forth the concrete and more terrible aspects of this reality. Such language can trigger all sorts of ideas, associations, existential involvement, and mystical responses that the straight prose found in most of the New Testament cannot achieve.

The letters to the seven churches in the Roman province of Asia (modern Turkey) identify the recipients of the book and give a broad indication of the historical situation. Some of the churches were experiencing persecution (2:10, 13), and it has been customary to assume that this persecution was quite intense and widespread. Revelation is then viewed as a "tract for the times," warning Christians against emperor worship and encouraging them to be faithful to Christ, even to death. Recent studies however question how intense, widespread, or sustained the persecution was, even under Emperor Domitian.[2] The primary occasion for the writing of the Book of Revelation must therefore be sought elsewhere.

The letters to the churches indicate that five of the seven had serious problems. The major problem seemed to be disloyalty to Christ; this may indicate that the major thrust of Revelation is not sociopolitical but theological. John is more concerned with countering the *heresy* that was creeping into the churches toward the close of the first century than with addressing the political situation. This heresy could well have been Gnosticism (see comments on 2:6).

Revelation is also commonly viewed as belonging to the body of non-biblical Jewish writings known as apocalyptic literature. The name for this type of literature is derived from the Greek word for "revelation," *apokalypsis*. The extrabiblical apocalyptic books were written in the period from 200 B.C. to A.D. 200. Scholars usually stress the similarities between the Apocalypse of John and these noncanonical books, such as the use of symbolism and vision, the mention of angelic mediators of the revelation, the bizarre images, the expectation of divine judgment, the emphasis on the kingdom of God, the new heaven and earth, and the dualism of this age and the age to come. Although numerous similarities

---

[2]For this and other substantiating evidence, the reader is referred to the author's larger and documented commentary on Revelation in Frank E. Gaebelein, ed., *The Expositor's Bible Commentary* (Grand Rapids: Zondervan Publishing House, 1981), vol. 12 (hereafter referred to as Johnson, EBC, 12).

exist, these are also some clear differences that must not be overlooked.[3]

Much more important than the Jewish apocalyptic sources is the debt John owes to the eschatological teaching of Jesus, such as the Olivet Discourse (Matt. 24–25; Mark 13; Luke 21). The parallelism is striking and certainly not accidental. (These connections are dealt with in more detail in EBC, 12; cf. introduction to 6:1ff.) In short, we believe that the ultimate source of John's understanding of the future as well as of his interpretation of the Old Testament lies not in his own inventive imagination but definitely in Jesus of Nazareth.

B. Unity, Authorship, and Canonicity

The Book of Revelation displays both the literary and conceptuaul unity to be expected in a book written by one author. This does not preclude the possibility that John, in expressing in written form the revelation given to him by Christ, used various sources, whether oral or written (cf. comments on 1:2). Yet, under the guidance of the Holy Spirit, who is of course the primary author, John has made these materials his own and imbued them with a thoroughly Christian orientation and content.

The earliest witnesses ascribe Revelation to John the apostle, the son of Zebedee. Dionysius, the distinguished bishop of Alexandria and student of Origen (d. ca. 264), was the first within the church to question its apostolic authorship, because the advocates of an earthly eschatological hope ("Chiliasts"), whom he opposed, appealed to Revelation 20. From the time of Dionysius, the apostolic origin of the book was disputed in the East until Athanasius of Alexandria (d. 373) turned the tide toward its acceptance. In the West, the book was widely accepted and was included in all the principal lists of canonical books from at least the middle of the second century on. The Reformation period witnessed a renewal of the earlier questions concerning its apostolic authorship and canonical status; thus Luther, offended by the contents of Revelation, declared that he regarded it as "neither apostolic nor prophetic."

From the internal evidence, the following things can be said about John as the author with some confidence.

1. He calls himself John (1:4, 9; 22:8). This is most likely not a pseudonym but rather the name of a person well-known among the Asian churches. Other than John the apostle, John the Baptist, and John Mark, the only John we know about is the disputed "John, the presbyter," the early-second-century Christian mentioned by Papias. (The John mentioned in Acts 4:6 is a highly unlikely candidate.)

2. This John of the Apocalypse identifies himself as a prophet (1:3; 22:6–10, 18–19) who was in exile because of his prophetic witness (1:9). As such, he speaks to the churches with great authority.

---

[3]For a discussion of these contrasts, see Johnson, EBC, 12, pp. 401–2.

3. His use of the Old Testament and Targums makes it virtually certain that he was a Palestinian Jew, steeped in the ritual of the temple and synagogue. He may also have been a priest.

The authorship of Revelation is admittedly problematic. On the one hand, the language and grammatical style are incompatible with the Gospel and the epistles of John; on the other hand, in its imagery, literary forms, liturgical framework, and symbolism there are notable similarities to the Gospel and the epistles. Early and widespread testimony attributes the book to the apostle John, and no convincing argument has been advanced against this view. Regardless of the problem of authorship, the church universal has come to acknowledge the Apocalypse as divinely authoritative, inspired Scripture.

C. Date and Purpose

Only two dates for Revelation have received serious support. An early date, shortly after the reign of Nero (A.D. 54–68), is allegedly supported by references in the book to the presecution of Christians, to the "Nero redivivus" myth (a revived Nero would be the reincarnation of the evil genius of the whole Roman Empire), to the imperial cult (ch. 13), and to the temple (ch. 11), which was destroyed in A.D. 70.

The alternate and more generally accepted date rests primarily on the early witness of Irenaeus (185), who stated that the apostle John "saw the revelation . . . at the close of Domitian's reign" (A.D. 81–96). Although the slender historical evidence on the whole favors this later date, the question as to when in the first century Revelation was written must be left open.

"In form it is an epistle, containing an apocalyptic prophecy; in spirit and inner purpose, it is a pastoral" (Swete). As a prophet, John is called to separate true from false belief—to expose the failures of the congregations in Asia. He desires to encourage authentic Christian discipleship by explaining Christian suffering and martyrdom in the light of the victory over evil won by Jesus' death and resurrection. John is concerned to show that the martyrs (e.g., Antipas; 2:13) will be vindicated. He discloses the end both of evil and of those who follow the beast (19:20–21; 20:10, 15) and describes the ultimate victory of the Lamb and of those who follow Him. John himself is centrally concerned with God's saving purpose and its implementation by Jesus. John writes to the church in every age so that they too may join him in confirming this witness of Jesus (1:9; 22:16). Sadly, because of an overemphasis on either the symbolic or the literal, and because of theological disagreements, the church has often been deprived of the valuable practical thrust of this book as through it God seeks to lead us into authentic Christian discipleship.

D. Interpretative Schemes

Four traditional ways of understanding Revelation 4–22 have emerged in the history of the church. In our day, additional views have been developed by combining elements from these four traditions.

1. *Futurist*

This view holds that, with the exception of chapters 1–3, all the visions in Revelation relate to a period immediately preceding and following the second advent of Christ at the end of the age. Therefore, the seals, trumpets, and bowls refer to events still in the future; the beasts of chapters 13 and 17 are identified with the future Antichrist, who will appear at the last moment in world history and will be defeated by Christ in His second coming to judge the world and to establish His earthly millennial kingdom.

Variations of this view were held by the earliest expositors, such as Justin Martyr (d. 164), Irenaeus (d. ca. 195), Hippolytus (d. 236), and Victorinus (d. ca. 303). After an eclipse of nearly ten centuries, during which time the allegorical method prevailed, the futurist view was revived in the late sixteenth century by Franciscus Ribera, a Spanish Jesuit. He held that the beast was the Antichrist of the end time and that Babylon was not Rome under papal rule but a degenerate Rome of a future age. Unlike many modern futurists, Ribera founded his views on a thorough appreciation of the historical backgrounds of Revelation and its language.

This futurist approach has enjoyed a revival of no small proportion since the nineteenth century and is widely held among evangelicals today. Its chief problem is that it seems to make all but the first three chapters of Revelation irrelevant to the contemporary church, a problem that becomes ever more pronounced when adherents of the futurist view affirm, as many do today, that the church will be removed from the earth before the events described in 6:1ff. occur.

2. *Historicist*

As the word implies, this view sees in Revelation a prophetic survey of history. It originated with Joachim of Floris (d. 1202), a monastic who claimed to have received on Easter night a special vision that revealed to him God's plan for the ages. He assigned a day-year value to the 1,260 days of the Apocalypse. In his scheme, the book is a prophecy of the events of Western history from the time of the apostles until Joachim's own time. In the various schemes that developed as this method was applied to history, one element became common: the Antichrist and Babylon were connected with Rome and the papacy. Later, Luther, Calvin, and other Reformers came to adopt this view. The primary reason this approach does not enjoy much favor today is the lack of consensus as to the identification of the historical periods.

3. Preterist

According to this view, Revelation deals with the time of its author; the main contents of chapters 4–22 are thus viewed as describing events wholly limited to John's own day. The beasts of chapter 13 are identified as imperial Rome and the imperial priesthood. This is the view held by many contemporary scholars, not a few of whom are identified with the liberal interpretation of Christianity. As a system, it did not appear until 1614, when a Spanish Jesuit named Alcasar developed its main lines. While they do not ignore the importance of the historical setting, those who accept Revelation as a book of genuine *prophecy* concerning events extending beyond the first six centuries are little attracted by this view.

4. Idealist

This method of interpreting Revelation sees it as being basically poetic, symbolic, and spiritual in nature. Indeed, it is sometimes called the spiritualist view—not, of course, in reference to the cult of spiritualism, but because it "spiritualizes" everything in the book. Thus Revelation does not predict any specific historical events at all; on the contrary, it sets forth timeless *truths* concerning the battle between good and evil that continue throughout the church age. As a system of interpretation, it is more recent than the other three schools. In general, the idealist view is marked by its refusal to identify any of the images with specific future events, whether in the history of the church or with regard to the end of all things. Undoubtedly, the book does reflect the great timeless realities of the battle between God and Satan and of divine judgment; undoubtedly, it sees history as being ultimately in the hand of the Creator. But certainly it also depicts the consummation of this battle and the triumph of Christ in history through His coming in glory.

Which view is the right one? Since each of these four views has been held by evangelicals, the issue is not one of orthodoxy but of interpretation. In recent years, many expositors have combined the stronger elements of the different views. The history of the interpretation of Revelation should teach us to be open to fresh approaches to the book, even when this attitude goes contrary to the prevailing interpretations. A careful exegesis of the text, uninhibited by prior dogmatic conclusions, is required for the fullest understanding of the Apocalypse.

This Bible Study Commentary will pay close attention to the historical situation of first-century Christianity in its Judeo-Greco-Roman setting. We do not, however, take the position that this emphasis necessarily leads to the conclusion that John's language and visions describe the political entities of imperial Rome or the imperial priesthood. Thus we feel that the preterist and, to a lesser extent, the preterist-futurist views are mistaken. On the other hand, we believe that John describes the final judgment and the bodily return of Christ to the earth. This means that in every age Revelation continues to encourage the church in persecution as well as to warn the church against the beast's satanically energized, multifaceted deception. Its language describes the deeper realities of the conflict between Christ's sovereignty and Satan's power rather than between mere temporary historical-political entities, whether past (such as Rome) or future. We have opted for a view that combines the futurist and the idealist schemes.

Revelation may then be viewed, on the one hand, as an extended commentary on Paul's statement in Ephesians 6:12: "For our struggle is not against flesh and blood, but against the rulers, against the authorities, against the powers of the dark world and against the spiritual forces of evil in the heavenly realms." On the other hand, it also reveals the final judgment upon evil and the consummation of God's kingdom in time and eternity.

E. Use of the Old Testament

Revelation is unique in its use of the Old Testament. While it does not contain a single direct quotation, there are hundreds of places where John alludes in one way or another to the Old Testament Scriptures. Swete states that of the 404 verses of the Apocalypse, 278 contain references to the Jewish Scriptures. Paul's epistles, by comparison, contain ninety-five direct quotations and possibly an additional one hundred allusions to the Old Testament.

John refers frequently to Isaiah, Jeremiah, Ezekiel, and Daniel, and also repeatedly to Exodus, Deuteronomy, and the Psalms. Especially important are John's christological reinterpretations of Old Testament passages. He does not simply use the Old Testament in its pre-Christian sense but often recasts the images and visions of the Old Testament. While there is an unmistakable continuity between the Old Testament revelation and the Apocalypse, the new emerges from the old as a distinct entity.

F. Structure

The main contents of Revelation are arranged in series of seven, some explicit, some implied: seven churches (chs. 2–3), seven seals (chs. 6–7), seven trumpets (chs. 8–11), seven bowls (chs. 16–18), seven last things (chs. 19–22). It is also possible to divide the contents around four key visions: (1) the vision of the Son of man among the seven churches (chs. 1–3); (2) the vision of the seven-sealed scroll, the seven trumpets, and the seven bowls (4:1–19:10); (3) the vision of the return of Christ and the consummation of this age (19:11–20:15); and (4) the vision of the new heaven and new earth (21–22).

G. Outline and Map

I. John's Introduction (1:1–8)
   A. Preface (1:1–3)
   B. Greetings and Doxology (1:4–8)

II. The Vision of the Son of Man Among the Seven Churches of Asia (1:9–3:22)
   A. The Son of Man Among the Lampstands (1:9–20)
      1. The historical occasion (1:9–11)
      2. The vision of the Son of Man (1:12–16)
      3. The voice and message of Christ (1:17–20)
   B. The Letters to the Seven Churches (2:1–3:22)
      1. To Ephesus (2:1–7)
      2. To Smyrna (2:8–11)
      3. To Pergamum (2:12–17)
      4. To Thyatira (2:18–29)
      5. To Sardis (3:1–6)
      6. To Philadelphia (3:7–13)
      7. To Laodicea (3:14–22)

III. The Vision of the Seven-Sealed Scroll, the Seven Trumpets, and the Seven Bowls (4:1–19:10).
   A. The Seven-Sealed Scroll (4:1–8:1)
      1. Preparatory: The throne, the scroll, and the Lamb (4:1–5:14)
      a. The throne (4:1–11)
      b. The scroll and the Lamb (5:1–14)
      2. The opening of the first six seals (6:1–17)
      3. First interlude (7:1–17)
      a. The 144,000 Israelites (7:1–8)
      b. The great white-robed multitude (7:9–17)
      4. The opening of the seventh seal (8:1)
   B. The First Six Trumpets (8:2–11:14)
      1. Preparatory: The angel and the golden censer (8:2–5)
      2. The sounding of the first six trumpets (8:6–9:21)
      3. Second interlude (10:1–11:14)
      a. The little book (10:1–11)
      b. The two witnesses (11:1–14)
   C. The Seventh Trumpet (11:15–14:20)
      1. The sounding of the seventh trumpet (11:15–19)
      2. The woman and the dragon (12:1–17)
      3. The two beasts (13:1–18)
      4. The Lamb and the 144,000 (14:1–5)
      5. The harvest of the earth (14:6–20)

D. The Seven Bowls (15:1–19:10)
  1. Preparatory: The seven angels with the seven last plagues (15:1–8)
  2. The pouring out of the seven bowls (16:1–21)
  3. The woman and the beast (17:1–18)
  4. The fall of Babylon the Great (18:1–24)
  5. Thanksgiving for the destruction of Babylon (19:1–5)
  6. Thanksgiving for the marriage of the Lamb (19:6–10)

IV. The Vision of the Return of Christ and the Consummation of the Age (19:11–20:15)
  A. The First and Second Last Things: The Rider on the White Horse and the Destruction of the Beast (19:11–21)
  B. The Third and Fourth Last Things: The Binding of Satan and the Millennium (20:1–6)
  C. The Fifth Last Thing: The Release and Final End of Satan (20:7–10)
  D. The Sixth Last Thing: The Great White Throne Judgment (20:11–15)

V. The Vision of the New Heaven and the New Earth and the New Jerusalem (21:1–22:5)
  A. The Seventh Last Thing: The New Jerusalem (21:1–27)
  B. The River of Life and the Tree of Life (22:1–5)

VI. John's Conclusion (22:6–21)

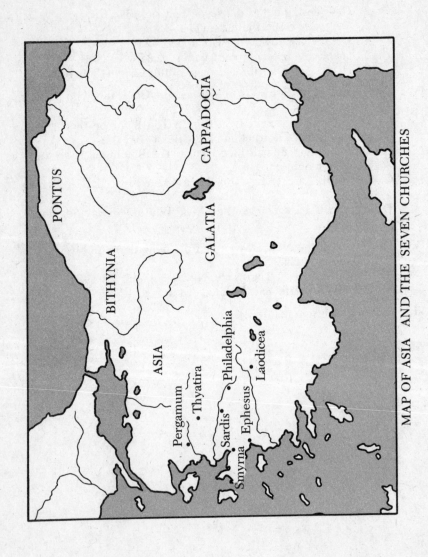

MAP OF ASIA AND THE SEVEN CHURCHES

John's Introduction

Chapter 1

John's Introduction
(Revelation 1:1–8)

The first three chapters of Revelation form a unit and are comparatively easy to understand. They are the most familiar part of the book and contain an introduction to the whole book (1:1–8); the first vision: the Son of Man among the seven lampstands (1:9–20); and the letters or messages to the seven churches in Asia (2:1–3:22).

The first eight verses introduce the whole book. They are freighted with theological content and detail. In a small commentary we can unfortunately only skim the surface. After a brief preface (vv. 1–3), John addresses the book to the seven churches of Asia in an expanded ancient letter form (vv. 4–8).

A. Preface (1:1–3)

Here we find a description of the divine source of the book (a "revelation of Jesus Christ"), a reference to the human author ("John"), and a statement that the book was meant for public congregational reading ("blessed is the one who reads").

The book is called the "revelation of Jesus Christ" (v. 1).[1] "Revelation" means "disclosure of what was formerly hidden, veiled, or secret." In the New Testament the word occurs exclusively in the sense of a divine disclosure. "Revelation" may refer to some present or future aspect of God's will (Luke 2:32; Rom. 16:25; Eph. 3:5), to persons (Rom. 8:19), or especially to the future unveiling of Jesus Christ at His return in glory (2 Thess. 1:7; 1 Peter 1:7, 13). This single occurrence of "revelation" in the Johannine writings refers not primarily to the appearing or revealing *of* Christ but rather, as the following words show, to the revelation *from* Jesus of "what must soon take place."

The content of the book comes from Jesus Christ. Yet even Christ is not the final author but the mediator who recieved the revelation from God

---

[1]Unless otherwise noted, all quotations are taken from the New International Version of the Bible.

the Father ("which God gave him to show"). John is the human instrument for communicating what Christ's messenger or angel has shown him (cf. 22:6, 8, 16). Through John the revelation is to be made known to the servants of God who constitute the churches (cf. 22:16).

"What must soon take place" implies that the revelation concerns events that are future (cf. Dan. 2:28–29, 45; Mark 13:7; Rev. 4:1; 22:6). But in what sense are we to understand that these events will take place "soon"? From the preterist point of view (cf. Introduction), "soon" means in John's day. Others translate "soon" as "quickly" (grammatically this is acceptable) and understand the author to describe events that will rapidly run their course once they begin. However, it is better to understand the word "soon" in the light of the words "the time is near" in v. 3 (cf. 22:10), although this does not make it necessary to follow the preterist interpretation of the book. In eschatology and apocalyptic literature, the future is always viewed as imminent without the necessity of intervening time (cf. Luke 18:8). The Book of Revelation itself makes it clear that "soon" does not preclude delay or intervening events. In chapter 6, for example, we hear the cry of the martyred saints: "How long, Sovereign Lord, holy and true, until you . . . avenge our blood?" They are told to "wait a little longer" (vv. 10–11). Therefore, "soon" means "imminent" in the eschatological sense. The church in every age has always lived with the expectancy of the consummation of all things in its own day. "Imminent" describes an event that is "possible any day, impossible no day."

Note the significance of angels in the worship of God, in the revelation of God's Word, and in the execution of His judgments on the earth. Angels are mentioned sixty-seven times in Revelation.

"Servant" (v. 2), used throughout the New Testament to describe the special representatives of the Lord Christ Himself, becomes a beautiful title of honor for God's people. The preface, then, presents five links in the chain of communication: God, Christ, His angel, His servant John, and those servants to whom John addressed his book.

In referring to his visions as the "word of God" (v. 2), John emphasizes his continuity with the prophets of the Old Testament as well as the apostles of the New Testament. The following passages show us John's concept of the Word of God: 1:9; 3:8, 10; 6:9; 12:11; 17:17; 19:9; 20:4. In 19:13 Jesus Himself is called "the Word of God." The church needs to be reminded that the neglected Book of Revelation is the very Word of God to us. While John's literary activity is present throughout, he claims that he actually "saw" in divinely disclosed visions that which he presents. And God Himself bears witness to the readers that these things are not the product of John's own mind (1:1–2; 21:5; 22:6; cf. 2 Peter 1:21).

"Testimony" is variously rendered "witness," "attestation," "validation," "verification." Grammatically, "the testimony of Jesus" can be the testimony "to" Jesus, i.e., John's own testimony *about* Jesus. However, the alternate grammatical sense—the testimony or validation *from* Jesus—is to be preferred. John thus testifies both to the Word of God received in the visions and to the validation of his message from Jesus Himself. The range of possible implications of the term in the following references is worthy of study: 1:9; 6:9; 12:11, 17; 19:10; 20:4; 22:16–20.

"The one who reads" (v. 3) reflects the early form of worship in which a reader read the Scriptures aloud on the Lord's Day. "Those who hear" are the people of the congregation who listen to the reading. "This prophecy" is John's way of describing his writing and refers to the entire Book of Revelation (10:11; 19:10; 22:7, 9–10, 18); we must remember that prophecy involves not only future events but also ethical and spiritual exhortations and warnings for today.

The benediction "blessed" (*makarios*), pronounced on the reader and on the congregation, emphasizes the importance of the message: they will be hearing not only John the prophet's words but actually the inspired word of Christ (Revelation contains six more beatitudes: 14:13; 16:15; 19:9; 20:6; 22:7, 14). John anticipated the full and immediate recognition of his message as worthy to be read in the churches as the Word of God coming from Christ Himself. In the ancient Jewish synagogue tradition in which John was raised, no such blessing was promised anyone who recited a mere human teaching, even if from a rabbi, while one who read Scripture performed a *mitzvah* (commanded act) and was worthy to receive a divine blessing.

All must listen carefully and "take to heart what is written" because "the time is near," the time or season for the fulfillment of the return of Christ (v. 7; cf. Luke 11:28; 21:8) and of all that is written in this book (cf. 22:10). Christ's return is always imminent—now as it has been since the day of His ascension (John 21:22; Acts 1:11).

A comparison of the Preface (1:1–3) with the Conclusion (22:6–21) shows that John throughout Revelation has followed a deliberate literary pattern. This should alert us to the possibility that the entire book was designed to be heard as a single unit in the public worship service. This should not in any way detract from the fact that John claims to have seen real visions ("saw," v. 2), which we may assume he arranged in this particular literary form for purposes of communication.

B. Greetings and Doxology (1:4–8)

John now addresses the recipients of his book: "To the seven churches in the province of Asia" (cf. v. 11; 2:1–3:22). Almost immediately he introduces an expanded form of the Christian Trinitarian greeting that turns into a doxology to Christ (vv. 5b–6) and is followed by a staccato exclamation calling attention to the return of Christ to the world (v. 7). The Father concludes the greeting with assurances of His divine sovereignty (v. 8).

The epistolary form of address immediately distinguishes this book from all other Jewish apocalyptic works (cf. Introduction). These seven churches actually existed in the Roman province of Asia (the western part of present-day Turkey), as the details in chapters 2 and 3 indicate (see comments on 2:1).

"Grace and peace" is the usual epistolary greeting that represents the bicultural background of the NT—Greek, "grace" and Hebrew, "peace." The source of blessing is described by employing an elaborate triadic formula for the Trinity:

"From him who is, and who was, and who is to come," i.e., the Father;
"From the seven spirits before his throne," i.e., the Holy Spirit;
"From Jesus Christ," i.e., the Son.

Then follows a threefold reference to the identity and function of Christ: "the faithful witness, the firstborn from the dead, and the ruler of the kings of the earth" (v. 5); and three indications of His saving work: "who loves us and has freed us from our sins . . . and has made us to be a kingdom and priests" (v. 6).

The Father. The descriptive name of the *Father* is "[he] who is, and who was, and who is to come." Each name of God in the Bible is replete with revelatory significance. This particular title is found only in Revelation (4:8; cf. 11:17; 16:5). It is generally understood to be a paraphrase of the divine name represented in the Old Testament by the Hebrew tetragrammaton YHWH (cf. Exod. 3:14). In 1:8 and 4:8 it is parallel with the divine name "Lord God, the Almighty." The tenses indicate that the same God is eternally present to sustain and encourage His covenant people through all the experiences of their lives.

The Holy Spirit. "And from the seven spirits before his throne" refers to the *Holy Spirit* rather than to angels. But why "seven spirits"? Some understand John to mean the "sevenfold spirit," i.e., the Holy Spirit in His fullness (NIV mg.). Borrowing from the imagery of Zechariah 4, where the ancient prophet sees a lampstand with seven bowls supplied with oil from two nearby olive trees, John seems to connect the church ("lampstands," v. 20) with the ministry of the Holy Spirit (3:1; 4:5; 5:6). The "seven spirits" represent the activity of the risen Christ through the Holy Spirit in and to the seven churches. This image brings great encouragement to the churches, for they serve God "'not by might nor by power, but by my Spirit,' says the Lord Almighty" (Zech. 4:6). Yet the image is also a sobering one because the history of each church (chs. 2–3) is an unfolding of that church's response to the Holy Spirit—"He who has an ear, let him hear what the Spirit says to the churches" (2:7, 11, et al.).

The Son. Finally, greetings come from the *Son*—"from Jesus Christ." John immediately adds three descriptive epithets and a burst of doxology to Him. He is first the "faithful witness." His credibility was proved in the past by His earthly life of obedience; it is proved in the present by His witness to the true condition of the churches; and it will be proved in the future by the consummation of all things in Him. Christ's being a reliable witness to God's kingdom and salvation (cf. John 7:7; 18:37; 1 Tim. 6:13)—even to the point of suffering death at the hands of the religious-political establishment of His day—is an encouragement to His servants who also are expected to be loyal to Him, even to *their* death (2:10; cf. Antipas, 2:13).

The fact that He is "the firstborn from the dead" brings further encouragement. As Christ has given His life in faithfulness to the Father's calling, so the Father has raised Christ from the dead, pledging Him as the first of a great company who will follow (cf. 7:13–14). Nowhere else does John refer to Christ as the "firstborn"; Paul uses the word in Romans 8:29 and Colossians 1:15, 18, and it is also found in Hebrews 1:6. In Colossians 1:18 it is associated with words of supreme authority or origin such as "head," "beginning" (cf. Rev. 3:14), and "supremacy." In Colossians 1:15 Paul refers to Christ as the "firstborn over all creation." This cannot mean that Christ was the first-created being but rather that He is the source, ruler, or origin of all creation. Christ's being the "firstborn" of the dead thus signifies not merely that He was the first in time to be raised from the dead but also that He is first in importance, having supreme authority over the dead (cf. 1:18). In Psalm 89:27 the same word is used of the Davidic king: "I will also appoint him my firstborn, the most exalted of the kings of the earth"; rabbinic tradition believed this to be a messianic reference.

Another title for Jesus, "the ruler of the kings of the earth," further connects John's thought with the psalm just quoted. Christ's rulership of the world is a key theme of Revelation (11:15; 17:15; 19:16). Jesus Christ is the supreme ruler of the kings of the earth. But who are the "kings of the earth" over whom Jesus Christ rules? John could mean the earthly rulers such as emperor Nero, in which case he affirms that even though Jesus is not physically present and the earthly monarchs appear to rule, in reality it is He, not they, who rules over all (6:15; 17:2). Another possibility is that Jesus rules over the defeated foes of the believers, e.g., Satan, the dragon, sin, and death (1:18). A third approach sees the believers as the kings of the earth (2:26–27; 3:21; cf. 11:6). All three ideas are true, so it is difficult to decide which was uppermost in John's mind.

Doxology to the Son. The mention of the person and offices of Christ leads John to a burst of praise to his Savior: "To him who loves us . . . be glory and power" (v. 5). In the *present*, Christ loves us. Through all the immediate distresses, persecutions, and even banishment, John is convinced that believers are experiencing Christ's continual care. Moreover, in the *past* Christ's love was unmistakably revealed in His atoning death, by which He purchased our release from the captivity of sin. Christ's kingly power is chiefly revealed in His ability to transform individual lives through His "blood" (i.e., His death; cf. 5:9; 7:14). Through His death on the cross, He defeated the devil, and those who follow Christ in the battle against the devil share this victory. "They overcame him [the devil] by the blood of the Lamb and by the word of their testimony" (12:11).

This transformation simultaneously involves the induction of blood-freed sinners into Christ's "kingdom" and priesthood. Of Israel it was said that they would be a "kingdom of priests and a holy nation" (Exod. 19:6; cf. Isa. 61:6). The Old Testament references as well as John probably refer to a "kingdom *and* priests" rather than a "kingdom *of* priests" (RSV). As Israel of old was redeemed through the Red Sea and was called to be a kingdom under God and a nation of priests to serve Him, so John sees the Christian community as the continuation of the Old Testament people of God, redeemed by Christ's blood and made heirs of His future kingly rule on the earth (5:10; 20:6). Furthermore, all believers are called to be priests in the sense that they are to offer spiritual sacrifices and praise to God (Heb. 13:15; 1 Peter 2:5). But while John sees the church as a kingdom, this does not mean that it is identical with the kingdom of God. Nor do the new people of God replace the ancient Jewish people in His purpose (cf. Rom. 11:28–29).

The Return of Christ. What Christ will do in the *future* is summed up in the dramatic cry: "Look, he is coming" (v. 7). This is a clear reference to the return of Christ (22:7, 12, 20). The preceding affirmation of Christ's rulership over the earth's kings and of the Christians' share in the messianic kingdom leads to tension between the believers' actual present condition of oppression and suffering and what seems to be implied in their royal and priestly status. So the divine promise of Christ's return is given by the Father, and the response of the prophet and the congregation follows in the words "So shall it be! Amen." Or we might think of Christ as saying, "So shall it be!" and the prophet and the congregation responding, "Amen" (cf. 22:20). The promise combines Daniel 7:13 with Zechariah 12:10. Daniel 7 provided a key focus for John throughout the book (there are no fewer than thirty-one allusions to it).

Christ's coming will be supernatural ("with the clouds") and in some manner open and known to all ("every eye"), even to those who "pierced him," i.e., put Him to death. "Those who pierced him" might be those historically responsible for His death, such as Pilate, Annas, Caiaphas, and the Jewish leaders of the Sanhedrin who pronounced Him guilty. And yet, when He comes, there will be mourning among "all the peoples of the earth." From the New Testament point of view, Pilate, Annas, Caiaphas, and the others were acting as representatives of all mankind in crucifying Jesus. While it is possible to see this mourning as a lament of repentance and sorrow for putting the Son of God to death, more probably it results from the judgment Christ brings upon the world.

The Father's Guarantee. God Himself now speaks and, with His own signature, vouches for the truth of the coming of Christ. Four of the many names of God that reveal His character and memorialize His deeds are given in this verse: "Alpha and Omega," "Lord God," "who is, and who was, and who is to come," and "the Almighty" (see v. 4 for comments on the second title). Alpha and omega are the first and last letters of the Greek alphabet; their meaning here is similar to "the First and the Last" in verse 17 and "the Beginning and the End" in 21:6 and 22:13. Only the Book of Revelation refers to God as "the Alpha and the Omega." God is the absolute source of all creation and history. Nothing lies outside of Him. Therefore, He is the "Lord God" of all and is continually present to His people as the "Almighty" (lit., "the One who has His hand on everything"; cf. 4:8; 11:17; 15:3; 16:7, 14; 19:6, 15; 21:22; 2 Cor. 6:18).

For Further Study

1. Identify the chief themes in the Introduction (1:1–8) that will reappear throughout the Book of Revelation.

2. What can be said about Jesus Christ, His person and work, from the Introduction (1:1–8)?

3. Locate the references to the Old Testament in 1:1–8. On the basis of these references, discuss how John views and uses the Old Testament.

4. How do you explain the phrases "soon take place" (v. 1) and "the time is near" (v. 3)? Can you relate your answer to the Christian today?

VISION ONE: *The Son of Man Among the Seven Churches of Asia*

Chapter 2

The Son of Man Among the Lampstands
(Revelation 1:9–20)

After a brief indication of the historical situation that occasioned it (1:9–11), John describes his vision of "someone, like a son of man," walking among seven golden lampstands (1:12–16). The person identifies Himself as the exalted Lord, Jesus Christ (1:17–18) and then explains the meaning of the symbolic vision (1:19–20). Finally, the Lord addresses a rather detailed and specific message to each of the seven churches in Asia (2:1–3:22).

A. The Historical Occasion (1:9–11)

The author again identifies himself as John and states where and when he received the vision and instructions concerning its divinely appointed destination. John stresses his intimate identification with the Asian Christians and the reason for his presence on Patmos.

1. *He was banished to Patmos* (1:9)

Patmos, one of the Sporades Islands, lies about thirty-seven miles west-southwest of Miletus, in the Icarian Sea. Its twenty-five square miles consist mainly of volcanic hills and rocky ground. It was one of the places to which the Romans banished their exiles. Eusebius mentions that John was banished to the island by Emperor Domitian in A.D. 95 and released eighteen months later by Emperor Nerva. John indicates that he was formerly on Patmos "because of the word of God and the testimony of Jesus" (cf. 1:2; 6:9; 20:4). He was not there to preach that Word but because of religious-political opposition to his faithfulness to it.

2. *He was one with the believers in Asia* (1:9)

John and the Asian believers share with Christ and one another the suffering or agony that comes because of faithfulness to Christ as the only true Lord and God (John 16:33; Acts 14:22; Col. 1:24; 2 Tim. 3:12). But they also share with Christ in His *kingdom* (power and rule). In one sense they already reign (1:6), albeit through suffering; yet, in another sense, they will reign with Christ in the eschatological manifestation of His kingdom (20:4, 6; 22:5).

Finally, as they look beyond their immediate distresses and put their full confidence in Christ, they share now in His royal dignity and power. Whether those distresses were imprisonment, ostracism, slander, poverty, economic discrimination, hostility, disruption of the churches by false prophets, or the constant threat of death from mob violence or judicial action, believers are to manifest their present kingship with Christ in their *patient endurance.*

Endurance is "the spiritual alchemy which transmutes suffering into royal dignity" (Charles). The Christians' witness and their radical love in all spheres of life produce the conflict with the powers of the world. Long-suffering is the mark of Christ's kingship in their lives (2:2, 19; 3:10; 13:10; 14:12; cf., e.g., Luke 8:15; 21:19; Rom. 2:7; 1 Cor. 13:7; Col. 1:11). At present, Christ's royal power does not crush opposition but uses suffering to test and purify the loyalty of His servants. His strength is revealed in their weakness (2 Cor. 12:9). Christians are called, as was John, to reign now with Christ by willingly entering into suffering conflict with the powers of this age.

3. His claim to prophetic inspiration (1:10–11)

"I was in the Spirit" describes John's experience of transport into the world of prophetic visions by the Spirit of God (4:2; 17:3; 21:10; cf. Ezek. 3:12, 14; 37:1; Acts 22:17). At least the first vision—if not the whole Book of Revelation—was revealed on "the Lord's Day." Since this is the only place in the New Testament where this expression is used, its identification is difficult. Some find a reference here to Easter Sunday, but most commentators, both ancient and modern, have taken the expression to mean Sunday, the first day of the week. Such a reference would bind the exiled apostle to the worshiping churches in Asia through his longing to be with them on Sunday.

John is to write down on a papyrus scroll what he sees and send it to the seven Asian churches. This writing would include the substance of the whole book, not just the first vision.

B. The Vision of the Son of Man (1:12–16)

Certain features of John's first vision are noted:

1. Beginning with verse 12, the vision extends as a unit through chapter 3. The quotation that begins in verse 17 is not closed till the end of chapter 3.

2. In this symbolic picture the glorified Lord is seen in His inner reality that transcends His outward appearance. The sword coming out of His mouth (v. 16) alerts us to this. In words drawn almost entirely from the imagery used in Daniel, Ezekiel, and Isaiah to depict God's majesty

and power, John uses hyperbole to describe the indescribable reality of the glorified Christ. These same poetic phrases reappear in the letters to the seven churches as well as throughout the rest of the book (14:2; 19:6, 12, 15).

3. The words of Christ present His absolute authority to address the churches. The vision (vv. 12–16) leads to John's transformed understanding of Jesus as the Lord of all through His death and resurrection (vv. 17–18).

1. *The golden lampstands* (1:12)

For the Old Testament tabernacle, Moses constructed a seven-branched lampstand (Exod. 25:31ff.). Later this lampstand came to symbolize Israel. Zechariah had a vision of a seven-branched golden lampstand fed by seven pipes, which was explained to him as the "eyes of the LORD, which range throughout the earth" (4:10). Zechariah's lampstand thus relates directly to the Lord Himself. Since other allusions to Zechariah's vision appear in Revelation (e.g., "seven eyes, which are the seven spirits of God," 5:6, and the "two witnesses" that are "the two olive trees," 11:3–4), it is logical to assume a connection with that vision here as well.

But there are problems in any strict identification. Christ tells John that the "seven lampstands are the seven churches" (v. 20) and that it is possible to lose one's place as a lampstand through a failure to repent (2:5). Therefore, the imagery represents the individual churches scattered among the nations—churches that bear the light of the divine revelation of the gospel of Christ to the world (Matt. 5:14). If Zechariah's imagery was in John's mind, it may mean that the churches, which correspond to the people of God today, are light bearers only because of their intimate connection with Christ, the source of the light, through the power of the Holy Spirit (1:4b; 3:1; 4:5; 5:6).

2. *The details of the vision* (1:13–16)

Evidently the words "someone 'like a son of man'" are to be understood in connection with Daniel 7:13 as a reference to the heavenly Messiah who is also human. Jesus preferred the title "Son of Man" for Himself throughout His earthly ministry, although on occasion He did not deny the appropriate use of "Son of God" (John 10:36; cf. Mark 14:61). Both titles are nearly identical terms for the Messiah. The early church, however, refrained from using "Son of Man" for Jesus except when there was some special connection between the suffering of believers and Christ's suffering and glory (e.g., Acts 7:56; Rev. 14:14).

"Dressed in a robe" (v. 13) begins the sevenfold description of the Son of Man. The vision creates an impression of the *whole* rather than of particular abstract concepts; it conveys awe, mystery, and deity. John saw

Christ as the divine Son of God in the fullest sense of the term. He also saw Him as fulfilling the Old Testament descriptions of the coming Messiah by using terms drawn from the Old Testament imagery of divine wisdom, power, steadfastness, and penetrating vision. The long robe and golden sash were worn by the priests in the Old Testament (Exod. 28:4) and may here signify Christ as the great High Priest to the churches in fulfillment of the Old Testament Aaronic priesthood or, less specifically, may indicate His dignity and divine authority (Ezek. 9:2, 11).

In an apparent allusion to Daniel, Christ's head and hair are described as "white like wool, as white as snow" (v. 14, cf. Dan. 7:9). To John, the same functions of ruler and judge ascribed to the "Ancient of Days" in Daniel's vision relate to Jesus. In Eastern countries, white hair commands respect and indicates the wisdom of years. This part of the vision may have shown John something of the deity and wisdom of Christ (cf. Col. 2:3). Christ's eyes were like a "blazing fire," a detail not found in Daniel's vision of the Son of Man (Dan. 7) but in Daniel 10:6. This simile is repeated in the letter to Thyatira (2:18) and in the vision of Christ's triumphant return and defeat of His enemies (19:12). It may portray either His penetrating scrutiny or fierce judgment.

"His feet were like bronze glowing in a furnace" (v. 15; cf. 2:18). His feet appeared like shining bronze, as if fired to white heat in a kiln. A similar figure of glowing metal is found in Ezekiel 1:13, 27; 8:2; Daniel 10:6. In both Ezekiel and Daniel the firelike brightness of shining metal is one of the symbols connected with the appearance of the glory of God. Revelation 2:18ff. may imply that the simile of feet "like burnished bronze" represents triumphant judgment on those who are unbelieving or unfaithful to the truth of Christ.

"His voice was like the sound of rushing [lit. 'many'] waters" describes the glory and majesty of God in a way similar to that in Ezekiel (1:24; 43:2). Anyone who has heard the awe-inspiring sound of a Niagara or Victoria Falls cannot but appreciate this image of God's power and sovereignty (Ps. 93:4). This same simile is found in 14:2 and 19:6.

"In his right hand he held seven stars" (v. 16). The right hand is the place of power and safety, and the "seven stars" are identified with the seven angels of the seven churches in Asia (v. 20). This is the only detail of the vision that is identified. The symbolism of the stars probably relates to the use of "angels" as those to whom the letters to the seven churches are addressed (chs. 2–3). Stars are associated in the Old Testament and in Revelation with angels (Job. 38:7; Rev. 9:1) or faithful witnesses to God (Dan. 12:3). The first letter (to Ephesus) includes in its introduction a reference to the seven stars (2:1), and in 3:1 they are associated with the "seven spirits of God."

John sees a "sharp double-edged sword" going forth from the mouth of Christ (v. 16). John uses this metaphor several times (1:16; 2:12, 16;

19:15, 21). The only scriptural parallel is found in Isaiah 11:4, where it is said that the Messiah will "strike the earth with the rod of his mouth" and "with the breath of his lips he will slay the wicked."

The sword is both a weapon and a symbol of war, oppression, anguish, and political authority. But John seems to perceive a startling difference in the function of this sword, since it proceeds from the *mouth* of Christ rather than being wielded in His hand. Christ will overtake the Nicolaitans at Pergamos and make war against them by the sword of his mouth (2:12, 16) and He will strike down the rebellious at His coming with such a sword (19:15, 21). The image definitely points to divine judgment but not to the type of power wielded by the nations. Christ conquers the world through His death and resurrection, and the sword is His faithful witness to God's saving purposes. The weapons of His followers are loyalty, truthfulness, and righteousness (19:8, 14).

Finally, the face of Christ is likened to "the sun shining in all its brilliance," a simile of Christ's divine glory, preeminence, and victory (Matt. 13:43; 17:2; cf. Rev. 10:1).

C. The Voice and Message of Christ (1:17–20)

1. *The Son of Man identified* (1:17–18)

These verses identify Christ to John and connect the vision of the glorified Christ (vv. 13–16) with His existence in history. The vision is seen in the light of the Eternal One who identifies Himself in these verses. "I fell at his feet as though dead" (v. 17) indicates that in the vision John actually saw a supernatural being and was stricken with trembling and fear, as the prophets before him had been (Ezek. 1:28; Dan. 8:17; 10:9). Christ immediately places His hand on John and assures him that he will not die: "Do not be afraid" (cf. 2:10; 19:10; 22:8; Matt. 17:6–7). The title "the First and the Last," which belongs to God in Isaiah 44:6 and 48:12 (where it means that He alone is God, the absolute Lord of history and the Creator), shows that in John's Christology Christ is identified with the Deity.

Christ is also "the Living One" in that He, like God, never changes (v. 18). This expression is probably a further elaboration of what it means to be "the First and the Last," viz., of all the gods He alone is able to speak and act in the world (Josh. 3:10; 1 Sam. 17:26; Ps. 42:2; Rev. 7:2). These divine qualities of Christ's person are now linked to His earthly existence in first-century Palestine—"I was dead, and behold I am alive for ever and ever!" John's whole view of Jesus and His kingdom revolves around the Cross and the Resurrection—a perspective that sets the tone for all the visions that follow.

Through His suffering, death, and resurrection Jesus won the right to have the "keys of death and Hades." Keys grant the holder access, and in ancient times the wearing of large keys was a mark of status in the community (cf. 3:7; 9:1; 20:1; 21:25). "Hades" refers to the Old Testament term *sheol* ("death" or "grave"). In the New Testament the word has a twofold usage: in some cases it denotes the place of all the dead (Acts 2:27, 31); in others, it refers to the place of the departed wicked (Luke 16:23; Rev. 20:13–14). Since Christ alone has conquered death and has Himself come out of Hades, He alone can determine who will enter death and Hades and who will come out of them—He has the "keys." The Christian can only see death as the servant of Christ.

2. The meaning of the vision (1:19–20)

John is told, "Write, therefore, what you have seen, what is now and what will take place later" (v. 19). Many think that Christ gives John a chronological outline as a key to the visions in the book. Others believe that verse 19 simply gives a general statement of the contents of all the visions throughout the book as containing a mixture of the "now" and the "later."

However, the Greek also allows for the rendering "what they mean" instead of "what is now," while "what will take place later" (lit. "after these") may refer to the later visions John received. John is then told to write down a description of the vision of Christ he has just seen, what it means, and what he will see afterward, i.e., not the end-time things, but the things revealed later to him—whether they are wholly future, wholly present, or both future and present depends on the content of the vision. This leaves the question open concerning the structure of the book and its chronological progression, as John may have intended.[1]

The first vision is called a "mystery" (v. 20). In the New Testament a "mystery" is something formerly secret but now revealed or identified (cf. 10:7; 17:7, 18). The seven stars represent the "angels of the seven churches." Who are the angels? There is no totally satisfactory answer to this question. The word for "angels" occurs sixty-seven times in Revelation and in every other instance refers to heavenly messengers, although occasionally in the New Testament it can mean a human messenger (Luke 7:24; 9:52; James 2:25 KJV).

A strong objection to seeing the "angels" as human messengers here is the fact that the word is not used that way anywhere else in apocalyptic literature. Furthermore, in early noncanonical Christian literature no historical person connected with the church is ever called an "angel." Another possibility is to identify the angels as a "way of personifying the prevailing spirit of the church" (Mounce). While this is an attractive approach to our Western way of thinking, it too lacks any supporting

---

[1]For a full discussion of the problems in this difficult verse, see the author's "Revelation," EBC, 12, p. 429.

evidence in the New Testament and especially in Revelation. Therefore, "angels" should be understood to refer here to the heavenly messengers who have been entrusted by Christ with responsibility for the churches and yet are so closely identified with them that the letters are addressed at the same time to these "messengers" and to the congregation (cf. the plural form in 2:10, 13, 23–24).

In 3:1 the stars are clearly linked with the seven spirits of God. Whatever may be the correct identification of the angels, the emphasis rests on Christ's immediate presence and communication through the Spirit to the churches. The reference to angels in the churches shows that the churches are more than a gathering of mere individuals or a social institution; they have a corporate and heavenly character (cf. 1 Cor. 11:10; Eph. 3:10; Heb. 1:14). "The seven lampstands are the seven churches" not only shows that the churches are the earthly counterpart of the "stars" but links the vision of Christ with His authority to rule and judge His churches.

For Further Study

1. Find Patmos on a map. Read the entry on "Patmos" in a good Bible encyclopedia. Are there contemporary parallels to John's banishment to Patmos as a religio-political prisoner? Cite several or point out the differences now from John's situation.

2. Why does the commentary insist that, although John actually received a divine revelation in the form of a vision, it is not appropriate to literalize the vision? What part of the vision especially shows that it is an interpretive vision and not a visual reproduction of what was revealed to John? (See comments on 1:13, 16.)

3. What special relationship of the glorified Christ to His people is revealed in the first vision of the book? How will this affect your Christian life this week?

Chapter 3

The Letters to the Seven Churches
(Revelation 2:1–3:22)

A. Introduction

Why these seven churches?

Why did John address these *seven* churches in particular? There were other churches in Asia at the close of the first century. The New Testament itself refers to congregations at Troas (Acts 20:5–12), Colosse (Col. 1:2), and Hierapolis (Col. 4:13). There may also have been churches at Magnesia and Tralles, since Ignatius wrote to them less than twenty years later.

It is difficult to say why the Lord selected these seven churches. Some have suggested that they were *prophetic* of the church ages throughout history (J. A. Seiss; *The Scofield Reference Bible* adopts this view in its notes). For example, Ephesus would represent the apostolic period until the Decian persecution (A.D. 250), followed by Smyrna, which represents the church of martyrdom extending until the time of Constantine (A.D. 316). However, after this initial agreement identifications become more difficult except for the last church: all agree that Laodicea is the final period of lukewarm apostasy. Yet the text itself provides no reason for holding this view. The churches are simply historical churches, typical of those found in every age. If the churches were genuinely prophetic of the course of church history rather than representative of churches in every age, those who held to the imminent return of Christ would have been quickly disillusioned once they realized this.

The reason *seven* churches were chosen and were placed in this order seems to be that seven is the number of completeness, which underlies the literary pattern of the book (cf. Introduction, p. 9). These seven churches contained typical or representative qualities of both obedience and disobedience that are a constant reminder to all churches throughout every age (cf. 2:7, 11, 17, 29; 3:6, 13, 22; esp. 2:23). Their order (1:11; 2:1f.) reflects the natural ancient travel circuit beginning at Ephesus and arriving finally at Laodicea (see map of the area).

2. *The literary pattern*

The letters are more in the nature of messages than separate letters.

Each message to an individual church was apparently also intended for the other six churches (2:7, 11, 17, etc., esp. 2:23). By comparing the similar components of all the letters, one may gain a fuller insight into their messages. Each message generally follows a common literary plan consisting of *seven* parts:

1. The *addressee* is given first, following a pattern common to all seven letters: "To the angel of the church in Ephesus write," etc.

2. Then the *speaker* is mentioned. In each case, some part of the great vision of Christ and of His self-identification (1:12–20) is repeated as the speaker identifies Himself; e.g., "These are the words of him who holds the seven stars in his right hand and walks among the seven golden lampstands" (2:1; cf. 1:13, 16). The introductory phrase "These are the words of him" is strongly reminiscent of the Old Testament formula for introducing the words of God to the congregation of Israel.

3. Next, the *knowledge* of the speaker is given. His is a divine knowledge. He knows intimately the works of the churches and the reality of their loyalty to Him, despite outward appearances. Each congregation's total life and the works they have embraced are measured against the standard of Christ's life. In two cases (Sardis and Laodicea) that assessment proves totally negative. The enemy of Christ's churches is the deceiver, Satan, who seeks to undermine the churches' loyalty to Christ (2:10, 24).

4. Following His assessment of the churches' accomplishments, the speaker pronounces His *verdict* on their condition in such words as "You have forsaken your first love" (2:4) or "You are dead" (3:1). Two letters contain no favorable verdict (Smyrna, Philadelphia) and two no word of commendation (Sardis, Laodicea); but since all seven letters would be sent to each church together with the entire Book of Revelation (cf. 1:11), we may assume that Christ intended that all the churches hear words of both commendation and blame. In the letters all derelictions are viewed as forms of inner betrayals of a prior relation to Christ. Each congregation as a whole is responsible for its individual members and for its leaders; each leader and each individual believer is at the same time fully responsible for both himself or herself and the congregation. This responsibility involves especially the problem of self-deception concerning good and evil, the true and the false, in situations where they are easily confused. The evil appears under the cloak of good, the good as apparent evil. Christ's verdict sets before each church the true criteria for leading it out of self-deception into the truth.

5. To correct or alert each congregation, Jesus issues a penetrating *command*. These commands further expose the exact nature of the self-deception involved. We are mistaken if we believe that the churches readily identified the heretics and heresies Christ describes. Because they were deceptions, they would not easily be recognized: the greater

the evil, the more deceptive the cloak. In the exposition of the letters, the commands must be carefully considered so as to determine precisely the nature of the various errors. The thrust of the commands is not consolation for persecuted churches but rather the opposite—John, like Jesus, was concerned to bring not peace but a sword.

6. Each letter contains the *general exhortation* "he who has an ear, let him hear what the Spirit says to the churches" (2:7, et al.); this exhortation is identical in all seven letters, but in the last four it follows rather than precedes the promise. The words of the Spirit are the words of Christ (cf. 19:10). Because the commands of Christ in the letters are somewhat ambiguous, they require the individual and the congregation to listen to the Spirit's voice that accompanies the words of Jesus if they are truly to realize the victory He considers appropriate for them. Even though the words of Christ referred initially to first-century churches located in particular places, by the continual relevance the Spirit gives them they transcend that time limitation and speak to all the churches in every generation.

7. Finally, each letter contains a *promise* of reward to the victor. These promises are often the most metaphoric and symbolic portions of the letters and thus in some cases present interpretative difficulties. Each is eschatological and correlates with the last two chapters of the book (21–22). For example, "the right to eat from the tree of life, which is in the paradise of God" (2:7) is parallel to "the tree of life" in 22:2; protection from "the second death" (2:11) finds its counterpart in 21:4: "There will be no more death," etc. Furthermore, the promises are echoes of Genesis 2–3: What was lost by Adam in Eden is more than regained by Christ. The words "I will give" or "I will make" identify Christ as the absolute source and donor of every gift. We are probably to understand the seven promises as different facets that combine to make up one great promise to believers: wherever Christ is, there will the "overcomers" be. Who are the "overcomers"? Certainly they are Christ's true disciples, those who are fully loyal to Him, and who are identified with Him in His suffering and death (1 John 5:4–5). Compare those who do not overcome in the letters (e.g., the "cowardly" 2:10, 13; the "sexually immoral," 2:14, 20; the "idolaters," 2:14, 20; and the "liars," 2:2, 9, 20; 3:9) with those in 21:8.

B. Messages to the Churches (2:1–3:22)

1. *To Ephesus* (2:1–7)

The church at Ephesus is addressed in the first letter. Ephesus was a crossroads of civilization. *Politically,* it had become the capital of the province of Asia and was known as "Supreme Metropolis of Asia." The Roman governor resided there. It was a "free" city, i.e., self-governed. Located on the western coast of Asia Minor, at the convergence of three great highways, Ephesus was the trade center of the area. It has been called "The Vanity Fair of the Ancient World."

Religiously, Ephesus was the center for the worship of the fertility goddess known in Greek as "Artemis," or Romanized as "Diana" (Acts 19:23ff.). The temple with its statue of Artemis was one of the seven wonders of the ancient world. Thousands of priests and priestesses were involved in her service. Many of the priestesses were dedicated to cult prostitution. (This may be related to "the practices of the Nicolaitans" in verse 6.) The temple also served as a bank for kings and merchants and as an asylum for fleeing criminals. To what extent the temple practices contributed to the general moral deterioration of the population cannot be assessed, but one of Ephesus' own citizens, the philosopher Heraclitus, said that the inhabitants of the city were "fit only to be drowned and that the reason he could never laugh or smile was because he lived amidst such terrible uncleanness." The church at Ephesus was probably founded jointly by Aquila, Priscilla, and (later) Paul (Acts 18:18–19; 19:1–10). The Ephesians were cosmopolitan and transient and the city had a history of cultural-political change; these factors may have influenced the apostasy of the congregation at Ephesus from its first love (cf. 2:4).

The *speaker* identifies Himself by a reference to the vision of chapter 1: "[he] who holds the seven stars in his right hand" (cf. 1:16). These words strike a note of reassurance, reflecting both Christ's protection and control of the church and His vital concern for it, while on the other hand the description of Christ as the One who "walks [travels] among the seven golden lampstands" contains a note of warning: He may journey to Ephesus to remove their lampstand (2:5).

The speaker's *knowledge* includes awareness of their activity, their present discernment of evil, and their patient suffering. The Ephesian Christians did not lack a serious and sustained commitment, even to the point of suffering for Christ's name: their "deeds," their "hard work" ("wearisome toil"), and their "perseverance" are underlined by the phrase "you have . . . endured hardships for my name, and have not grown weary" (v. 3). Paul attributes the same threefold activity to the Thessalonians and adds to each quality its motivating source: "faith," "love," and "hope" (1 Thess. 1:3).

Christ also knows that doctrinal discrimination accompanies the toil and patience of the Ephesians: they "cannot tolerate wicked men." These "wicked men" are not the pagans in Ephesus but false brethren who "claim to be apostles but are not." It is not easy, however, to determine precisely who these people were, what they taught, or how the church "tested" them. An "apostle" is one who is sent as a representative of another and bears the full authority of the sender. In the New Testament, the word is applied first to the original circle of the Twelve (Mark 3:14; Acts 1:2, 26), who had a special place historically in laying the foundation of the church (Eph. 2:20; Rev. 21:14). But the New Testament further broadens this original circle to include men such as Paul (Gal. 1:1), Barnabas (Acts 14:14), James the brother of Jesus (Gal. 1:19), and others (cf. Rom. 16:7). The name was applied to those who were authentically and specifically called by Christ to be His authoritative spokesmen.

Miracles were the signs of apostolic authority (2 Cor. 12:12; Heb. 2:4), but miracles may also accompany false prophets (Mark 13:22; 2 Thess. 2:9; 2 Tim. 3:8; Rev. 13:13–14). Thus it was necessary to "test the spirits to see whether they are from God, because many false prophets have gone out into the world" (1 John 4:1). Beyond their denial of Jesus as Lord, these self-proclaimed apostles also sought selfish advantage through their claims (2 Cor. 11:5, 13; 12:11).

The apostolic fathers shed light on the question whether the authoritative function of apostles continued after the first century. In no case do the many references to apostles in the writings of Clement of Rome, Ignatius, Barnabas, and the Shepherd of Hermas relate to any recognized apostles other than those associated with the New Testament. The Fathers apparently understood the special apostolic function to have ceased with the end of the apostolic era.

About fifteen years after John wrote Revelation, Ignatius wrote to the church of Ephesus and commended them for refusing to give a "home" to any heresy. Thyatira had failed (2:20ff.), but the Ephesians had won the victory over false teachers—they had heeded Paul's earlier warning (Acts 20:28–30).

The speaker's *verdict* shows, on the other hand, that however much had been gained at Ephesus by resisting the false apostles, not all was well. They had "forsaken," or "let go," their "first love" (v. 4). This was a serious defect that, if uncorrected, would result in the loss of their position as light bearers (v. 5). The majority of commentators take the first love to refer to the original Christian love the Ephesians had for one another. Paul's exhortation to the Ephesian elders to "help the weak" (Acts 20:35) and the warm commendation he gives them in their early years for their fervent love of one another (Eph. 1:15) may lend some support to this view.

Other commentators, however, see the "first love" as a reference to the inner devotion to Christ that characterized their earlier commitment, like the love of a newly wedded bride for her husband. This interpretation is supported by the fact that in the letters to the other churches Christ complains of problems of inner betrayal of Him. Neither view necessarily eliminates the other. Loving devotion to Christ can be lost in the midst of active service, and certainly no amount of orthodoxy can be a substitute for love for one another. "First" love would suggest that they still loved, but with a quality and intensity unlike that of their initial love.

The speaker's *command* further exposes the problem and offers a way to correct the fault. The imperatives are instructive: "Remember. . . . Repent . . . do" (v. 5). The Ephesians (like the Sardians, 3:3) are called on to reflect on their earlier works of fervent love, to compare them with the present situation, to ponder how far they have fallen from their former devotion and enthusiasm, to humbly "repent" (totally change) before God, and to do the former works motivated by love. These imperatives are all part of a single response that would keep the Ephesians from the judgment of Christ, a judgment that would effectively remove them as His representatives in the world.

How many individuals and churches today stand at this same cross-roads? Do we sense the importance to Christ not only of honoring His name by our true confession but also of reflecting His life by our loving relationship to others? This threat of loss of light bearing (or witness) applies without doubt equally to the other four churches to whom a similar exhortation to repent is given (Pergamos, Thyatira, Sardis, and Laodicea).

Christ adds a further commendation concerning the Ephesians' hatred of the practices of the Nicolaitans (cf. 2:15)—a hatred directed at the practices, not at the people themselves (cf. Ps. 139:21). It is difficult to determine exactly who the Nicolaitans were and what they taught. Etymologically the name means "to conquer [or 'consume,'] the people." Did they call themselves by this name or is it a derogatory title Christ applied to them? The similarity between the meaning of this name and that of the Balaamites in 2:14–15 may suggest either identity with this group or similarity to their teachings (see comments on 2:14–15).[1]

On the *general exhortation* and the meaning of "overcomes" (v. 7), see the introduction to this section (2:1). The overcomer is *promised* access to the "tree of life, which is in the paradise of God." The "tree of life" is first mentioned in Genesis 2:9 as one of the many trees given to Adam and Eve for food and was off-limits to them after their fall into sin (Gen. 3:22, 24). It is last mentioned in Revelation 22:19.

Rabbinic and Jewish apocalyptic works mention that the glorious age of the Messiah would be a restoration of Edenic conditions as they existed before the Fall (see also Isa. 51:3; Ezek. 36:35; cf. Ezek. 28:13; 31:8–9).

---

[1]Information about the Nicolaitans is limited, ambiguous, and based on John's references here in Revelation. Irenaeus claims that John wrote his Gospel to thwart the teaching of the Gnostic Cerinthus, whose error was similar to the earlier kind of teaching known as Nicolaitanism. Seeing the sect as a heresy would agree with the references in 2:14 and 2:20, which warn against mixing Christian faith with idolatry and cult prostitution. Fiorenza identifies the group as Gnostics and summarizes the problem well: "The Nicolaitans are according to Revelation a Christian group within the churches of Asia Minor and have their adherents even among the itinerant missionaries and the prophetic teachers of the community. They claim to have insight into the divine or, more probably, into the demonic. They express their freedom in libertine behavior, which allows them to become part of their syncretistic pagan society and to participate in the Roman civil religion." Others understand the Nicolaitans as Christians who still showed devotion to the emperor by burning incense to his statue or image (William M. Ramsay).

Jewish thought joined the concepts of the renewed city of God, the tree of life, and the paradise of God. In the noncanonical Jewish apocalyptic book, the Testament of Levi, it is promised that God (or Messiah) "shall open the gates of Paradise, and shall remove the threatening sword against Adam, and he shall give the saints to eat from the tree of life, and the spirit of holiness shall be on them" (18:10-11).

"Paradise" is a Persian loanword meaning "a park" or "a garden." The Greek Old Testament uses it to translate the Hebrew expression the "garden" of Eden (Gen. 2:8-10). John seems to reinterpret the Jewish idea of Paradise. First, Jesus Christ is the restorer of the lost Paradise (22:1-4, 14)—He gives access to the tree of life. But Paradise means to be with Him in fellowship rather than the idea of a hidden paradise with its fantastic sensual delights. The tree of life conveys symbolically the truth of eternal life or the banishment of death and suffering (22:2). Those at Ephesus who truly follow Christ in deep devotion and thus experience the real victory of Christ will share the gift of eternal life that He alone gives.

2. To Smyrna (2:8-11)

Smyrna (modern Izmir) lay almost due north of Ephesus at a distance of about forty miles. The city was exceptionally beautiful and large (ca. 200,000 pop.) and ranked with Ephesus and Pergamum as "First of Asia." Known as the birthplace of Homer, it was an important seaport that commanded the mouth of the Hermus River valley. Smyrna was a wealthy city where learning, especially in the sciences and medicine, flourished. An ancient city (third millennium B.C.), allegedly founded by a mythical Amazon who gave her name to it, Smyrna repeatedly sided with Rome in different periods of her history, and thus earned special privileges as a free city and assize (self-governed) town under emperor Tiberius and his successors. Among the beautiful, paved streets traversing the city from east to west was the "Golden Street," along which stood the temples of Apollo, Asclepius, and Aphrodite, with the temples of Cybele and Zeus at either end.

Smyrna was also a center of the emperor cult, having won from the Roman Senate in A.D. 23 (over eleven other cities) the privilege of building the first temple in honor of Tiberius. Under Domitian (A.D. 81-96) emperor worship became compulsory for every Roman citizen under threat of death. Once a year a citizen had to burn incense on the altar to the bust of Caesar, after which he was issued a certificate. Such an act was probably considered more an expression of political loyalty than of religious worship, and all a citizen had to do was burn a pinch of incense and say, "Caesar is Lord." Yet most Christians refused to do this. Perhaps nowhere was life for a Christian more perilous than in this city of zealous emperor worship. About sixty years later (ca. 156), Polycarp was burned alive at the age of eighty-six as the "twelfth martyr in Smyrna." His words have echoed through the ages: "Eighty-six years have I served Christ, and He has never done me wrong. How can I blaspheme my King who saved me?"[2] A hostile faction of the large Jewish community at Smyrna was prominent in Polycarp's death and no doubt also troubled the church in John's day (2:9).

The *speaker* identifies himself as "[he] who is the First and the Last, who died and came to life again" (v. 8; cf. comments on 1:17–18). The "First and Last" might remind those suffering persecution and rejection from their countrymen (vv. 9–10) that the One they belong to is the Lord of history and the Creator. He is in control regardless of appearances of evil. Ramsay suggests that the term may allude by contrast to Smyrna's claim to be the "first" of Asia in beauty and loyalty to the emperor. But Christians at Smyrna were concerned with Him who is truly first in everything.

He who is "the First and the Last" is also the One "who died" (lit., "became a corpse") and "came to life again." To a congregation threatened by imprisonment and death, the Prisoner who died and came back to life again can offer the crown of life to other executed prisoners and protect them from the second death (vv. 8, 10–11). There may also be an allusion here to the history of the city of Smyrna, which had been destroyed in the seventh century B.C. and rebuilt in the third century B.C.

The speaker's *knowledge* is threefold: (1) He knows their "afflictions" (v. 9)—a word translated "persecution" in verse 10. (2) He knows their "poverty." This can only mean material poverty, because the speaker (Christ) immediately adds, "yet you are rich" (toward God). We do not know why this church was so poor in such a prosperous city. Perhaps the high esteem in which the emperor cult was held in the city produced economic sanctions against Christians who refused to participate. In Smyrna, economic pressure may have been the first step toward persecution. Even today, loyalty to their Lord sometimes entails economic loss for Christians (cf. 3:17). (3) The risen Lord also knows "the slander of those who say they are Jews and are not, but are a synagogue of Satan." A certain faction within the Jewish community (not the whole community) used malicious untruths ("slander") to incite persecution of the impoverished saints in Smyrna. "They say they are Jews but are not" shows that even though these men claimed descent from Abraham, they were not his true descendents because they did not have faith in Christ, the "Seed" of Abraham (Gal. 3:16, 29). These unbelieving and hostile Jews probably viewed the Jewish Christians in Smyrna as heretics of the worst

---

[2]A modern-day parallel to the predicament of Christians faced with the demand to worship the Roman emperor occurred when the Japanese occupied Korea in 1937–40 and ordered Christians to worship at their Shinto shrines. Many Christians refused and were imprisoned and tortured.

sort, deserving ridicule and rejection. Whether the "true" Jews are now Christians in general or those Jews in Smyrna who became Christians is open to debate (cf. comments on 7:4).

"But are of the synagogue of Satan" reveals for the first time in Revelation the ultimate source of the persecution of Christians—Satan. Many further references to the archenemy of the followers of Christ are found throughout the book (2:13; 3:9; 9:11; 12:9–10, 12; 13:4; 20:2, 7, 10). In fact, he is one of the principal actors in the apocalyptic drama. While Satan is the author of persecution and wicked men are his instruments, God remains sovereign in that He will give "the crown of life" to those who are "faithful, even to the point of death" (v. 10). "Synagogue of Satan" refers, then, to certain hostile Jews in ancient Smyrna who, motivated by Satan, slandered the church there. The term should never be indiscriminately applied to all Jewish synagogues.

The speaker's *command* immediately follows since no *verdict* of fault is found (v. 10). The prospect of further and imminent suffering may have made the believers at Smyrna fearful: "Do not be afraid of what you are about to suffer" (lit. "Stop being afraid . . ."). The risen Christ reveals that some of them will be imprisoned by the Devil in order to test them, and they will have ten days of persecution—whether by Jews or pagans is not stated. The testing will show where their true loyalty lies. Christ offers a faithful and suffering church further trial and suffering, even "to the point of death." The "ten days" may be ten actual days, or it may be a Semitism for an indeterminate but comparatively short period of time (cf. Neh. 4:12; Dan. 1:12). In the first-century Roman world, prison was usually not correctional but the prelude to trial and execution, hence the words "Be faithful, even to the point of death."

For those who would face martyrdom out of loyalty to Christ there was to be a "crown of life" given by Christ Himself. The Christians at Smyrna would be very familiar with the term "the crown of Smyrna," which alluded to the beautiful skyline formed around the city by the "hill Pagos, with the stately public buildings on its rounded sloping sides." The "crown" usually referred to a garland of flowers worn chiefly in the worship of pagan gods such as Cybele or Bacchus, who were pictured on coins with a crown of battlements. Faithful servants of the city appeared on coins with laurel wreaths on their heads. As the patriots of Smyrna were faithful to Rome and to their crown city, so Christ's people are to be faithful to death to Him who will give them the imperishable crown of life (James 1:12; 1 Peter 5:4).

The *general exhortation* is identical to those in the other letters. The *promise* to those who overcome is that they "will not be hurt at all by the second death." Death was a real possibility for these believers. But greater than the fear of physical death should be the fear of God's eternal judgment (Luke 12:4–5). The "second death" is a well-known Targumic expression, but it does not occur in the Old Testament or elsewhere in Jewish literature. Even though death was the outcome of Adam's sin, in Christ there is a complete reversal for man (Gen. 2:16–17; Rom. 5:15ff.). Since the messianic believers at Smyrna were under attack by some in the Jewish community, it was reassuring indeed to hear the Lord Himself say that His followers would not be harmed by the second death—the lake of fire (20:14; 21:8).

3. To Pergamum (2:12–17)

The inland city of Pergamum lay about sixty-five miles north of Smyrna along the fertile valley of the Caicus River. Pergamum held the official honor of being the provincial capital of Roman Asia, though this honor was in fact also claimed by Ephesus and Smyrna. Among its notable features were its beauty and wealth; its library of nearly 200,000 volumes (second only to the library of Alexandria); its famous sculpture; its temples to Dionysus, Athena, Asclepius, and Demeter and the three temples of the emperor cult; its great altar to Soter Zeus; and its many palaces. The two main religions seem to have been the worship of Dionysus, the god of the royal family symbolized by the bull, and of Asclepius, the savior god of healing, represented by the snake. The latter made Pergamum the "Lourdes of the ancient world" (Charles). Tradition also records that King Eumenes II (197–159 B.C.) planned to build a library in Pergamum to rival the one in Alexandria. Ptolemy Epiphanes of Egypt (205–182 B.C.) took action to stop this venture by cutting off the export of papyrus. It was this embargo that forced Eumenes to develop vellum or parchment ("from Pergamum"), a writing material made from animal skins. Josephus mentions a Jewish community at Pergamum.

The *speaker* identifies Himself as "[he] who has the sharp, double-edged sword" (v. 12; cf. comments on 1:16; cf. Isa. 49:2). In dealing with the Pergamum congregation, divided by deceptive teaching, the risen Lord will use this sword to fight against the Balaamites and the Nicolaitans (v. 16). It is interesting that Rome had given Pergamum the rare power of capital punishment (*ius gladii*), which was symbolized by the sword. The Christians in Pergamum were thus reminded that though they lived under the rule of an almost unlimited imperium they were citizens of another kingdom—that of Him who needs no other sword than that of His mouth (Caird).

The speaker's *knowledge* is searching: He knows that they live in a hostile and difficult place—"where Satan has his throne" (v. 13). This certainly refers to the fact that Pergamum was a center of the worship of pagan gods and especially of the emperor cult: the first temple in the empire in honor of Augustus was established in A.D. 29 at Pergamum because it was the administrative capital of Asia. In succeeding years the city boasted of being the official warden (*neokoros*, lit., "temple sweeper") of the "temple where Caesar was worshiped." Others see in "Satan's throne" a reference to the altar of Savior Zeus or to the center of worship of Asclepius. Pergamum was an idolatrous city where declaring oneself to be a Christian who worshiped the one true God and Savior, Jesus Christ, would certainly have provoked hostility.

Furthermore, the risen Lord knew their loyalty to Him in all that He is revealed to be ("my name"), even when "Antipas, my faithful witness . . . was put to death in [their] city." Nothing further is known about Antipas than the meaning of his name, "against all." The proximity of the name "Satan" before and after Antipas in verse 13 makes it virtually certain that his death was instigated by the enmity of pagans in Pergamum. He may have been the first or most notable of Pergamum's martyrs. Christ pays this hero of the faith a noble tribute: "faithful witness"—words that John applies to Christ Himself in 1:5. Satan tries to undermine loyalty to Christ by persecution; Christ strengthens that loyalty by commending those who are true to Him and by exposing those who are deceitful.

The speaker's *verdict* reveals that the church in Pergamum was divided. Some had followed Antipas and did not deny Christ's name or their faith in Him (v. 13). Others held to the teaching and practice of the Balaamites and Nicolaitans, which Christ hates (2:6). Since the name "Balaam" can mean in Hebrew "to conquer the people," which is the same as the meaning of the Greek "Nicolaitans," and since they are mentioned together in this letter, both groups may be closely related. In fact, the error introduced into the church at Thyatira through the teaching of the woman Jezebel may also be similar; in both letters the more deadly effects of the error are described as "eating food sacrificed to idols and committing sexual immorality" (2:14, 20).

The Old Testament names "Balaam" and "Jezebel" serve to alert the church community to the insidious nature of the teaching that had until now not been recognized as evil. Since Satan's chief method is deception, his devices are not known until they are clearly pointed out. Christ exposes error here by identifying the false teachers in Pergamum with clear-cut evil such as that of Balaam and Jezebel. Balak, king of Moab, could not succeed in getting the seer Balaam to curse Israel directly. But Balaam devised a plan whereby the daughters of the Moabites would seduce the Israelite men and lead them to sacrifice to their god the Baal of Peor, and to worship him (Num. 25:1ff.; 31:16; cf. 2 Peter 2:15; Jude 11). So God's judgment fell on Israel because of fornication and idolatry. What Balak was not able to accomplish directly, he achieves through Balaam's deception. While the Ephesians recognized the Nicolaitan error (v. 6), Pergamum and Thyatira were apparently deceived by it; it was an unconscious subversion. What Satan could not accomplish at Smyrna or Pergamum through intimidation, suffering, and death from outside the church, he achieved from within.

The combination of "food sacrificed to idols" and "sexual immorality" may refer to the common practice of participating in the sacrificial meal of the pagan gods (cf. 1 Cor. 10:19–22) and indulging in sexual intercourse with temple priestesses in cult prostitution. This is the more normal way to understand the term "sexual immorality" in the context of the pagan gods. Some feel, however, that the term refers to spiritual unfaithfulness and apostasy from Christ (cf. Isa. 1:21; Ezek. 23:37). But the prevalence of sexual immorality in first-century pagan society makes it entirely possible that some Christians at Pergamum were still participating in the holiday festivities and saw no wrong in indulging at the "harmless" table in the temples and in the sexual excitement everyone else was enjoying (cf. 1 John 5:21).

The speaker's *command* includes both a call to the whole congregation to repent and a special threat to the heretical members if they do not repent (v. 16). Since those who did not indulge in these things tolerated their practice on the part of some of the church's members, they, along with the guilty, needed to repent. If those at Pergamum will not heed the word of Christ's warning, that word from His mouth will become a "sword" to fight against the disloyal. (Curiously, Balaam himself was slain by the "sword"; Num. 31:8.) The words "I will soon come to you" should be understood as a coming "against" the congregation in judgment, as in verse 5, not as a reference to Christ's second coming.

The *promise* to the overcomer includes three difficult symbols: "hidden manna," "a white stone," and "a new name" (v. 17). The "hidden manna" is reminiscent of the manna hidden in the ark of the covenant by Moses (Exod. 16:33–34; Heb. 9:4). Since this jar of manna was to remind the Israelites of God's grace and faithfulness in the wilderness (Ps. 78:24), the thought here may be similar. In apocalyptic Jewish teaching, however, the messianic era will see the restoration of the hidden wilderness manna: "And it shall come to pass at that self-same time (in the days when the Messiah comes) that the treasury of manna shall again descend from on high, and they will eat of it in those years" (2 Baruch 29:8; Sibylline Oracles 7:149). To those at Pergamum who refused the banquets of the pagan gods, Christ will give the manna of His great banquet of eternal life in the kingdom (John 6:47–58).

The "white stone" is a puzzle. It has been variously related to voting pebbles, an inscribed invitation to a banquet, a victory symbol, an amulet, or a counting pebble. It seems best to connect the stone with the manna and see it as an allusion to an invitation that entitled its bearer to attend one of the pagan banquets.

The "new name . . . known only to him who receives it" (v. 17) is either the name of Christ Himself, now hidden from the world but to be revealed in the future as the most powerful of names (3:12; 14:1), or the believer's new name or character changed through redemption (Isa. 62:2;

65:15). Pritchard cites an Egyptian text that tells of the goddess Isis plotting to learn the secret name of the supreme god Re to gain his hidden power for herself. The one who knew the hidden name received the power and status of the god who revealed it. This name was therefore jealously guarded by the god. This background would fit the context here in Revelation: to Christians tempted to compromise their loyalty to Christ to gain the favor of the pagan gods, Christ generously offers Himself and the power of His name so that those who have faith in Him may overcome.

4. To Thyatira (2:18–29)

On the inland route about forty-five miles due east of Pergamum was the city of Thyatira. Although not a great city, it was nevertheless important through its commerce in wool, linen, apparel, dyed stuffs, leatherwork, tanning, and excellent bronzework. Associated with its commerce was an extensive network of trade guilds or labor unions, that must have played a prominent role in the social, political, economic, and religious life of the city. Each guild had its own patron deity, feasts, and seasonal festivities that included sexual revelries. Religiously, the city was unimportant, although the worship of Apollo and Artemis (Diana) was prominent. Acts 16:14 mentions that Lydia, a proselyte, came from the Jewish settlement at Thyatira. She was a distributor of garments made with the purple dye known today as "Turkey red" and was no doubt a member of the dyers' guild. It has been suggested that some of Paul's converts at Ephesus went out and evangelized Thyatira (Acts 19:10).

The *speaker* of this fourth letter, the longest of the seven, identifies Himself as "the Son of God, whose eyes are like blazing fire and whose feet are like burnished bronze" (v. 18; cf. comments on 1:14–15). The expression "Son of God" appears only here in the book. It is a designation for the Messiah, almost equivalent to the more frequently used title "Son of Man," and probably anticipates the quotation from the messianic second Psalm in verse 27, which implies the term. But the name might also have captured the attention of those who were enticed by the emperor cult into calling Caesar the Son of God. Christ's eyes are here described as "blazing fire," perhaps an allusion to the sun-god, Apollo, who was worshiped at Thyatira. More likely, however, it refers to His penetrating discernment of the false prophetess Jezebel (v. 23). The feet of Christ, which are like burnished bronze, would no doubt have special significance to the bronze workers at Thyatira.

The speaker's *knowledge* of the Thyatirans' work is essentially twofold: he knows their love and their faithfulness (v. 19). Their love manifests itself in "service" and their faithfulness in "perseverance" during trial. Their present state reflects outstanding progress, but there is a perilous flaw in this church.

The speaker's *verdict* reveals that the congregation has allowed a prophetess (a false one, according to Christ's assessment) to remain in the church and to continue to teach the saints to indulge in "sexual immorality" and to "eat food sacrificed to idols" (v. 20). The genuine gift of prophecy was highly respected in the early church; prophets were often elevated to leadership along with apostles, teachers, and elders (1 Cor. 12:28; Eph. 4:11). Women also received the genuine gift of prophecy (Luke 2:36; Acts 21:9; 1 Cor. 11:5). Prophets generally brought direct revelation from God in the form of teaching as well as occasional predictions of the future (Acts 11:27).

This supposedly Christian woman at Thyatira claims to have been a "prophetess," gifted as such by the Holy Spirit. She must have been elevated to prominence in the church because of her unusual gifts. But only a small minority see through her pious deception (v. 24); the rest either follow her or ignore her views without objecting to her presence in the church. In order to expose her true character, she is labeled "Jezebel"—the name of the Canaanite wife of Israel's King Ahab. Jezebel had not only led Ahab to worship Baal but through Ahab had promulgated her teachings of idolatry throughout Israel (1 Kings 16:31–33; 2 Kings 9:22).

We must not, however, press the similarity too far. As this wicked and deceptive woman in the Old Testament led Israel astray and persecuted the true prophets of God, so this woman at Thyatira entices the servants of God to abandon their exclusive loyalty to Christ. Her teaching is no doubt similar to that of the Nicolaitans and Balaamites at Ephesus and Pergamum. While most commentators prefer to see this "sexual immorality" as spiritual adultery (i.e., idolatry), the possibility of cultic fornication should not be ruled out for reasons cited above (cf. 2:14).

Christ's *verdict* continues. His strongest accusation is not directed against Jezebel's perversion, serious as that is, nor even against her successful deception of fellow Christians, but against her refusal to repent (vv. 21–22). Although Christ has dealt with her over a period of time, she will not change her ways or her thinking. The Lord, therefore, will judge Jezebel by two swift acts. She will be "hurled" (NIV, "cast") into a bed, and her children will be put to death. The "bed" or "couch" can refer to a bed used for resting, or to the couches on which the participants at idol-feasts reclined. Others suggest a bed of sickness or suffering, seen as an act of God's visitation or judgment. On a bed she sinned, on a bed she will suffer; and those who committed adultery with her will also "suffer intensely."

As in the case of Jezebel, Christ's strongest threat to the offenders concerns not their sin but their reluctance to repent. The Lord is walking among His churches. He judges evil, but He also offers deliverance to those who have fallen, if they repent and stop doing Jezebel's deeds.

To those who follow Jezebel ("her children") and refuse to repent, a fatal judgment will be meted out by the Lord Christ: "I will strike her children dead" (v. 23; lit., "I will kill her children with death"—perhaps a Hebrew idiom denoting "pestilence"; cf. 6:8) Some understand "her children" to refer to her actual children, born of her sexual sins, rather than to her followers. This cannot be decided with certainty. Whatever the exact nature of the judgment, it is announced beforehand by Christ so that when it takes place not only Thyatira but "all the churches will know that I am he who searches hearts and minds," since they too will read the same letter and will later hear of the historical outcome. The Old Testament ascribes omniscience to God alone (Ps. 7:9; Prov. 24:12; Jer. 17:10). There is nothing in our thoughts or desires that is hidden from Christ's penetrating gaze (Heb. 4:12–13). Our only safety from judgment is in repentance. The risen Lord does not stop with searching hearts and minds but brings recompense according to deeds: for faithfulness, reward; for unfaithfulness, judgment.

Christ's only *command* to the church at Thyatira was probably meant for the minority who had sufficient insight to see through Jezebel's deception. They are simply told, "hold on to what you have" (i.e., their insight into Jezebel's teaching and evil deeds) till Christ returns (v. 25). This small group may have been nearer His standard than any other group mentioned in Revelation, because they could discriminate between authentic and spurious worship.

The reference to "Satan's so-called deep secrets" (v. 24) is ambiguous. It may refer to what the heretics believed to be the "deep things of God" (cf. 1 Cor. 2:10), i.e., the secret knowledge of God reserved only for those initiated into the heretical teaching. The words "so-called" would then be a mocking remark of John's—"the so-called deep things of God, which are in fact of Satan" (Bruce).

However, it is preferable to take the "deep secrets of Satan" as the actual phrase Jezebel used. But how could she lure Christians by using such a term? The reasoning of some in the early church (the Nicolaitans) may have gone something like this: The only effective way to confront Satan is to enter his strongholds; the real nature of sin can be learned only by experience, and therefore only those who have really experienced sin can truly appreciate grace. Thus by experiencing the depths of paganism ("the deep secrets of Satan"), one would be better equipped to serve Christ or to be an example of freedom to his brothers (cf. 1 Cor. 8:9–11). Thus the sin of Jezebel was deadly serious because of the depths of its deception. Only a few perceived where the teaching was leading.

"Until I come" (v. 25) is the first of several references to the second coming of Christ in these letters (cf. 1:7).

The *promise* to the overcomer is twofold: "authority over nations" and the gift of "the morning star" (vv. 26–28). It contains one important modification of the regular overcomer's formula. Added to the words "to him who overcomes" is "and does my will to the end" (lit., "who keeps my works until the end"). It reminds us of Jesus' statement in His great eschatological discourse that "he who stands firm to the end will be saved" (Matt. 24:13), and of Paul's words to the Colossians about continuing in the faith "established and firm" (Col. 1:23). The proof of authentic trust in Jesus is steadfastness of belief and continuance in the will of God till Christ returns or death comes.

The first promise is a fulfillment of Psalm 2, which is messianic and tells how the Father gave the Messiah the rule over the nations of the world. This psalm plays an important part in John's thinking about Christ (11:18; 12:5; 19:15). The coming reign of the Messiah over the world is to be shared with His disciples (1:6; 3:21; 20:6; 1 Cor. 6:2). In the pre-Christian apocryphal Psalms of Solomon, the same psalm is used with reference to the Messiah and the Jews who will reign with Him (17:23–24). Here in verses 26–27 its use seems to indicate that the overcomers will participate with Christ in fulfilling the promise of Psalm 2:9. There is a paradox in the combination of the mild word "rule" (lit., "to shepherd") with the harsh words "with an iron scepter; he will dash them to pieces like pottery" (cf. comments on 19:11ff.). The prospect of such a reversal of their present experience of oppression and persecution would be a constant encouragement to suffering Christians.

Second, the overcomers in Thyatira are promised "the morning star" (v. 28). Some link this expression to Christ Himself (cf. 22:16). Believers would then receive Christ as their very life. Or it may refer to the Resurrection in the sense that the morning star rises over the darkness of this world's persecution and offers victory over it. Perhaps a combination of the two thoughts is intended. The promise of Christ's return is like the "morning star" (2 Peter 1:19). (See 22:16, where Jesus calls Himself "the bright Morning Star," in apparent reference to His return.)

In this fourth letter and in the three that follow, the *general exhortation* comes at the very end (v. 29); in the first three letters it precedes the promise (cf. introduction to the seven letters).

5. To Sardis (3:1–6)

Sardis was about thirty miles south of Thyatira. Its location commanded the trade of the Aegean Islands and the military road through the important Hermus River valley. Sardis enjoyed prominence as a commercially prosperous and militarily strategic city throughout its history. The city's topography was notable for the acropolis, the temple of Artemis, and the necropolis. The acropolis rose about eight hundred feet above the north section of Sardis and was virtually impregnable because of its rock walls, which were nearly vertical, except on the south side. The acropolis, the site of the original city, became a refuge for the inhabitants in time of siege.

Only twice in the history of Sardis was this fortress ever captured, though attacks on it were frequent. When Cyrus attacked it in the sixth century B.C., a shrewd Persian soldier observed a Sardian descending the winding path on the south side to retrieve his fallen helmet. Unknown to the soldier, the Persians followed his path back up to the summit and captured the whole city, taking them by surprise. There was a similar occurrence when Antiochus attacked Sardis about two hundred years later.

The temple of Artemis (possibly Cybele), although never finished, equaled in size the famous temple of Artemis in Ephesus.

A third feature of Sardis was the impressive necropolis, or cemetery, of "a thousand hills" (modern Bin Tepe), so named because of the hundreds of burial mounds visible on the skyline some seven miles from Sardis.

Sardis retained its wealth into the first two centuries of the Christian Era, but its political brilliance as the capital city of Asia under the Persian Empire lay in the past. The luxurious living of the Sardians led to moral decadence. Herodotus (fifth century B.C.) wrote despairingly of Sardis and its people as "the tender-footed Lydians, who can only play on the cithara, strike the guitar, and sell by retail." Sardis was a city of peace, not the peace won through battle, but "the peace of the man whose dreams are dead and whose mind is asleep, the peace of lethargy and evasion." A great wool industry flourished at Sardis; this may account for Christ's reference to clothing (v. 4).

The *speaker* identifies Himself as "[he] who holds the seven spirits of God and the seven stars" (v. 1; cf. comments on 1:4 and 1:16, 20; 2:1). To the Sardians Christ reveals Himself as the One who controls the seven spirits of God. If the Sardian church is strong, it is because Christ has sent His Spirit to encourage and quicken the Sardian believers; if they are dead like the city in which they live, it is because He has withdrawn His Spirit from them in judgment. Yet the faithful minority at Sardis (v. 4) can count on the divine power of Christ to sustain, give life, and mobilize them to do His will even though the majority are dead. (On the "seven stars," cf. comments on 2:1.)

The speaker's *knowledge* of the church in Sardis reveals their true condition. He knows their "deeds." It is not clear whether this alludes to their past accomplishments, which gave them their reputation of being alive, or to their present deeds, which are not those Christ seeks from them. This latter view is supported by verse 2, where He mentions their deeds again and says that they are incomplete. He also knows that, although they claim to be a healthy Christian church, in reality they are "dead."

How does a church die? Why does Christ use this expression for Sardis, even though the churches in Thyatira and Laodicea also had serious problems? Sardis had known greatness as a royal city, but now it was nothing; its citizens were living off past fame. Apparently the same spirit had affected the church. Their loyalty and service to Christ were in the past; now they were nothing. It may be that they had so made peace with the society in which they lived that the offense of the Cross had ceased and they were no longer in jeopardy of life or vulnerable to suffering. Further facts emerge when we consider the series of commands in verses 2–3. Death was a special preoccupation of the Sardians, as witnessed by the impressive necropolis seven miles from the city. What had been a part of the pagan rites had also crept into the church. But again this work of the enemy came through deception. The Sardian church was for the most part a duped church.

The *command* "Wake up!" or "Be (constantly) watchful" is a call to reverse their attitudes radically (v. 2). The congregation must be alerted to the seriousness of the situation, which is dire but not totally hopeless. Immediate steps are to be taken to "strengthen what remains." Some persons and things are salvageable if quick and decisive action is taken. Otherwise, death will follow.

The Sardians are in danger of judgment because Christ has not found their deeds to be "complete ['full,' 'fulfilled,' 'filled up to the measure'] in the sight of my God": they do not measure up to the standard Christ sets. In the other letters, works acceptable to Christ are love, faithfulness, perseverance, keeping Christ's words, and not denying His name.

Like the church in Ephesus, the Sardians must remember what they "have received and heard" (v. 3). What they "received" was the apostolic tradition of the gospel; what they "heard" were probably the teachings of the apostles and prophets who brought the gospel to them. Unlike the church at Philadelphia (v. 8), the Sardians were not holding to the word of Christ, and repentance was the only way out of certain and final death for them. They were to repent by restoring the gospel and the apostolic doctrine to a position of authority over their lives, and by once again obeying ("keep," "watch") the truth of Christ's word. Today's church needs to hear this challenge to take the word of Christ seriously. Unless the church at Sardis repents, Christ says, He will come to them in judgment "as a thief"—i.e., by surprise, just as Sardis had been attacked and defeated by Cyrus long before. "As a thief" should probably be taken as referring not to the Second Coming but to Christ's coming against them (opposing them) in judgment (cf. His threat to the church in Ephesus in 2:5).

While the majority had departed from obedience to Christ, a few at Sardis remained true (v. 4). They had not "soiled their clothes." In Sardis, with its wool industry, those with soiled garments were removed from the public list of citizens. In the pagan religions it was forbidden to approach the gods in garments that were soiled or stained. Soiling here then appears to be a symbol for mingling with the pagan life and thus defiling the purity of one's relation to Christ (14:4; 1 Cor. 8:7; 2 Cor. 7:1; 11:2; Jude 23). To "walk with Christ" symbolizes salvation and fellowship with Him—something the others at Sardis had forfeited through their sin (1 John 1:6-7). "White" garments are symbolic of the righteousness, victory, and glory of God (3:18; 6:11; 7:9, 13f.; 19:14). This passage shows that not all faithful Christians were martyrs and that we cannot make emperor worship the sole source of the problems of the early Christians. Ironically, the Sardians were occupied with their outward appearance, but they were not concerned with inner purity toward Christ and their outward moral life in a pagan society.

The overcomer's *promise* is threefold and grows out of the reference to white clothing (v. 5).

1. "Like" the faithful Sardian Christians who will receive white clothes from Christ, the others there who overcome the stains of pagan society will similarly be dressed in white.

2. Furthermore, the pure relationship to Christ is permanently guaranteed: "I will never erase his name from the book of life." In ancient cities the names of citizens were recorded in a register till their death; then their names were erased or removed from the book of the living. This same idea appears in the Old Testament (Exod. 32:32-33; Ps. 69:28; Isa. 4:3); the idea of being recorded in God's book of the living (or the righteous) later came to mean belonging to God's eternal kingdom or possessing eternal life (Dan. 12:1; Luke 10:20; Phil. 4:3; Heb. 12:23; Rev. 13:8; 17:8; 20:15; 21:27). Christ's statement that He will never blot out or erase the overcomer's name from the book of life is the strongest affirmation that death can never separate us from Christ and His life (Rom. 8:38-39). A person enrolled in the book of life by faith remains in it by faithfulness and can be erased only by disloyalty. There is some evidence that a person's name could be removed from the city register before death if he were convicted of a crime. In the first century, Christians who were loyal to Christ were under constant threat of being branded political and social rebels and of then being stripped of their citizenship. But Christ offers them eternal, safe citizenship in His everlasting kingdom if they only remain loyal to Him.

3. Finally, to the overcomer Christ promises to "acknowledge his name before the Father and his angels." "Acknowledge" is a strong word for confession before the courts. It is Christ's confession of our name before the Father and His angels (implying our fellowship with Him) that assures our heavenly citizenship (Matt. 10:32; Luke 12:8).

What ultimately counts, then, is not our acceptance by this world's society but that our relationship to Christ is genuine and not disloyal, and hence will merit His approbation in the coming kingdom.

Again, the *general exhortation* comes last (v. 6), as in the previous letter (cf. introduction to the seven letters).

6. *To Philadelphia* (3:7–13)

About twenty-five miles southeast of Sardis, on the high plateau along the Hermus River valley, lay the important city of Philadelphia (modern Alasehir). A main highway ran through the city, connecting Smyrna (about a hundred miles due west) with northeast Asia, Phrygia, and the east. Furthermore, the imperial post road of the first century A.D., which went from Rome via Troas, Adramyttium, Pergamum, and Sardis to the east, passed through this valley and Philadelphia. So situated, Philadelphia became a strong fortress city. To the northeast was a vine-growing district, which, along with textile and leather industries, contributed greatly to the city's prosperity.

Philadelphia was established by the Pergamenian King Attalus II (159–138 B.C.), who had been given the epithet "Philadelphus" ("brother lover") because of his loyalty to his brother. The city was to be a mission city for disseminating Greco-Asiatic culture and language in the eastern part of Lydia and in Phrygia. It succeeded in part, as attested by the fact that the Lydian language ceased to be spoken in Lydia by A.D. 19 and Greek became the only language in the region. But beyond this, Philadelphia had not been successful in converting the Phrygians.

According to Strabo, the whole region was earthquake prone. In A.D. 17 a major earthquake destroyed Philadelphia, Sardis, and ten other cities. Strabo visited the city shortly afterward and found the inhabitants living in tents outside the city. Indeed, many people preferred to live in the rural area surrounding the city, while those who continued to live in the city left it at the slightest sign of a tremor.

After the devastating earthquake, Tiberius came to the peoples' aid and had the city rebuilt. In gratitude the citizens renamed it Neocaesarea ("New [city of] Caesar"). Later the name was changed to Flavia (A.D. 70–79), and this, along with Philadelphia, continued to be its name throughout the second and third centuries A.D. Later, the establishment of the emperor cult in the city earned it the title "Neokoros," or Temple Warden" (ca. 211–17). In the fifth century, it was nicknamed "Little Athens" because of its proliferation of festivals and pagan cults, but whether this indicates something of its early period is uncertain. Since wine was one of the city's important industries, some have assumed that the worship of Dionysus was prominent.

Although nothing is known about the origin of the Philadelphian church, in A.D. 100–160 the church prospered under the ministry of a prophetess named Ammia, whose prophetic gift was universally recognized as ranking with that of Agabus and of the four daughters of Philip. Long after all the surrounding country had succumbed to the Turks and come under Muslim control, Philadelphia held out as a Christian center until 1392.

The letter to the church in Philadelphia begins with the *speaker* identifying Himself as "[he] who is holy and true, who holds the key of David. What he opens, no one can shut; and what he shuts, no one can open" (v. 7). Each of these identifications calls attention to Jesus as the true Messiah. "Holy and true" relates to God Himself and describe aspects of His presence among us (cf. 6:10). Holiness is the attribute of God whereby we sense the presence of the "Wholly Other," the One who says, "I am God, and not man—the Holy One among you" (Hos. 11:9). He is the "True One" in that He is wholly trustworthy and reliable in His words and actions. These titles would encourage this congregation, for whom Christ has only commendation, to go on in their faithfulness despite their "little strength" (v. 8), in contrast to those described in verse 9.

The "key of David" alludes to Isaiah 22:20ff. Keys were normally held by the king himself, unless delegated to another. The use of the name "David" points to Christ as the Messiah, who alone determines who will participate in His kingdom and who will be turned away: "He opens, no one can shut; . . . he shuts, no one can open." This may allude to the claims of certain Jews at Philadelphia who argued that they, not the heretical Nazarenes, would inherit the kingdom of David (v. 9) and who thus excluded the followers of Jesus. But the true Messiah, Jesus, will exclude them!

Here the *knowledge* of the speaker and his *verdict* blend together in untarnished praise, as in the letter to Smyrna (v. 8). Between the declaration "I know your deeds" and the words "you have little strength, yet you have kept my word and have not denied my name" is the somewhat awkward interjection "See, I have placed before you an open door that no one can shut."

Christ, who has absolute authority from the Father, has opened a door for the Philadelphians that even their enemies cannot close. But an open door to what? Some see an allusion here to Philadelphia as a missionary city that had been effective in spreading Hellenism in the region. The statement then refers to the fact that the witness of the church in Philadelphia will be effective in spite of this opposing "gospel" of Hellenism and in spite of their small strength (1 Cor. 16:9; Col. 4:3). Others feel that verse 8 refers to Christ's opening the door to His kingdom for those who love Him and thus reinforces the statement in verse 7 about opening and shutting.

It could be argued that a parenthetical reference to the future missionary activity of the church is out of place between parts of a sentence that commend the church for its steadfastness in the past. The context therefore strongly favors the second view. The serious problem at Sardis (v. 3) was not found in Philadelphia: "You have kept my word."

They have been faithful to the gospel and the apostles' teaching even during the trial of their faith alluded to in the words "and have not denied my name" (cf. 2:13).

Those opposing the witness of the congregation are characterized as "those who are of the synagogue of Satan, who claim to be Jews though they are not, but are liars" (v. 9). The words are similar to those spoken to the church in Smyrna (cf. comments on 2:9). The "synagogue of Satan" appears to describe a Jewish element that vehemently denied Jesus as the Messiah and actively persecuted those who made this claim. In the view of Jews like John and Paul, a true Jew is one who has found forgiveness and life in Jesus the Messiah, while a false Jew is one who rejects Jesus and those who believe in Him and openly persecutes them; "such a man is the antichrist" (1 John 2:22).

But Christ will make those who have persecuted the followers of Jesus as heretics acknowledge that God is indeed with the church in Philadelphia and that they are not heretics but God's people. We catch a glimpse here of the ever-widening gap between Judaism and Christianity toward the end of the first century. The church is the true people of God, loved by Christ, and in a real sense inheritors of the covenant promises made to the people of God in the Old Testament (Isa. 43:4; 45:14; 49:23; 60:14). In these Old Testament passages it is the Gentiles, or heathen nations, who bow before Israel and acknowledge that God is with them. But in this letter Christ reverses these roles: His followers are the people of God, and Jewish unbelievers are the pagans who come and acknowledge the love of the Messiah for the church! There is, however, no indication of when or how this will happen. Some see this as a fulfillment of Paul's expectation of the conversion of "all Israel" (i.e., of the majority of the Jewish people) at some future time (Rom. 11:25–26; cf. esp. v. 28).

Against this view, however, is the fact that the context seems to point to retribution on Christ's enemies rather than their conversion. Be that as it may, underlying verse 9 is the same truth Paul expressed in Philippians 2:10–11: "At the name of Jesus every knee should bow, . . . and every tongue confess that Jesus Christ is Lord, to the glory of God the Father." Some will do this joyfully and some without repenting (cf. 6:12–17).

There is another promise given the church in Philadelphia. Though not part of the promise to the overcomers (v. 12), it, like the special promises to Smyrna and Sardis (2:10; 3:4), may be taken as a promise to all the churches. Some, including the NIV, translate the phrase "since you have kept my command to endure patiently" (lit., "kept the word of my patience"), inferring that the "word of my patience" means the command of Christ to endure suffering, or to endure till He returns (Luke 21:19; cf. Heb. 10:36). Others translate it as "the word enjoining Christ's patient endurance" (Ladd). In that case it would refer to an apostolic teaching encouraging Christians to endure the contrariness of a sinful world after the pattern of Christ's own endurance (2 Thess. 3:5; Heb. 12:3). The Greek text slightly favors the latter translation, although the former is also possible.

The promise "I will also keep you from the hour of trial that is going to come upon the whole world to test those who live on earth" presents two problems: the identification of the "hour of trial" and the precise meaning of the phrase "keep you from the hour of trial." Both problems relate directly to the ongoing debate among evangelicals concerning the Tribulation-Rapture question.[3] Because of their theological ramifications, an adequate discussion of these two problems would require more space than a small commentary allows; we will therefore limit ourselves to the following points:

a. The phrase "those who live on the earth" is repeated a number of times in Revelation and refers not to believers but to unbelievers who are the objects of God's wrath—i.e., the worshipers of the beast (6:10; 8:13; 11:10; 12:12; 13:8, 12, 14; cf. Isa. 24; Jer. 13:12–14).

b. Much confusion may be avoided by clearly identifying "the hour of trial" as the wrath of God upon unbelievers.

c. Christ promises immunity, then, not from trial or persecution in general, but from a specific type of trial (God's wrath) that is aimed at the rebellious on the earth.

d. While some interpreters feel that this immunity will be granted to the believers who are on earth during this "hour of trial," to this writer the most natural way to understand the expression "kept from" the hour of something that will be worldwide is not "to be preserved through it," but "to be kept from being present when it happens."

In any event, we have here a marvelous promise of Christ's protection for those who have protected His word by their loving obedience.[4]

Here the words of Christ "I am coming soon" (v. 11; cf. 22:7, 12, 20) are not a threat of judgment but a promise of Christ's second coming, similar to the promise the faithful Christians in Thyatira received (2:25). The testing that faced the Philadelphians was not the same as that facing the unbelieving world (v. 10). Loyal disciples must face one type of conflict, the world and those who live in it quite another. Some such conflict is envisioned when Christ says, "Hold on to what you have, so that no one will take your crown." They had kept His word and had not denied His name in the face of persecution. Either Satan or men could rob them of

---

[3]According to a number of interpreters, the "hour of trial" is a time of intense trouble, known as the eschatological "day of the Lord" or the "Great Tribulation," that will befall the world before the coming of Christ (Dan. 12:1; Joel 2:31; Mark 13:14; 2 Thess. 2:1–12; Rev. 14:7). Many of these interpreters understand the promise to the overcomers that they will be "kept from the hour" to mean that they will be removed from the earth (Rapture) before the Great Tribulation begins.

[4]For a fuller discussion of this verse and its problems, see Johnson, EBC, 12, pp. 454–6.

their "crown" (see comments on 2:10) by diverting them from exclusive loyalty to Jesus.

The *promise* to the overcomer is again twofold and relates to the past and present experience of the inhabitants of the city. First, Christ will make the overcomer a "pillar in the temple of my God" (v. 12). As stated, the city was constantly threatened by earthquakes. Often the only parts of a city left standing after a severe quake were the huge stone temple columns. Christ promises to set believers in His temple (the future kingdom?) in such a secure position that no disturbance can ever force them out.

Moreover, a faithful municipal servant or a distinguished priest was sometimes honored by having a special pillar, inscribed with his name, added to one of the temples. This may well be the sense of the second promise, "I will write on him the name of my God and the name of the city of my God, the New Jerusalem, . . . and . . . my new name." The inscribed name then signifies identification, ownership, and recognition. To those who have "little strength" (little influence) because of being ostracized, Christ promises recognition in His kingdom worthy of the most noble hero of any society.

Remembering how in days past the name of their city was changed twice (see introduction to this letter), the Philadelphians would be impressed that God Himself (not the emperor) had chosen to identify Himself with them and to insure their citizenship in the New Jerusalem (cf. 21:2ff.; Ezek. 48:35). Christ's "new name" could be either the unknown name that He alone knows, signifying His absolute power over all other powers (19:12), or the new name of Christ given to the believer, reflecting Christ's ownership through redemption (Isa. 62:2; 65:15).

The *general exhortation* follows the promise (v. 13). (See introduction to the seven letters.)

7. *To Laodicea* (3:14–22)

Laodicea was about forty-five miles southeast of Philadelphia and about one hundred miles due east of Ephesus. Along with Colosse and Hierapolis, it was one of the cities in the fertile Lycus valley. The great Roman road stretching from the coast at Ephesus to the inland of Asia ran straight through its center, making Laodicea an important center of trade and communication. In addition, its wealth came from the production of a fine quality of famous glossy black wool—whether dyed or natural in color is not known. The city's banking assets were considerable, as evidenced by the fact that Cicero cashed huge bank drafts in Laodicea. So wealthy was Laodicea that after the great earthquake of A.D. 17, which destroyed it, the people refused imperial help in rebuilding the city, choosing rather to do it entirely by themselves.

Laodicea had a famous school of medicine; and a special ointment for

the cure of eye defects, known as "Phrygian powder," was either manufactured or distributed here, as were ear ointments. Near the temple of
the god associated with healing. Men Karou (later identified with
Asclepius), was a market for trading all sorts of goods. Zeus, the supreme
god, was also worshiped in the city.

Ramsay notes that Laodicea is difficult to describe because no one thing
stands out. There were no excesses or notable achievements to distinguish it. It was a city of bankers and finance, which had learned to compromise and accommodate itself to the needs and wishes of others. The
Laodiceans did not zealously stand for anything.

A six-mile-long aqueduct brought Laodicea its supply of water from the
south. The water came either from hot springs and was cooled to
lukewarm or came from a cooler source and warmed up in the aqueduct
on the way. For all its wealth, the city had poor water. A large and
influential Jewish population resided there. The church in Laodicea may
have been founded by Epaphras (Col. 4:12–13).

The *speaker* identifies himself by means of a threefold affirmation: "The
Amen, the faithful and true witness, the ruler of God's creation" (v. 14).
The Hebrew word behind the Greek *amēn* means the acknowledgement
of that which is sure and valid. It is a word of human response to divine
truth or action. Jesus is the "Amen" in the sense that He is the perfect
human response to the divine promises (cf. Isa. 65:16). Jesus' response to
God's will was the perfect response of obedience and suffering; He is
therefore the "faithful and true witness" (cf. comments on 1:5, 9; 2:13).
The same thought is expressed by Paul in 2 Corinthians 1:20: "For no
matter how many promises God has made, they are 'Yes' in Christ. And so
through him the 'Amen' is spoken by us to the glory of God." In one
sense, all Christians are called to be "little amens" after the example of
Christ.

"Ruler" ("source," "origin") further amplifies the "Amen." Paul uses
the same word in Colossians 1:18 to describe Christ as the source or origin
of all creation (not the first created; cf. Prov. 8:22; John 1:3), no doubt to
correct a heresy. Since Colosse was a neighboring city of Laodicea, it is
not improbable that the same heresy was also affecting the church at
Laodicea. When Christ addresses a church that is failing in loyalty and
obedience, He is to them the "Amen" of God in faithfulness and in true
witness, the only One who has absolute power over the world because He
is the source and origin of all creation (1:17; 2:8; 22:13).

Sadly, the speaker's *knowledge* reveals an unqualified condemnation of
the Laodicean church (vv. 15–16). The *verdict* is the opposite of the
church's self-perception and expectations. Their deeds were "neither cold
nor hot" (v. 15). The expression "cold nor hot" may refer to their lack of
zeal (v. 19) or to their uselessness, for Christ says, "I wish you were either
one or the other" (lit., "either cold or hot"). There is good reason why we

should not try to take this phrase to mean that Christ wishes that they were either spiritually cold (i.e., unsaved or hostile) or spiritually hot (i.e., alive and fervent). In the first place, it is inconceivable that Christ would want people to be spiritually cold, or unsaved and hostile. Furthermore, the metaphor of "hot" and "cold" to indicate "spiritual temperature," though familiar to us, would have been completely foreign to first-century Christians. The two adjectives in "neither hot nor cold" should be understood together as equivalent to "lukewarm" (v. 16). That is to say, they were useless to Christ because they were complacent, self-satisfied, and indifferent to the real issues of faith in Him and of discipleship.

Since the city of Hierapolis, seven miles north of Laodicea, had famous hot springs, it may be that similar springs were located south of Laodicea and affected the temperature of the water supply. "I am about to spit ['vomit'] you out of my mouth" seems to allude to the lukewarm water. "Cold" could refer to the useful cool water located at Colosse, less than ten miles away. "Hot" would remind the Laodiceans of the beneficial hot springs at Hierapolis. Yet Laodicea, for all its wealth, had an insipid water supply—one that induced vomiting! Christ detests a Laodicean attitude of compromise, one that seeks easy accommodation and peace at any cost. With such a condition He must deal harshly. To be a Christian means to be useful to Christ.

The deeper problem in the Laodicean church was not simply their indifference. It was their ignorance of their real condition: "You say, 'I am rich; I have acquired wealth and do not need a thing'" (v. 17). Observe the way this indictment is related to the general condition of the populace at large—rich in material possessions and self-sufficient. The spirit of the surrounding culture had crept into the congregation and had paralyzed their spiritual life. But did they claim to be materially rich or spiritually rich? Since it is difficult to see how a Christian community would boast of material wealth, many prefer the latter interpretation. Yet the Laodiceans may have interpreted their material wealth as a blessing from God and thus have been deceived as to their true spiritual state. In any case, they had misread their true condition.

Christ's revelation of the Laodiceans' actual state shatters their illusions and calls them to repentance. "But you do not realize that you are wretched, pitiful, poor, blind and naked" (v. 17). The first two characteristics—"wretched" and "pitiful"—should probably be linked together, while the latter three explain this twofold condition in more detail (cf. v. 18). They are not, as they thought, rich and without need; they are pitifully wretched and in great need, being "poor, blind and naked." (Conversely, Jesus said to the church at Smyrna, "I know. . . . your poverty—yet you are rich!" 2:9.) "Lukewarmness," then, may not refer to the laxity of Christians but rather to the condition of not really knowing

Christ as Savior and Lord and thus being useless to Him. The early church father Origen (d. 254) likewise understood the passage to refer not to lapsed Christians but to the unregenerate.

The *commands* of Christ correspond exactly to the self-deceptions of the Laodiceans. Gold, a source of the city's wealth, was to be bought from Christ and to become the true wealth of the spiritually poverty-stricken Laodiceans. Their shameful nakedness was to be clothed, not by purchasing the sleek, black wool of Laodicea, but by buying from Christ the white clothing that alone can cover shameful nakedness (16:15). For those who were blind to their true condition, the "Phrygian powder" was useless (cf. introductory comments). They needed to buy salve from Christ so that they could truly see. The reference to buying would recall the famous market near the temple of Men Karou, where the commodities manufactured at Laodicea could be bought, along with imports from other areas. But to what do gold, white clothes, and salve symbolically refer? Minear suggests the following:

> The only cure for poverty-stricken disciples was to purchase from Christ gold which is refined in the agonies of the shared passion. For their nakedness (did Hans Christian Anderson find here the theme of "The Emperor's New Clothes"?) the only recourse was to buy such clothes as the naked Christ had worn on the cross. The blindness of self-deception could be cured only by understanding the correlation between Christ's love and his discipline. These three purchases constitute a substantial definition of the kind of zeal and repentance which was the burden of all John's prophecies. The thrust of these commands moves in the direction of rigorous warning. They are tantamount to saying "Open your eyes" and "Carry your cross." This letter argues against the widespread assertion of many interpreters to the effect that John's chief concern was to provide consolation to a persecuted church. Nearer the mark would be the opposite assertion; that John, like Jesus, was concerned to bring not peace but a sword.

The three figures all point to the Laodiceans' need of authentic salvation through Christ.

Even though the state of a church such as that in Laodicea verges on disaster, all is not lost if there are those in it who will receive Christ's loving rebuke and come back to Him (v. 19). Christ's statement "I rebuke and discipline" speaks of His love (Prov. 3:12; 1 Cor. 11:32; Heb. 12:6): He "spits" out those He does not love and "rebukes" ("reproves," "convicts") and disciplines those who hear His voice. The difference between the expelled and the disciplined lies in their response: "So be earnest ['zealous,' 'enthusiastic'] and repent." The Laodiceans' repentance would come from a rekindling of their loyalty to Christ.

To those who hear the words of rebuke, Christ extends an invitation to dine with Him (v. 20). Some older commentators see in the "door" a reference to the new age that will dawn at the advent of Christ (cf. Matt. 24:33; James 5:9); the challenge then is to be ready to enter the banquet of

Christ at His return. This view, however, does not seem to fit the immediate context, nor does it agree with other New Testament teaching on the Lord's return.

Others hold that the figure represents Christ standing at the door to the hearts of the members of the congregation at Laodicea. Christ will come and have fellowship with anyone who hears His voice of rebuke and thus proves himself Christ's friend by zeal and repentance. "Eating" refers to the main meal of the day, which in the Orient is an occasion for having intimate fellowship with the closest of friends. It is through the Holy Spirit that Christ and the Father come to have fellowship with us (John 14:23).

While most commentators have taken this invitation as addressed to lapsed, half-hearted Christians, the terminology and context (v. 18) suggest that these Laodiceans were for the most part mere professing Christians who lacked the essential prerequisite for true discipleship, authentic conversion to Christ. Verse 20 is therefore more evangelistic than admonitory.

The *promise* to the overcomer concerns the sharing in Christ's future reign in the eschatological kingdom: "I will give [him] the right to sit with me on my throne" (v. 21). Such a joint reign with Christ has already been referred to earlier (1:6, 9; 2:26–27) and also appears later on (5:10; 20:4–6). The kingdom reign is also a theme in other New Testament writings (Luke 22:28–30; Rom. 8:17; 2 Tim. 2:12). As Christ overcame through His suffering and death (John 16:33) and entered into the highest honor God could bestow, that of being seated at His "right hand" of sovereignty (Mark 16:19; Acts 2:22ff.; Rev. 22:1), so believers who suffer with Christ even to the point of death will share in the honor of Christ's exalted position. The distinction between the Father's throne and Christ's throne is no mere rhetoric. On the contrary, it differentiates two aspects of God's program in history (1 Cor. 15:24–28). Christ is reigning now, for there is a sense in which the eschatological or messianic kingdom of God was inaugurated with Christ's earthly ministry, death, and resurrection. But the promise here, as elsewhere in the New Testament, foresees a final earthly consummation of the kingdom that awaits the return of Christ.

The *general exhortation* (v. 22) closes the seventh letter (cf. introduction to the seven letters).

For Further Study

1. Construct a chart of the seven churches that compares each church listed vertically at the left with each of the seven features of the messages listed horizontally (e.g., addressee, addressor's description, speaker's knowledge, etc.).

2. Look up the cities where the seven churches are found in a good Bible dictionary and find as many allusions to each city's history and character in the seven letters as seems warranted. What can be inferred from these close relationships?

3. Summarize the false teaching and practices referred to in the various messages to the churches.

4. Which churches seem to parallel most closely the overall emphasis of the evangelical church in America? Local churches with which you are familiar? Why?

5. Summarize the teaching in the seven messages concerning authentic Christian discipleship. What kinds of things in our lives please Christ?

6. Identify as many clearly symbolic elements in the letters as you can. Does this give you any clue to the author's way of communicating? Can you see possible connections with images and themes later in the book?

7. With the help of a good Bible dictionary, study "Gnosticism" and "Cult prostitution."

VISION TWO: *The Seven-Sealed Scroll, the Seven Trumpets, and the Seven Bowls*

Chapter 4

The Seven-Sealed Scroll
(Revelation 4:1–8:1)

In view of the elaborate use of imagery and visions from 4:1 through the end of Revelation and the question how this material relates to chapters 1–3, it is not surprising that commentators differ widely in their treatment of these chapters. One problem is that of interpretation: *What* do the imagery and visions mean? Another problem involves chronology: *When* do these things take place? Furthermore, does John interpret his frequent Old Testament images in exact accordance with their Old Testament sources, or does he freely reinterpret these images? What is symbolic and what is literal? Answers to such questions will determine the interpreter's approach. Since few of these questions are capable of dogmatic answers, there is a need for tolerance of divergent approaches in the hope that the Spirit may use open-minded discussion to lead us further into the meaning of the Apocalypse.

A. The Throne, the Scroll, and the Lamb (4:1–5:14)

Chapters 4–5 form one vision consisting of two parts: the throne (ch. 4) and the Lamb and the scroll (ch. 5). Actually, the throne vision (chs. 4–5) and the breaking of all seven seals (chs. 6–8:1) form a single, continuous vision and should not be separated; indeed, the throne vision (chs. 4–5) should be viewed as dominating the entire vision of the seven-sealed scroll (4:1–8:1), and, for that matter, the rest of the book (cf. 14:1; 22:3).

1. *The throne* (4:1–11)

Seeing a "door standing open in heaven," John is told, "come up here" (cf. Ezek. 1:1, where the prophet says he saw the heavens opened). A new view of God's majesty and power (throne) is disclosed to John so that he can understand the events on earth that relate to the seven-sealed vision (cf. 1 Kings 22:19). For the first time in Revelation, the reader is introduced to the frequent interchange between heaven and earth found in the remainder of the book. What happens on earth has its inseparable heavenly counterpart.

Chapter 4 focuses on the throne vision that provides the setting for the dramatic action of the slain Lamb in chapter 5. There is a connection between this throne vision and the vision of the glorified Christ in 1:10–16. Here we are told that John heard the same voice speaking to him that he "had first heard speaking . . . like a trumpet" (cf. 1:10). The words of the messenger relate to what has just transpired: "I will show you what must take place after this" ("next", i.e., after the time of the historical churches in Asia, or after the first vision; see comments on 1:19).

There is no good reason for seeing the invitation to John to come up into the opened heaven as a symbol of the rapture of the church. Some have so interpreted it and have inferred that the absence of the word "church" in Revelation 4:1–22:15 and the continued references to the "saints" indicate that at this point the church departs from the earth. But "church" or "churches" in Revelation always stands for the historic seven churches in Asia and not for the universal body of Christ. Since 4:1–22:15 concerns the believing community as a whole, it would be inconsistent with John's usage to find the narrower term "church" in this section (cf. 3 John 6, 9–10).

Finally, it is significant that the visions that continue to the end of the book contain references to the throne, the book, the crowns, the four living creatures, the twenty-four elders, and the victory of the Lamb. In all this, the center of focus appears to be the five hymns of praise that begin in 4:8 and continue through chapter 5.

Chapter 4 is above all a vision of the royal throne of God. The prophet ascends "in the Spirit" to see the source of all that will happen on earth (v. 2; cf. 1:10). The events that will take place will all be an expression of the throne's purpose—nothing happens, nothing exists in the past, present, or future apart from God's intention. Whatever authority is given to an angel or to a horseman is given by God. The throne symbolizes God's majesty and power. Yet His majestic transcendence is fully safe-guarded—John does not attempt to describe the "someone sitting on" the throne (cf. 1 Kings 22:19; 2 Chron. 18:18; Ps. 47:8; Isa. 6:1ff.; Ezek. 1:26–28).

The minerals "jasper" and "carnelian" portray the supernatural splen-dor of God, while the "rainbow, resembling an emerald" conveys the impression of God's encircling brilliance (cf. Ezek. 1:27–28). But we need not find symbolism in each element of the vision; it is enough to allow the archetypical imagery to create the impression of transcendent glory. Whether John intends God's judgment to be part of the symbolism of the throne vision (cf. Ps. 9:4, 7) is not clear. What is unmistakably clear is that all—whether elders, angels, lamps, seas of glass, or living creatures—centers on the throne and the One who sits on it, "who lives for ever and ever" (v. 9).

John also sees "twenty-four elders" (v. 4). It would be helpful if we could ask an interpreting angel, "Who are the elders?" There are at least thirteen different views of their identity, ranging from the twenty-four ruling stars (or judges) in the heavens to the simple figure of wholeness and fullness. The following passages are pertinent to the elders' identification: 4:9–11; 5:5–14; 7:11–17; 11:16–18; 12:10–12; 14:3; 19:4.

The elders are always associated with the "four living creatures" (4:6ff.) and engage in acts of worship of God and the Lamb. While not entirely ruling out the elders' possible representative or symbolic significance (a view held by many good expositors), the view that the elders are a class of heavenly spirit beings belonging to the general class of angels and living creatures seems more compelling. From this viewpoint, the "angels," the "twenty-four elders," and "the four living creatures" all designate actual supernatural beings involved with the purpose of God on earth and His worship in heaven. They are always distinguished from the "saints" (5:8; 11:17–18; 19:1–4).[1]

In the Bible "twelve" appears to be the number of divine government—twelve months in the lunar year, twelve tribes of Israel, twelve apostles, twelve gates in the New Jerusalem, twelve angels at each gate, twelve foundations, twelve thousand sealed from each tribe, twelve thousand stadia (the length, width, and height of the New Jerusalem), etc. Multiples of twelve—such as twenty-four, etc.—probably have a similar significance. Thrones are related to the heavenly powers in Colossians 1:16. In Revelation, "white" clothing generally belongs to the saints, but it relates to angelic beings elsewhere in the New Testament (e.g., John 20:12). While the "crowns of gold" are likewise usually related to the redeemed, here they refer to the royal dignity of those so closely associated with the throne of God (cf. 1 Kings 22:19; Ps. 89:7). Golden crowns are referred to in 4:4, 10; 9:7; 14:14.

"Flashes of lightning, rumblings and peals of thunder" (v. 5) coming from the throne are symbolic of God's awesome presence and the vindication of the saints; they occur with slight variation four times in Revelation (4:5; 8:5; 11:19; 16:18; cf. Exod. 19:16; Ezek. 1:13; Ps. 18:13–15). On the expression "seven blazing lamps," see comments on 1:4 (cf. Ezek. 1:13).

"A sea of glass, clear as crystal" simply adds to the magnificence of the scene (15:2). Caird considers the "sea of glass" identical to the "sea" in Revelation 13:1 and 21:1 and identifies it as "a reservoir of evil". But a sea "of glass" may be an intentional inversion of this sea imagery (cf. Exod. 24:10; Ezek. 1:22, 26). The mirrorlike reflecting quality could symbolize the fact that before the sight of God all is revealed: "Everything is uncovered and laid bare before the eyes of him to whom we must give account" (Heb. 4:13).

---

[1]The discussion concerning the identity of the twenty-four elders hinges in part on the question of the correct text of 5:10. See footnote on p. 77.

The "four living creatures" should be linked with Isaiah's seraphim and Ezekiel's cherubim (cf. Isa. 6:3; Ezek. 1:5–25; 10:1–22). They, like the elders and angels, are heavenly creatures of the highest order, involved with the worship of God and His government. "Covered with eyes" may give the impression of their exceeding knowledge of God, while the faces of a "lion," "ox," "man," and a "flying eagle" suggest qualities that belong to God, such as royal power, strength, spirituality, and swiftness of action. Each of the creatures mentioned is the chief of its class. Together they embody the reflection of God's nature as the fullness of life and power. Their six wings (cf. Isa. 6:2) give the impression of unlimited mobility in fulfilling God's commands. Their position "in the center, around the throne" suggests that one is before, one behind, and one on either side of the throne (Beckwith). The four living creatures appear throughout Revelation (cf. 5:6, 8, 14; 6:1ff.; 7:11; 14:3; 15:7; 19:4).

The four living creatures ceaselessly proclaim the holiness of God in hymnic fashion: "Holy, holy, holy" (v. 8; Isa. 6:3). In Hebrew, the repetition of a word adds emphasis, while the rare double repetition designates the superlative and here thus calls attention to the infinite holiness of God—the quality of God felt by creatures in His presence as awesomeness or fearfulness (Ps. 111:9: "Holy and awesome is his name"). The living creatures celebrate God's holiness and power as manifested in His past, present, and future activity. Such holiness cannot tolerate the presence of evil (21:27). (On these titles of God, see comments on 1:4, 8.) The trisagion ("Holy, holy, holy") is used as a liturgical expression in both ancient Jewish and Christian worship. Its Christian liturgical use does not, however, reach back to the first century.

This hymn is the first, not only of the five sung by the heavenly choirs in chapters 4–5, but also of a number of others in Revelation (4:8, 11; 5:9–10, 12, 13; 7:12, 15–17; 11:15, 17–18; 12:10–12; 15:3–4; 16:5–7; 18:2–8; 19:2–6). These hymns are very important: they relate to the interpretation of the visions and provide a clue to the literary structure of Revelation. The first two hymns are addressed to God, the next two to the Lamb, and the last one to both. There is also a gradual increase in the size of the choirs: the last hymn is sung by "every creature in heaven and on earth and under the earth" to "him who sits on the throne and to the Lamb" (5:13).

The second hymn praises God for His creation and is sung by the twenty-four elders (vv. 9–11). When the living creatures confess the truth of God's holy deeds, the response of this highest order of God's heavenly creatures is to relinquish their crowns of honor before the feet of Him who alone is "worthy" of "glory and honor and power," because He alone (no man, not even the emperor) is the source and stay of every created thing (Pss. 33:6–9; 102:25; 136:5ff.).

The expression "by your will they were created and have their being"

(v. 11) presents a translation difficulty because the Greek text has two different tenses ("they were" [NIV, "having their being"], imperfect; "they were created," aorist). Although a number of possible explanations have been advanced, Alford's remains the best: the imperfect tense describes the *fact* of their existence, while the aorist captures the sense of the *beginning* of their existence. Consequently, the phrase might be translated thus: "Because of [not 'by'] your will they continually exist and have come into being."

2. The scroll and the Lamb (5:1–14)

This chapter is part of the vision that begins with chapter 4 and continues through the opening of the seven seals (6:1–8; cf. introduction to ch. 4). Its center of gravity lies in the three hymns addressed to the Lamb (vv. 9, 12, 13). They beautifully combine the worship of the Lamb (hymns one and two) with the worship of the One who sits on the throne (hymn three, which is addressed to both God and the Lamb). The movement of the whole scene focuses on the slain Lamb as He takes the scroll from the hand of the One on the throne. The actions of all other participants are described in terms of worship directed to the Lamb and the One on the throne. The culminating emphasis is on the worthiness of the Lamb to receive worship because of His death.

a) The seven-sealed scroll (5:1–4)

John sees "in the right hand of him who sat on the throne a scroll with writing on both sides and sealed with seven seals" (v. 1). Papyrus codices (which were like books as we know them) did not originate until the second century A.D., or perhaps the late first century. In ancient times, papyrus rolls were used for public and private documents. Usually the writing, arranged in vertical columns, was on one side only—the inside. Occasionally both sides of a scroll were used; in that case it was called an "opisthograph." Such double-sided writing was for private use, in contrast to the usual scrolls with writing on only one side, which were sold. The importance of establishing the scroll rather than codex character of the document lies in the interpretation of the opening of the seals. If the book was a codex, the seals could have been opened and portions of the book disclosed one at a time; a scroll, however, could be opened only after *all* the seals were broken.

Scrolls, or folded sheets, were sealed with blobs of wax impressed with a signet ring to protect the contents or guarantee the integrity of the writing. Only the owner could open the seals and disclose the contents. Original documents were usually sealed; copies were not. Sealed documents were kept hidden while unsealed copies were made public (Rev. 22:10).

As to the identity and significance of the scroll, there are a number of different views.

1. Ancient Roman wills or "testaments" were sealed with six seals, each of which bore a different name of the sealer and could only be opened by him. This has led some to identify the scroll as the testament of God concerning the promise of the inheritance of his future kingdom.

2. Others see the scroll as containing, like Ezekiel's scroll, "words of lament and mourning and woe" (Ezek. 2:9–10) and depicting the future judgment of the world.

3. Still others find the significance to be the progressive unfolding of the history of the world. As each successive seal is opened, the further contents of the book are revealed.

4. Some connect the scroll with a "title-deed" (Jer. 32:10–14). It is the "title-deed" to creation that was forfeited by sin in Genesis. By His redeeming death Christ has won the authority to reclaim the earth.

Each of these views has merit and may provide elements of truth for the background of the striking imagery in these chapters. Yet each view is vulnerable to criticism. Only from Revelation itself can the content and nature of the scroll be determined. Since the seals hinder the opening of the scroll until all are broken, we may assume that the seals are preparatory to the opening of the scroll and the disclosure of its contents (cf. Isa. 29:11).

The following internal evidence relating to the contents of the scroll may be noted:

1. Just prior to the opening of the seventh seal, we read in connection with the events under the sixth seal, "For the great day of their [i.e., of the One sitting on the throne and the Lamb] wrath has come, and who can stand?" (6:17).

2. When the seventh seal is opened (8:1–5), no immediate events as such follow on earth—except for an earthquake—as in the first six seals, unless the opening of the seventh seal includes the blowing of the seven trumpets of judgment (8:6–11:15). This appears to be precisely the case.

3. The seventh trumpet likewise is not immediately followed by any specific events on earth (11:15ff.), except for an earthquake and a hailstorm (11:19). However, just before the seventh trumpet is sounded, we read, "The second woe has passed; the third woe is coming soon" (11:14). When the seven angels prepare to pour out "the seven last plagues," symbolized by the bowls, we read that with these bowls "God's wrath is completed" (15:1, 7). Thus it seems reasonable to identify the content of the seventh trumpet with the seven bowls of judgment (chs. 16–19).

4. Furthermore, frequent references to the events of the seals, trumpets, and bowls appear throughout the remaining visions in Revelation (cf. 19:19ff.; 20:4; 21:9), indicating that the contents of the seven-sealed

scroll ultimately include the unfolding of the consummation of the mystery of all things, the goal or end of all history, for both the overcomers and the worshipers of the beast. In 10:7 we are told that in the days of the sounding of the seventh trumpet "the mystery of God will be accomplished, just as he announced to his servants the prophets." From this it may be concluded that the scroll contains "the mystery of God" that the Old Testament prophets foretold (cf. comments on 10:7); the "seals" conceal this mystery, which only Christ can disclose (Dan. 12:9; Rev. 10:4), of how God's judgment and His kingdom will come. In 11:15, when the final trumpet sounds, heavenly voices say, "The kingdom of the world has become the kingdom of our Lord and of his Christ," indicating that the scroll also contains the announcement of the inheritance of Christ and of the saints who will reign with Him (5:10).

The scroll, then, is not only about judgment or about the inheritance of the kingdom. Rather, it contains the announcement of the consummation of all history—how things will ultimately end for all people: judgment for the world and the final reward for the saints (11:18). Christ alone, as the Messiah, is the executor of the purposes of God and the Heir of the inheritance of the world. He obtained this by His substitutionary and propitiatory death on the cross (5:9).

A mighty angel shouts out a challenge for anyone to come forth who is "worthy" to open the great scroll and its seals. All creation in heaven and on earth and under the earth stands motionless and speechless. No one is worthy to open the scroll, i.e., no one has the authority and virtue for such a task (vv. 2–4). If the scroll contains both the revelation and the implementation of the final drama of history, then John's despair can be appreciated. In this vision, the execution of events on earth is ascribed to the Lamb. As the seals are broken and the roll opened, salvation history unfolds until history culminates in the kingdom reign of the Messiah over the whole earth. History, then, has its center in Jesus Christ and its goal in His triumphant reign over all the powers of the world.

b) *The messianic King-Lamb* (5:5–7)

John's sorrow is assuaged. One of the elders announces that there is One who has "triumphed" ("overcome," "conquer," "win a victory"—the same word as in 2:7; 3:21; et al.). He has triumphed because of His death (v. 9). Two titles are used of the One who is worthy—"the Lion of the tribe of Judah" and "the Root of David." Both are familiar Old Testament messianic titles (Gen. 49:9–10; cf. Isa. 11:1, 10; Jer. 23:5; 33:5; Rev. 22:16), but they are linked together only here and in the Qumran literature. In Jewish apocalyptic literature contemporary with John, the figure of a lion was used to designate the conquering Messiah who would destroy Rome (4 Ezra 11:58).

As John looks to see the mighty Lion (the conquering warrior-Messiah from the Root of David) he sees instead the striking figure of a "Lamb" ("a

young sheep") as if it had been slaughtered, standing in the center of the
throne court (v. 6). This new image portrays sacrificial death and links the
Messiah to the Old Testament passover lamb (Exod. 12:5f.; Isa. 53:7; John
1:29, and 36; Acts 8:32; 1 Peter 1:19). Here John joins the Old Testament
royal Davidic Messiah and the Suffering Servant of Isaiah (Isa. 42–53).
Both prophetic themes come together in Jesus of Nazareth, the true
Messiah. "As if it had been slain" ("with its throat cut") could refer to the
"marks of death" the living Lamb still bore or to His appearance "as if
being led to the slaughter," i.e., "marked out for death." The "lamb"
metaphor dominates John's thought in the rest of the book (e.g., 6:1ff.;
7:9ff.; 12:11; 13:8; 21:9).

The "eyes" are more explicitly identified as the "seven spirits of God
sent out into all the earth," probably a symbolic reference to the divine
Holy Spirit who is sent forth by Christ into the world (1:4; 4:5). The
teaching of the fourth gospel is similar: the Spirit is sent forth to exalt
Christ and to convict the world of sin (John 14:26; 15:26; 16:7–15).

Next the Lamb acts: "He came and took the scroll" (v. 7). The Greek
conveys a dramatic action in the tense of the verb "took": "He went up
and took it, and now he has it!" Symbolically, the One on the throne thus
authorizes the slain messianic King to execute His plan for the redemption of the world, because in and through the Lamb, God is at work in
history for the salvation of humanity. Observe that this dramatic act of
seizing the scroll is not itself the act of victory referred to in verse 6 and
later in verse 9. Christ's victorious death on the cross is the basis of His
authority to redeem the world and to take and open the seven-sealed
scroll.

c) Three hymns of redemption (5:8–14)

The Lamb's act calls forth three hymns of praise (vv. 9, 12, 13) from the
living creatures and elders. John sees them fall down in worship before
the Lamb as they had earlier done before the One on the throne (4:10),
thus acknowledging the deity of the Lamb. They have "harps," which are
the "lyres" used for the older psalmody (cf. e.g., Pss. 32:3; 98:5) but will
now be used for the "new song" of praise to the Lamb (v. 9; 15:2–3).

The "bowls full of incense" represent the "prayers of the saints"
(8:3–4). Prayer in this scene is not praise but petition. Why would John
mention the saints on earth as petitioning God? In 6:10 the martyrs are
seen as calling to God for His judgment on those who killed them, and in
8:3–4 the prayers of the saints are immediately connected with the trumpets of God's judgment. These prayers, then, are evidently for God's
vindication of the martyred saints. And since verse 10 refers to the coming
kingdom, it may be that the prayers are petitions to God to judge the
world and to extend His kingdom throughout the earth (Luke 18:7–8).
"Saints" here, as elsewhere in the New Testament and the rest of Revela-

tion, is the normal term for the rank and file of Christians, i.e., those set apart for God's purposes (2 Cor. 1:1; Phil. 1:1; Rev. 11:18; 13:7, 19; 19:8; 22:21).

The three hymns interpret the symbolism of the scroll and the Lamb. The number of singers increases from twenty-eight in verse 8 to every creature in all creation in verse 13. The first two hymns are songs of praise to the Lamb, whereas the last is praise to both the One on the throne and the Lamb (v. 13). The first hymn (vv. 9–10) is called a "new" song because there was never any like it before in heaven (cf. comments on 14:3).

"You are worthy" ("comparable," "equal to," "deserving") refers to the qualifications of this person who alone has won the right to take the scroll and open its seals (v. 9). His worthiness for this task was won by His loving sacrifice on the cross—"because you were slain." This must be understood as a direct reference to the earthly death of the human Jesus of Nazareth. It is no mythological death or salvation. Like other New Testament writers, John views the death of Jesus as a redeeming death—"and with your blood [or 'by the price of your blood'] you purchased [or 'redeemed'] men for God."

The death of Jesus broke the stranglehold of the "powers and authorities" over the creation and produced a great victory liberating mankind (Col. 2:15). It is this victory, obtained through suffering and death, that entitles Christ to execute the unfolding of the mystery of God's consummation of history. The centrality of the Cross and its meaning as a redemptive act come repeatedly to the fore and should dominate throughout our understanding of Revelation (1:5; 5:12; 7:14; 12:11; 13:8; 14:4; 15:3; 19:7; 21:9, 23; 22:3, et al.). Jesus' death secured a salvation universally available to all classes and peoples of the earth—"every tribe and language and people and nation" (cf. 7:9).

The Lamb's right to open the scroll rests also on the fact that He has made the ransomed into a "kingdom" and made them "priests" (to serve God in praise; v. 10; cf. Heb. 13:15–16). Christians "will reign on the earth" with Christ because they have been given "kingly authority" through His death (1:6; 20:4–6). While not excluding the present reign of believers, the reference to "the earth" is best taken to refer to the future eschatological kingdom reign of Christ.[2]

Now John sees a new feature in the vision: "thousands upon thousands, and ten thousand times ten thousand" angels surrounding the throne (vv. 11–12). The vision is similar to Daniel's vision of the countless multitude before the Ancient of Days (Dan. 7:10). The imagery suggests the infinite

---

[2]Verses 9–10 contain two alternate ancient textual traditions. Some texts read ". . . you purchased us" (v. 9) and ". . . you made us to be a kingdom" (v. 10). Other manuscripts omit the "us" from both v. 9 and v. 10 and read "You purchased men for God" (v. 9) and ". . . you made them to be a kingdom" (v. 10). It is a difficult question to settle with certainty, but this commentary follows the shorter texts and views the elders as angels. See Johnson, EBC, 12, p. 470

honor and power of the One who is at the center of it all. The angels shout their song of praise to the Lamb who was slain (cf. Heb. 1:6). Their sevenfold shout rings out like the sound from a huge bell—"power . . . wealth . . . wisdom . . . strength . . . honor . . . glory . . . praise [lit. "blessing"]." All these are intrinsic qualities of Christ except the last, which is the expression of the creatures' worship. Elsewhere the same qualities are ascribed to God Himself (5:13; 7:12). The sevenfold accumulation of these attributes by angel choirs is a Qumran liturgical method for creating the feeling of God's majesty and glory (7:12; 4QSL).

Finally, far beyond the precincts of the throne, an expression of praise and worth arises from the whole created universe to the One on the throne and to the Lamb (vv. 13–14). John beautifully blends the worship of the Father (ch. 4) and the worship of the Son (5:8–12) together. In appropriate response, the living beings utter their "Amen" (cf. comments on 3:14), and the elders fall down in worship.

B. Opening of the First Six Seals (6:1–17)

The opening of the seals continues the vision begun in chapters 4 and 5. Now the scene shifts to events on earth. Before the exposition of each of the seals, it will be helpful to consider their overall meaning. As we have already seen (cf. comments on 5:1), the scroll itself involves the rest of Revelation and has to do with the consummation of the mystery of all things, the goal or end of history for both the overcomers and the worshipers of the beast. But what relationship do the seals have to this mystery? Are the events of the seals representative and simultaneous world happenings that occur throughout the church age? Do they occur sequentially? Are they part of the final drama or merely preparatory?

With the opening of the fifth seal, the martyrs cry out, "How long, . . . until you judge the inhabitants of the earth?" and are told to wait "a little longer" (vv. 10–11). And when the sixth seal is opened, the judgment appears to be imminent (v. 17); this seems to indicate that there is a time progression in the seals. The writer of this commentary tentatively suggests that the seals represent events preparatory to the final consummation. Whether these events come immediately before the end or whether they represent general conditions that will prevail throughout the period preceding the end is a more difficult question.

The seals closely parallel the signs of the approaching end times spoken of in Jesus' Olivet Discourse (Matt. 24:1–35; Mark 13:1–37; Luke 21:5–33). In these passages the events of the last days fall into three periods: (1) the period of false Christ, wars, famines, pestilences, earthquakes, and death, called "the beginning of birth pains" (Matt. 24:8); (2) the period of the Great Tribulation (Matt. 24:21; NIV, "great distress"); and (3) the period "immediately after the distress of those days," when the sun, moon, and stars will be affected and Christ will return (Matt.

24:29–30). This parallel to major parts of Revelation is too striking to be ignored. Thus the seals would correspond to the "beginning of birth pains" in the Olivet Discourse. The events are similar to those occurring under the trumpets (8:2–11:19) and bowls (15:1–16:21), but they should not be confused with those later and more severe judgments. Moreover, in the eschatological reckoning of time (cf. comments on 1:1), the events immediately preceding the end can stretch out over the whole age of the church, from John's time until now, and can still be viewed as "next" (4:1) in the sense that the "last days" began in the first century and are still continuing (cf. 1 John 2:18).

1. The first four seals: four horsemen (6:1–6)

The first four seals are distinct from the last two in that they describe four horses of different colors with four riders who are given different powers over the earth. The imagery of these four seals reflects Zechariah 1:8ff. and 6:1–8. In Zechariah's visions, the horsemen and chariots are divine instruments of judgment on the enemies of God's people, while the colors represent the four points of the compass. This may also be the best interpretation of the horses and their riders in Revelation 6, where each is sent by Christ through the instrumentality of the living creatures. The emphatic call "Come!" (vv. 1, 3, 5, 7) should not be viewed as addressed either to John or to Christ but rather to each of the horsemen. An analogy may be a first-century amphitheater or circus with various charioteers being summoned forth into the arena by the call "Come!" or "Go forth!"

a) The first seal: a white horse (6:1–2)

The identification of the first rider has given interpreters great difficulty: Does the rider on the white horse represent Christ and the victory of the gospel or the Antichrist and the forces of evil? In favor of the first identification are the striking similarity of this rider to the portrayal of Christ in 19:11–16, the symbolism of white which throughout Revelation is associated with righteousness and Christ (e.g., 1:14; 2:17; 3:4–5, 18; 4:4; 7:9, 13–14; 20:11), and the references in the Olivet Discourse to the preaching of the gospel throughout the world before the end (Matt. 25:14).

Support for the identification of the white horse with the Antichrist and his forces is the parallelism with the other three horses, which are instruments of judgment. The rider on the white horse in 19:11–16 is "Faithful and True" and "with justice he judges and makes war," in contrast to the rider in 6:2, who is not faithful and true and who wages war for unjust conquest. As for the Lamb, He opens the seals and would not be one of the riders. Moreover, it would be inappropriate to have an angelic being call forth Christ or His servants. Again, the "bow" would most naturally be connected with the enemy of God's people (Ezek. 39:3; cf. Rev. 20:7–8). Finally, the first event mentioned in the Olivet Discourse is the rise of "false Christs and false prophets" (Matt. 24:24).

The problem of the identity of the rider on the white horse may be solved either way, depending on the presuppositions one brings to the passage. The evidence, however, seems to favor slightly the second solution, which identifies the white horse with the Antichrist and his forces that seek to conquer the followers of Christ. John sensed that these persecutions were already present in his day and that they would culminate in a final, more severe form (1 John 2:18; Rev. 13:7).

Each of the first four seals, then, represents conflict aimed at Christians to test them and to sift out false disciples (6:10). This interpretation need not necessarily eliminate the fact that the seals may also refer to judgments on mankind in general, but since the fifth seal stresses the cry of the martyred Christians, probably the thought of Christian persecution belongs also in the first four seals. Each of them unleashes events that separate false belief from true. The destruction of Jerusalem is a case in point (Luke 21:20ff.). The white horse is released to conquer. As he goes forth, judgment falls on the unbelief of Israel (Luke 21:22–23), while at the same time there is a testing of believers to separate the chaff from the wheat (cf. Luke 21:12–19).

The bow in this context suggests forces opposed to Christians (cf. Matt. 24:5). A "crown" refers to victorious conquest (cf. 19:12, where Christ wears "many crowns"). "He was given" is the formula for the sovereign permission to carry out acts that, from a human point of view, seem contrary to God's character but nevertheless accomplish His will (cf. 13:5, 7, 15). Thus the rider on the white horse may also point to the attacks of the false Jews (2:9; 3:9), to the assault on Christians by pagan religionists, to the persecutions by Rome, as well as to all future, limited victories over the church by Satan (cf. 2:13; 12:17).

While verse 2 would be sobering for first-century believers, it would also encourage them, provided they understood that the Lamb had permitted their testing and suffering. In the midst of seeming defeat from their enemies, they could trust that He would ultimately be the victor (17:14).

b) The second seal: a red horse (6:3–4)

The second horseman is war and bloodshed. He rides on a steed whose "fiery red" color symbolizes slaughter (2 Kings 3:22–23). He is given a "large sword" because the number of those he kills is so great (cf. 13:10, 14). John may have thought of Nero's slaughter of Christians, the martyrdom of Antipas (2:13), or perhaps of those slain under Domitian's persecutions (cf. Matt. 10:34; 24:9).

c) *The third seal: a black horse* (6:5–6)

The third horseman is poverty and famine. He rides on a "black horse" and symbolizes the effects of war and bloodshed: sorrow, mourning, and desolation (Isa. 50:3; Jer. 4:28; Lam. 5:10 KJV). In the rider's hand is a "pair of scales." A voice is heard interpreting its significance in economic terms: "a quart of wheat . . . and three quarts of barley for a day's wage" (v. 6; lit., "for a denarius," a Greek coin). This amount implies inflation and famine conditions (Matt. 24:7). A quart of wheat would supply an average person one day's sustenance. Barley was used by the poor to mix with the wheat.

The expression "Do not damage the oil and wine" (v. 6) is less clear. Some view oil and wine as luxuries not necessary for bare survival: the rich would have them while the poor were starving (cf. Prov. 21:17). Others take oil and wine as showing the extent of the famine, since a drought affecting the grain may not be severe enough to hurt the vines and olive trees. Moreover, oil and wine are staple foods in the East, both in dearth and in prosperity (e.g., Deut. 7:13; Hos. 2:8, 22). In this view, the third seal brings poverty and partial, though not extremely severe famine. As Mounce notes, "This interpretation is in harmony with the increasing intensity of the three cycles of judgment. The fourth seal affects 'the fourth part of the earth' (6:8), the trumpets destroy a third (8:7, 8, 10, 12), and the destruction by the bowls is complete and final (16:1ff.)"

d) *The Fourth seal: a green horse* (6:7–8)

The fourth seal reveals a rider on a "pale horse." "Pale" denotes a yellowish green, the light green of a plant, or the paleness of a sick person in contrast to a healthy appearance. This cadaverous color fits in well with the name of the rider—"Death." This probably refers to the death resulting from pestilence, or plague, which often follows famine (cf. Jer. 14:12; Ezek. 5:17; 14:21; Luke 21:11). "Hades was following close behind him [Death]"—whether on foot, on the back of the same horse, or on a separate horse, Scripture does not say. (On "Hades" cf. comments on 1:18.) There seems to be an increasing intensity in the judgments as they are carried out by various agencies—the sword (human violence), famine, plague, and now the wild beasts of the earth.

2. *The fifth seal: the martyred saints* (6:9–11)

The fifth seal leaves the metaphor of the horsemen and discloses a scene of martyred saints under the altar crying out for justice on those who killed them. They are told to wait a little longer until their fellow servants are also killed. Who are these martyrs? They are referred to again in 18:24 as "all who have been killed on the earth" and in 20:4 as "those who had been beheaded." In 13:15 they are referred to as those who refused to worship the image of the beast and were "killed." Some also take the group seen in 7:9ff. as martyred saints in heaven. At any rate, the question arises why the martyrs alone receive so much attention, rather than all suffering or persecuted Christians. John may be referring to all those who so faithfully follow Christ that they may be characterized as the slain of the Lord. They may or may not actually suffer physical death for Christ, but they have (like John) so identified themselves with the slain Lamb that they have in effect already offered up their lives ("because of the word of God and the testimony they had maintained"; cf. 1:2, 9; Rom. 8:36).

John says that he saw the "souls" of those slain (v. 9). This is generally understood to mean the disembodied souls of these saints. However, the Greek word *psychē* has various meanings and probably stands here for the actual "lives" or "persons" who were killed rather than for their "souls." They are seen by John as persons who are very much alive though they have been killed by the beast. "Under the altar" places the scene in the temple of heaven. In 8:3, 5 and 9:13, "the altar" is the golden altar of incense that stood in the tabernacle in front of the Most Holy Place (Exod. 30:1ff.; Heb. 9:4); the other references in Revelation to "altar" also can be understood as referring to this altar of incense (11:1; 14:18; 16:7). If this is the altar John saw, the prayers of the saints would be for God's vindication of the martyrs of Christ (cf. Luke 18:7-8). On the other hand, some understand this to be the brazen altar of burnt offering and see in the imagery the blood of the martyrs at its base or "under the altar." But if the symbolism was sacrificial, it would be more natural to read "on" the altar, not "under" it.

The martyred address God as "Sovereign Lord" (v. 10). This term implies "ownership" and is used elsewhere in the New Testament to denote slave masters (1 Tim. 6:1; 1 Peter 2:18), God (Luke 2:29; Acts 4:24), or Jesus Christ (2 Peter 2:1; Jude 4). (On the phrase "holy and true," cf. comments on 3:7.) The martyrs cry for God's vengeance on the evildoers. The word "avenge" relates everywhere in the Old Testament and in the New Testament to the idea of punishment or retribution. These saints are following the teaching of Paul in Romans 12:19: "Do not take revenge, my friends, but leave room for God's wrath, for it is written: 'It is mine to avenge, I will repay,' says the Lord." Though believers are forbidden to take revenge, God will vindicate His elect by punishing those who killed them (Luke 18:7f.; 2 Thess. 1:8).

The martyrs are each given a "white robe" as an evidence of their victory and righteousness before the Judge of all the earth, who will speedily avenge their deaths (v. 11). They are to wait a "little longer"—in God's estimate but a fleeting moment, though for us it may stretch out for ages (cf. 12:12; 20:3). The expression "until the number of their fellow servants . . . was completed" is usually taken to mean that the number of either the martyred or their companions on earth who will be killed will be completed (so the NIV). However, the verb "completed" may also mean "complete their course," or "fulfill their Christian calling," which will also involve martyrdom. In any event, what constitutes the essence of Christian discipleship in John's eyes should not be overlooked. As Lilje says, "Every believer in Christ ought to be prepared for martyrdom; for Christians . . . cannot express their priestly communion with their Lord more perfectly than when they accept the suffering and the glory of martyrdom."

3. The sixth seal: the final judgment is imminent (6:12-14)

The sixth seal is broken by the Lamb, and John witnesses eschatological signs heralding the imminent, final Day of the Lord so often described in Scripture (e.g., Isa. 2:10, 19, 21; 13:10; 34:4; Jer. 4:29; Ezek. 32:7-8; Joel 2:31; 3:15; Zeph. 1:14-18; Matt. 24:29; Luke 21:11, 25-26). The signs are threefold: (1) the great earthquake and its storm affecting the sun and moon, (2) the stars falling, and (3) the terror on earth (vv. 15-17). It is difficult to know how literally the whole description should be taken. Some of the events are described from the standpoint of ancient cosmology—e.g., the stars fall to earth like figs from a shaken tree, the sky rolls up like a scroll, and the firmament, suspended like a roof over the earth, is shaken by the great earthquake.

The scene, whether taken literally or figuratively, is one of catastrophe and distress for the inhabitants of the earth. As later biblical authors seized on the earlier imagery of the theophany on Sinai to describe appearances of God to man (e.g., Hab. 3:3ff.), so John utilizes the archetypal imagery of the Old Testament to describe this terrible visitation of God's final judgment on the earth. In much the same manner as we would describe a chaotic situation by saying "all hell broke loose" (though not intending to be taken in a strictly literal sense), so the biblical writers use the language of cosmic turmoil to describe the condition of the world when God comes to judge the earth (v. 17). Earthquakes are mentioned in Revelation 8:5; 11:13, 19; 16:18 and disturbances of the sun, moon, and/or stars in 8:12; 9:2; 16:8. Of course, actual physical phenomena may also accompany the final judgment.

Verses 15-17 record the terror of all classes of people at these events and at the wrath of God and the Lamb. "The kings of the earth, the princes [dignitaries], the generals" describes the powerful; "the rich, the mighty" describes the affluent and the heroes; finally, "every slave and every free man" indicates the widest possible range of political distinctions. Since all kinds of people are included, we cannot say that God's wrath is directed only at the powerful, at the rich, or at false Christians. His judgment will fall on all who refuse to repent and instead worship demons and idols and persecute Christ's followers (9:20-21; 16:6, 9).

The pleas of the people for the rocks and mountains to fall on them (v. 16) is also found in Old Testament contexts of God's judgment (Isa. 2:19, 21; Hos. 10:8). It expresses the desire to be buried under the falling mountains and hills so as to escape the pains and terrors of the judgment. Jesus said that in this way the inhabitants of Jerusalem would cry out when God's judgment fell on the city in A.D. 70 (Luke 23:30).

The "wrath" ("anger") of the Lamb is not only a new metaphor but a paradoxical one. Lambs are usually gentle. But this Lamb shows "wrath" against those who have refused His grace (cf. John 5:27). Henceforth the wrath of God and of the Lamb is a continuing theme in Revelation and is described under the images of the trumpets and bowls (11:18; 14:7, 10, 19; 15:1, 7; 16:1, 19; 19:15). Moreover, God's wrath is a present historical reality as well as an eschatological judgment (cf. Rom. 1:18ff.; 2:5). So great is the day of destruction that "who can stand?" (cf. Joel 2:11; Nah. 1:6; Mal. 3:2).

C. First Interlude: The 144,000 Israelites and the White-Robed Multitude (7:1–17)

The change in tone from the subject matter in the sixth seal as well as the delay until 8:1 in opening the seventh seal indicate that chapter 7 is a true interlude. John first sees the angels who will unleash destruction on the earth restrained until the 144,000 servants of God from every tribe of Israel are sealed (vv. 1–8). Then he sees an innumerable multitude clothed in white standing before the throne of God, who are identified as those who have come out of the "great tribulation" (vv. 9–17). This chapter is in many respects one of the most difficult and yet most important in the book. Lilje calls the whole picture one of the most glorious in the entire Apocalypse. It probably functions both prospectively and retrospectively in that it casts light on chapter 6 as well as on chapters 8–11.

The principal difficulty in chapter 7 centers around the identification of the 144,000 (vv. 1–8) and the identification of the innumerable multitude (vv. 9–17). Is the reference to the tribes of Israel symbolic, representative, or literal? What is the "great tribulation" (v. 14)? Are those described in 7:9ff. martyrs? There is considerable divergence of opinion about these questions.

1. The 144,000 sealed Israelites (7:1–8)

a) The seal (7:1–3)

The "four angels" at "the four corners of the earth" hold back "the four winds of the earth" to keep them from blowing on the earth until the servants of God are sealed on their foreheads (v. 1). The expression "the four corners of the earth" was used in antiquity among the Near Eastern nations much as we use "the four points of the compass." Since nowhere in Revelation do we read that the four winds actually blow they may be taken as representing the earthly catastrophes that occur under the trumpets and bowls (cf. chs. 8 and 16).

Another angel comes from the "east" (possibly from Jerusalem or Zion, to emphasize its mission of salvation?) and calls to the four others not to release their destruction until the servants of God have a "seal" on their foreheads (v. 2). Such a seal surely indicates ownership by God and the Lamb (14:1). Furthermore, a seal may offer protection or security for its bearers. Such seems to be the emphasis in 9:4, where the demonic forces are told to harm "only those people who did not have the seal of God on their foreheads." Only protection from demonic forces is involved in the sealing, rather than escape from physical harm from the plagues or from the Antrichrist, or protection from spiritual apostasy.

The matter may be clarified by examining what happens to those who, by contrast, have the "mark" of the beast (13:16–17): while those who do not have the mark of the beast face severe socio-economic sanctions, those who have the mark of the beast are not only identified as beast worshipers but become the objects of the irreversible wrath of God (14:9, 11). This implies, by contrast, that those who have "the seal of God" are God worshipers and will be the objects of His abiding grace. In 16:2, the bowl of God's wrath appears to be directed exclusively toward those who have the mark of the beast, thus excluding those with the seal of God (cf. 16:6). Those having the mark of the beast are deluded by the beast (19:20), implying that the sealed of God are not thus deceived. Finally, the martyred group is seen just prior to their resurrection and thousand-year reign with Christ and are described as not having the mark of the beast or worshiping him (20:4).

In the light of these passages, we may say that the "sealed" are the people of God and that their sealing must be related to their salvation as in the comparable figure used by Paul (2 Cor. 1:22; Eph. 1:13; 4:30; cf. 4 Ezra 6:5). This is also evident in 14:3–4, where the sealed are described as those who were redeemed from the earth as firstfruits to God (cf. Rom. 8:23; James 1:18).

Furthermore, while the seal may not protect the sealed against harm inflicted by human agency (13:7; 20:4), they are protected from the divine plagues (16:2). It is clear that the protection from famine, pestilence, and sword afforded the sealed in the apocryphal Psalms of Solomon (15:6, 9) cannot also apply to John's sealed, since they are beheaded (20:4). As for the Old Testament background of the problem, Ezekiel 9:4–7 may well be primary. In this passage a divine messenger with stylus in hand was to go through the apostate Jerusalem of Ezekiel's day and put a mark on the foreheads of those who deplored the faithless idolatry of the Israelites. Those so marked were the faithful and true servants of God in contrast to the professed but false servants who had abandoned Him. The sealed would be spared in the divine slaughtering of the rebellious inhabitants of the city.

This passage concerning God's sealing would have the effect of assuring the people of God of His special concern and plan for them. Even when facing persecution and martyrdom at the hand of the beast, they can be certain that no plague from God will touch them but that they will be in His presence forever because they are His very own possession. Therefore, the seal on the forehead is equivalent to the divine mark of ownership that elsewhere in the New Testament refers to the presence of the Holy Spirit (2 Cor. 1:22; Eph. 1:13; 4:30). This act of God will fulfill the promise to the Philadelphian church: "Since you have kept my command to endure patiently, I will also keep you from the hour of trial that is going to come upon the whole world to test those who live on the earth" (3:10). Consequently, those thus sealed must be Christians and not unconverted Jews or Gentiles.

b) *Identification of the 144,000* (7:4)

John next gives the number of those sealed—144,000—and their identification: "From all the tribes of Israel." There are two principal views regarding this identification: (1) The number and the tribal identifications are to be taken literally and refer to 144,000 Jewish Christians who are sealed (to protect them from destruction) during the time of the Great Tribulation; (2) John uses the language of the new Israel and thus refers to the completed church composed of Jews and Gentiles.

In support of the first view is the normal usage of "Israel" in the New Testament as referring to the physical descendants of Jacob. The "twelve tribes" (vv. 5–8) would most naturally be understood to refer to the historical Israel and not to the church. Thus, in this first view, John would symbolically describe the beginning of what Paul foretold in Romans 11:25–29 as the salvation of "all Israel."

In support of the second view, which identifies Israel with the church, is the fact that the New Testament identifies the followers of Christ as "Abraham's seed" (Gal. 3:29), as "the true circumcision" (Phil. 3:3), and as the "Israel of God" (Gal. 6:16). Furthermore, John himself earlier in Revelation made a distinction between the true Jew and the false (cf. 2:9; 3:9), which could imply that here in chapter 7 he also refers to the true Israel or the church. Additional support for this view is found if there is a unity between the first and second groups in chapter 7, groups that otherwise must be treated as distinct and unconnected. This view seems preferable to us (see comments on 7:9–17).

By the middle of the first century, Paul made a distinction between the true, spiritual Jew and the physical descendants of Abraham (Rom. 2:28–29; 9:8). Only those Jews who recognized Jesus as Messiah could rightly be called "Israel" in the strictest sense (Rom. 9:6), though the term might be used with qualifications to refer to the physical descendants of Jacob ("Israel after the flesh," 1 Cor. 10:18 KJV). Peter likewise described the church (Jew and Gentile) in terms drawn from the Old Testament that historically describe the true people of God among the Jewish descendants ("holy priesthood . . . chosen people . . . royal priesthood . . . holy nation," 1 Peter 2:4, 9). Moreover, even Gentiles who received Jesus as the Messiah and Lord were considered "Abraham's seed" (Gal. 3:29) and the true "circumcision" (Phil. 3:3).

Earlier in the Book of Revelation, John has already made a distinction between Jews who were Jews in name only and not true Jews because they did not acknowledge Jesus as Lord (2:9; 3:9). Also, the Old Testament image of the people of Israel as a kingdom and priests to God is used by John of the followers of Jesus (1:6). Similarly, many of the promises to the victors in the churches of Asia (chs. 2–3) are fulfillments of Old Testament promises given to the true people of Israel. In Christ's rebuke to the churches, we have the Old Testament imagery of "Balaam" and "Jezebel," describing error that had influenced not the Old Testament Israel but the New Testament church. In chapter 12, it is again difficult to decide whether the "woman" represents the ancient Jewish covenant people or the New Testament followers of Jesus. In Revelation 21:9–21, the church is called the "bride, the wife of the Lamb"; she is identified with the New Jerusalem, and on its twelve gates are inscribed the "names of the twelve tribes of Israel." Even in the Gospel of John, Jesus is the "true vine," which many commentators understand to be an allusion to the vine that decorated the temple entrance and stood as a symbol for Israel (cf. Isa. 5:1ff. with John 15:1ff.). Jesus claims to be the true Israel; His followers, the branches, would then be related to the true Israel (cf. Rom. 11:17–24). All this simply suggests the possibility that in John's mind the followers of Jesus (14:4) are the true servants of God, the Israel of God (cf. John 11:51–52).

The identification of the 144,000 with the whole elect people of God who will face the Great Tribulation, including both Jews and Gentiles, does not negate Paul's teaching that the majority of the Jews themselves will one day be brought back into a relationship of salvation before God. John simply is not dealing with Paul's emphasis at this point in Revelation (but cf. 11:2f.).

The number 144,000 is obviously obtained by adding together 12,000 from each of the twelve tribes of Israel (vv. 5–8). Earlier in Revelation (cf. 4:4), twenty-four (a multiple of twelve) serves as a symbolic number. The same multiple of "thousand" is found again in the size of the Holy City: "He measured the city with the rod and found it to be 12,000 stadia in length, and as wide and high as it is long" (21:16). Thus, 12,000 is symbolic of completeness and perfection. Even the wall is "144 cubits" (twelve times twelve; 21:17). The tree of life bearing "twelve crops of fruit, yielding its fruit every month" (i.e., twelve months; 22:2) further supports the view that John intends the number twelve to be taken symbolically and not literally. By 144,000 he signifies the sealing of *all* or the *total* number of God's servants who will face the Great Tribulation.

Those who are sealed come from "all the tribes of Israel," and this emphasizes even more the universality and comprehensiveness of the Christian gospel. Whereas in first-century Judaism there were many sects with exclusive tribal claims to being the true Israel, for the followers of Jesus all such sectarianism is broken down and all groups, regardless of race, culture, religious background, or geographical location, are accepted before God (7:9; 14:4). There is an exclusivism in Revelation, but it is based on loyalty to Christ, not on historical or liturgical continuity.

c) *Tribal enumeration* (7:5–8)

John goes even further. He enumerates each of the twelve tribes and their number: "From the tribe of Judah 12,000 were sealed," etc. Why was it necessary to provide this detailed enumeration? And why this particular selection of tribes? In answering these difficult questions, some facts about the list should be noted. John places Judah first, evidently to emphasize the priority of the messianic King who came from the tribe of Judah (Rev. 5:5; Heb. 7:13–14). Nowhere in the tribal listings of the Old Testament does Judah come first, except in the space arrangement of the wilderness camp (Num. 2:3ff.); this exception may itself be linked with the messianic expectation through Judah (Gen. 49:10; 1 Chron. 5:2). John's priority of Judah is comparable to the emphasis placed in late Judaism on the tribe of Levi (the priestly tribe). It is significant that John includes Levi among the other tribes in the comparatively unimportant eighth place and thus gives no special place to the Levitical order.

The selection of tribes and their order as given here by John are unique. The Old Testament has no fewer than twenty variant lists of the tribes; these lists include anywhere from ten to thirteen tribes, although the number twelve is predominant (cf. Gen. 49; Deut. 33; Ezek. 48). The grouping of twelve may be a way of expressing the corporate identity of the elect people of God as a whole and may be maintained—even artificially at times—to preserve this identity (cf. the need to make up the "twelfth" apostle when Judas fell, Acts 1:25–26). John omits Dan (which elsewhere is always included) and Ephraim. In order to maintain the ideal number twelve with these omissions, he must list both Joseph and Manasseh as tribes. This is peculiar, because the tribe of Joseph is always mentioned in the other lists by either including Joseph and excluding his two sons, Ephraim and Manasseh (Gen. 49), or by omitting Joseph and counting the two sons as one tribe each (Ezek. 48). Not until the Levitical priesthood gains more prominence is the tribe of Levi omitted from the lists and replaced by the two sons of Joseph.

Various efforts have been made to solve the enigma of John's list and especially to explain the absence of the tribe of Dan. As yet, we have no completely satisfactory solution. The early church held that the Antichrist would arise from the tribe of Dan. Furthermore, in the Old Testament Dan was associated with idolatry (Judg. 18:18–19; 1 Kings 12:29–30). This may be the clue. If John sought to expose Christian idolatry and beast worship in his day by excluding Dan from the list of those sealed, it may also be possible to explain on the same basis why Manasseh and Joseph were chosen to fill up the sacred number rather than Manesseh and Ephraim: In the Old Testament Ephraim was also explicitly identified with idolatry (Hos. 4:17). Since Dan comes first in the tribal listing of the restored eschatological Jewish community (Ezek. 48), while John's list puts Judah first, it may be that John's list describes the church rather than ethnic Israel.

It is important to note that John does not equate the 144,000 with all members of the tribes: "144,000 from all tribes of Israel. . . . From the tribe of Judah 12,000 were sealed," etc. If John had the actual Jewish Israel in view, this use of "from" would indicate an election from the whole nation. On the other hand, if he intended to imply something about the church, his language might indicate God's selecting the true church out "from" the professing church. This thought has been mentioned earlier (cf. 2:14ff., 20ff.; 3:16ff.) and is supported by Ezekiel 9:4–7, where the seal identified the true servants of God among the professing people of God (see comments on 7:2–3). Paul stated the same thought when he wrote, "Nevertheless, God's solid foundation stands firm, sealed with this inscription: 'The Lord knows those who are his,' and 'Everyone who confesses the name of the Lord must turn away from wickedness'" (2 Tim. 2:19).

The description of the judgments under the sixth seal (6:12ff.) ended with the question, "The great day of their wrath has come, and who can stand?" (6:17). Chapter 7 answers this question by implying that only the true servants of God, who are divinely sealed, can be protected from the wrath of God and the Lamb.

2. The great white-robed multitude (7:9–17)

John now sees a great multitude from every nation and cultural background, standing before the throne of God and clothed in white robes. They are identified by the angel as those "who have come out of the great tribulation" (v. 14). Again, the question is that of identity. They are not the Gentiles who are saved in the Tribulation in contrast to the Jews in vv. 1–8, because they are described as coming from every nation and tribe and language, which would mean both Jews and Gentiles. Are they, then, martyrs who have given their lives in the Great Tribulation and have been slain by the beast? If so, are they the reminder of those to be killed referred to when the fifth seal is opened (6:11)? Are they the complete group of martyrs? Or do they represent the whole company of the re-deemed in Christ as seen in glory?

Although there is no direct statement that the great multitude are martyrs, there are some indications of this: (1) they are seen in heaven "before the throne" (v. 9) and "in his temple" (v. 15); (2) they are de-scribed as those "who have come out of the great tribulation" (v. 14). Thus it is assumed that, since they have died in the Great Tribulation, they have most likely been martyred, because the Tribulation will be a time when many of the saints are killed (17:6; 18:24; 19:2; 20:4, etc.).

The multitude would not be the whole company of the martyred throughout history but only those who were victims of the persecution by the beast during the Great Tribulation; they are probably those future martyrs referred to under the fifth seal as those "who were to be killed as they had been" (6:11).

The identification of this second group is related to the identification of the first one (vv. 1–8). Some argue that the two groups must be different because the first is numbered, the second innumerable; the first is limited to Jews, the second refers to every nation. These objections are not serious if we recall the exposition of verses 1–8, where it was noted (1) that the number of the sealed was symbolic and not literal and (2) that the delineation of the twelve tribes was John's deliberate attempt to universalize the election of God. Thus, what some have seen as contrasts may actually be designed to complement each other and show the con-tinuity between the two groups. Furthermore, we should bear in mind that John does not see any group at all in verses 1–8 but merely hears the number of the sealed, whereas in verses 9–17 he actually sees a group and describes what he sees and hears. Therefore, the unity of both groups can be maintained and verses 9–17 understood as the interpretative key to the 144,000. John's vision then leaps ahead to a scene in heaven after the Great Tribulation has run its course and views the glorified Tribulation saints as being in God's presence, at rest from their trial, and serving Him continually.[3]

---

[3]As to debate about the Rapture and the Great Tribulation, two slightly different variations of the more literal Jewish identity of those in verses 1–8 and the relationship of this first group to the second (vv. 9ff.) are quite popular today. Some see the 144,000 as the select group of Jews who will be converted to Jesus shortly after the rapture of the church to heaven. These Jewish evangelists will preach the gospel to the world during the Tribulation. As a result of their preaching, a great multitude of Gentiles will be converted to Christ (A.C. Gaebelein).

Others, accepting a posttribulational view of the church's rapture, understand the 144,000 as a literal Jewish remnant preserved physically through the Tribulation and converted immediately after the Rapture. They will constitute the beginning of the restored Jewish Davidic Kingdom at the inception of the millennial reign of Christ on the earth (R. Gundry).

The Bible speaks of three different types of tribulation or distress, and it is important to distinguish between them:

1. There is tribulation that is inseparable from Christian life in the world (John 16:33; Acts

a) *The cosmopolitan group* (7:9–14)

"A great multitude . . . from every nation, tribe, people and language" pictures what has been called a "polyglot cosmopolitan crowd" (v. 9). Similar fourfold descriptions of the members of the Christian community or of the inhabitants of the world also occur in Revelation 5:9; 11:9; 13:7; 14:6; 17:15. "Standing before the throne and in front of the Lamb" signifies their position of acceptance and honor as God's true servants (cf. v. 15) and reminds us of the continuity of this vision with the earlier vision of the throne and the Lamb (chs. 4–5). Since this group represents the redeemed saints, it appears to complete the full circle of participants before the throne begun in chapter 4.

Their "white robes" impress John and are an important feature of the vision (vv. 9, 13–14). We cannot fail to connect them with the white robes given to the martyrs under the fifth seal (6:11). The white robes symbolize salvation and victory (v. 10), and those who wear them obtained them by "[washing] their robes and [making] them white in the blood of the Lamb" (v. 14). This implies that they were true recipients of Christ's redemption in contrast to others who, though professing belief in Christ, were not genuine overcomers (cf. 3:5–6, 18).

"The blood of the Lamb" connotes here more even than the reference to the sacrificial death of Jesus (5:9): it also suggests faithful witness in following Jesus in His death (2:13; 12:11).

"Palm branches" are referred to only one other time in the New Testa-

---

14:22; Rom. 5:3; 2 Tim. 2:11–12; 1 Peter 4:12; Rev. 1:9; 2:10, etc.). All Christians during all ages participate in tribulation, thus sharing in the continuing sufferings of Christ (Col. 1:24).

2. The Bible also speaks of an intense tribulation that will come on the final generation of Christians and climax all previous persecutions. Daniel 12:1 refers to such a time: "There will be a time of distress such as has not happened from the beginning of nations until then." Jesus likewise predicts such an unprecedented persecution: "For then there will be great distress, unequaled from the beginning of the world until now—and never to be equaled again" (Matt.. 24:21). Paul's mention of "the rebellion" and "the man of lawlessness" surely refer to this same period (2 Thess. 2:3ff.). In Revelation this more intense persecution is mentioned in 7:14; 11:7–10; 13:7; 16:6; the events under the fifth seal should perhaps also be included here (6:9–11). This future tribulation is distinguished from previous persecutions of the church in its intensity, in its immediate connection with Christ's second coming, and in the presence of the Antichrist.

3. Scripture also speaks of a future time of God's intense wrath on unbelievers. Revelation refers to this as "the great day of their wrath" (6:17) and "the hour of trial that is going to come upon the whole world to test those who live on the earth" (3:10). Such wrath from God comes especially under the trumpets and bowls (8:2ff.; 16:1ff.). Paul refers to this punitive action of God in 2 Thessalonians 1:6–10, probably drawing on the teaching of Jesus in the Olivet Discourse (Matt. 24). While for Christians the Great Tribulation may be concurrent with a portion of the period of God's wrath on the rebellious, this final and more intense judgment of God seems to *follow* the Great Tribulation itself and is directly connected with the coming of Christ (Matt. 24:29; Rev. 6:12ff.; 19:11ff.).

In the following pages this commentary will endeavor to consistently distinguish these three types of trouble or tribulation. The discussion will therefore not fit neatly into any of the current evangelical schemes. Thus the reader will be the final judge whether the arguments at each turn are convincing or not.

ment, in connection with the Passover celebration (John 12:13). Moses decreed that palms should be used at the Feast of Tabernacles (Lev. 23:40); later they were also used on other festal occasions (1 Macc. 13:51; 2 Macc. 10:7). Jewish coins of the period from 140 B.C. to A.D. 70 frequently contain palms and some have the inscription "the redemption of Zion." Palms were emblems of victory: in John 12 they denote the triumph of Christ, while here in Revelation the reference is to the victory of the servants of Christ.

In accord with the literary symmetry of chapters 4–7, this group also expresses their worship of the King and the Lamb (v. 10). Their praise to God is for His "salvation." Since the same word is elsewhere associated with the final manifestation of God's power and kingdom (12:10; 19:1), here it may also denote God's final victory over sin and the principalities of this world that crucified Christ and that kill His true disciples (cf. Isa. 49:8; 2 Cor. 6:2).

Finally, the angelic hosts respond to the cry of the redeemed (v. 10) with "Amen" and voice their praise and worship of God for the salvation given to men (vv. 11–12; cf. Luke 15:10). Compare this doxology with 5:12–13.

Here and in 5:5 are the only references in Revelation to an elder speaking individually, a fact that supports the view that the elders in Revelation are angels and not a symbolic group representing the church (see comments on 4:4). Thus, after the manner of the Old Testament apocalyptic passages, the interpreting angel (elder) asks concerning the white-robed throng, "Who are they, and where did they come from?" (vv. 13–14; cf. Dan. 7:15–16; Zech. 1:9, 19; 4:1–6).

The reference to the washed robes should be viewed in relation to 3:4, where soiled clothes represent defection from Christ through unbelief and worship of false gods (cf. 21:8). On the "great tribulation," see footnote on pages 90–91.

b) *A glimpse of heaven* (7:15–17)

The following verses describe the activity and condition of the true servants of God in their future and eternal relation to the Lamb. The scene is one of the most beautiful in the Bible. Those who have washed their robes in the blood of the Lamb are described as being before the throne of God without fear or tremor, fully accepted by the divine Majesty, continually serving God in praise and worship.

The reference to the "temple" of God (v. 15) raises the question whether this scene describes the final state of the saints or an intermediate state, since 21:22 tells us that the New Jerusalem has no temple. However, the language used in verses 15–17 (esp. v. 17) seems to depict the same condition as that of the saints in chapters 21 and 22 (cf. 21:3–4, 6; 22:1). Since 7:15 relates to worship, it would be appropriate to refer to the presence of God and the Lamb as "in" the temple. In 21:22, however, the future existence of the people of God is described as a city; and in that glorious city, unlike the pagan cities of the present world, there will be no special temple in which to worship God because God Himself and the Lamb will be present everywhere.

"He . . . will spread his tent over them" (v. 15) calls to mind the shekinah presence in the Old Testament tabernacle and temple (Exod. 40:34–38; 1 Kings 8:10–11; cf. Ezek. 10:4, 18–19) and later in Jesus (John 1:14), and also the idea of a permanent residence (Rev. 21:3). Never again will these people endure torment. They have the supreme protection of the living God Himself.

The condition described in verse 16 contrasts with the earthly experience of those who suffered much for their faith (cf. Heb. 11:37–38): starvation, thirst, and the burning desert are now forever past. There may be an allusion here to Isaiah 49:10, which places the time of relief from such distresses in the days of Messiah's kingdom. There also is a contrast to what the four horsemen bring (6:1–8; cf. Matt. 24:7).

We have in verse 17 a beautiful pastoral figure—that of the Lamb shepherding His people (cf. John 10:1–8; Heb. 13:20; 1 Peter 2:25). It is not due to some perfect environment but through the presence and continual ministry of the Lamb that their sufferings are forever assuaged. Whereas on earth their enemies may have tormented them, now the Lamb guides them: "He will lead [the same verb is used of the Holy Spirit in John 16:13] them to springs of living water." In contrast to the burning thirst experienced in their tribulation, they now will enjoy the refreshing waters of life. In the future life the saints thus will not know stagnation, boredom, or satiation (Ps. 23:1f.; Jer. 2:13; Ezek. 47:1–12; Zech. 14:8).

Finally, even the sorrowful memory of the pain and suffering of the former days will be mercifully removed by the Father: "God will wipe away every tear from their eyes" (cf. 21:4). Tribulation produces tears, but like a tenderhearted, devoted mother, God will wipe each tear from their eyes with the eternal consolations of glory itself. Never again will they cry out because of pain or suffering. Only through the Resurrection can all this become a reality (Isa. 25:8; 1 Cor. 15:54).

c) *The opening of the seventh seal* (8:1)

After the long interlude of chapter 7, the sequence of the opening of the seals is resumed with the opening of the seventh and final seal, which provides both the conclusion of the seals and a preparation for the seven trumpets. The praises ordinarily heard uninterruptedly in heaven (4:8) now cease: "There was silence in heaven for about half an hour." Most interpreters understand the silence to refer to the awesome silence before the great storm of God's wrath on the earth. But in John's view heaven is quieted to hear the cries for deliverance and justice of God's persecuted servants (6:10): even heaven's choirs are subdued to show God's concern for His persecuted people in the Great Tribulation (8:4; cf. Luke 18:2–8).[4] (Concerning the relationship between the seals, trumpets, and bowls, see comments on 8:6.)

For Further Study

1. Using either Strong's or Young's concordance, look up all the references to "throne" and "lamb" in the Book of Revelation from chapter 6 onward. How significant are these concepts?

2. What can be learned about true worship from observing the heavenly worship in chapters 4 and 5?

3. Study the relationship between the five hymns in chapters 4 and 5 and the vision descriptions that precede and follow each of them. What is the relationship?

4. Can you find parallels between the events described under the first five seals (ch. 6) and any contemporary events in the world? Events affecting primarily Christians?

5. Study the close parallelism between Matthew 24:1–31 (Olivet Discourse) and Revelation 6:1–17. Does this seem deliberate?

6. Explain how the "sealing" image (7:1–8) and the glorious picture of heaven in 7:15–17 might help Christians now who are being persecuted for their faith.

7. How important should the Rapture-Great Tribulation question be among evangelicals?

---

[4] A Jewish teacher states, "In the fifth heaven are companies of angels of service who sing praises by night, but are silent by day because of the glory of Israel," i.e., that the praises of Israel may be heard in heaven.

Chapter 5

The First Six Trumpets
(Revelation 8:2–11:14)

A. The Angels and the Golden Censer (8:2–5)

While the seven seals are opened by the Lamb Himself, the judgments of the seven trumpets and the seven bowls (15:1) are executed by seven angels.[1] Before the trumpet judgments are executed, another angel enacts a symbolic scene in heaven. He takes a golden censer filled with incense and offers the incense on the altar in behalf of the prayers of all God's people (vv. 3–4). Earlier, in connection with the martyred saints (6:9), John mentioned the altar that was near God's presence. A strong assurance is here given to the suffering followers of Christ that their prayers for vindication are not forgotten: God will speedily vindicate them and avenge their enemies' assaults. So close is the altar to God that the incense cloud of the saints' prayers rises into His presence and cannot escape His notice (cf. Ps. 141:2).

The censer or firepan is now used to take some of the burning coals from the altar and cast them to the earth (v. 5). Symbolically, this represents the answer to the prayers of the saints through the visitation on earth of God's righteous judgments: God next appears on earth in a theophany. The language, reminiscent of Sinai with its thunder, lightning, and earthquake, indicates that God has come to vindicate His saints (Exod. 19:16–19; Rev. 4:5; 11:19; 16:18).

B. The First Six Trumpets (8:6–9:21)

The relation of the seals to the trumpets and the bowls (v. 6). Two questions confront the interpreter at this point: (1) what is the relationship of the trumpets to the preceding seals and the following bowls? and (2) are the events described symbolic or more literal? In answer to the first question, there are two basic options: either the series are parallel and thus simultaneous, or they are sequential or successive. It is not

---

[1] In the noncanonical Jewish book of 1 Enoch 20:2–8, reference is made to seven angels who stand before God and are named Uriel, Raphael, Raguel, Michael, Saraqael, Gabriel (cf. Luke 1:19), and Remeil. John many not have these in mind, but the offering up of the prayers of the saints was in Jewish thought connected with archangels (Tobit 12:15; Levi 3:7).

possible to decide with certainty for either of these views, since each contains elements of truth. Both sequential and parallel elements are evident. This commentary has already argued that the first five seals precede chronologically the events of the trumpets and bowls (see comments on 6:1). But the sixth seal seems to take us into the period of the outpouring of God's wrath that is enacted in the trumpet and bowl judgments (6:12–17).

The *sequential* factors are as follows: (1) there is a rise in the intensity of the judgments (only a part of earth and people are affected in the trumpets, but all are affected under the bowls); (2) there is a difference in the sequence and content of the events described in each series; (3) the reference to those not sealed in 9:4 (fifth trumpet) presupposes the sealing of 7:1–8; (4) the statement in 8:1–2 implies that the trumpets follow the seals: "When he opened the seventh seal, . . . I saw the seven angels . . . to them were given seven trumpets"; (5) the bowl judgments are directly called the "last plagues" because with them God's wrath is "completed" (15:1), indicating the prior trumpet judgments. When the seventh bowl is poured out, the words "It is done" are spoken (16:17).

On the other hand, there are *parallelisms*. The sixth and seventh seals (6:12ff.), the seventh trumpet (11:15ff.), and the seventh bowl (16:17ff.) all seem to depict events associated with the second coming of Christ. The parallelism of these last events may indicate that all three series (seals, trumpets, bowls) are parallel in their entirety, or that there is a partial recapitulation or overlap. But the text seems to demand some type of sequential understanding and hence rules out a complete parallelism.

The main question is whether the parallelism indicates that the events described under the sixth and seventh seals, the seventh trumpet, and the seventh bowl are identical or merely similar and hence really sequential. Here the following points are relevant: (1) the sixth seal takes us into the period of God's wrath on the beast worshipers but does not actually advance beyond that event to refer to the coming of Christ (6:12–17); (2) the seventh seal introduces the trumpet judgments, which run their course, and the seventh trumpet seems to bring us into the kingdom of Christ (11:15–18); (3) The seventh bowl likewise brings us to the consummation and the return of Christ (if we keep in mind that the description of Babylon's destruction is an elaboration of events under the seventh bowl, 16:17ff.; 19:11ff.).

It has been correctly noted that the "third woe" (9:12; 11:14) is never fulfilled by the seventh trumpet, unless, that is, the contents of the seventh trumpet are the seven bowls, which then constitute the "third woe." This is another way of saying that there is some limited recapitulation or overlap in the seventh seal and the first trumpets and in the seventh trumpet and the first bowls. This might be called a *telescopic view* of the seals, bowls, and trumpets. Further support for this view is also found in observing that interludes come between the sixth and seventh seals and between the sixth and seventh trumpets but not between the sixth and seventh bowls, which would be expected if the trumpets were strictly parallel to the bowls (see diagram).

DIAGRAM OF THE SEALS, TRUMPETS, AND BOWLS

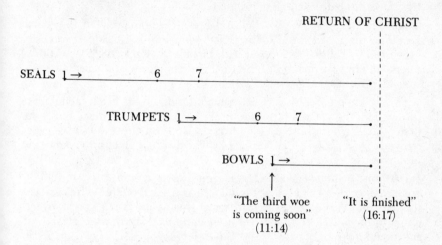

RETURN OF CHRIST

SEALS 1→   6   7

TRUMPETS 1→   6   7

BOWLS 1→

"The third woe   "It is finished"
is coming soon"   (16:17)
(11:14)

The second problem concerns the *literalness* of the events described under each trumpet. The crucial question is not literal versus nonliteral but what did John intend? Some things may need to be understood more literally and others symbolically. For example, the reference to the army of 200 million (9:16–19) can hardly be literal (cf. comments on 9:16). Either the number is figurative, or the army refers to demonic powers rather than human soldiers. It is also difficult to take literally the reference to the eagle that speaks human words (8:13). While there is no way to settle this problem finally, the exposition will attempt to steer between a literal approach and a totally symbolic one.

1. *The sounding of the first six trumpets* (8:6–9:19)

As in the seals, there is a discernible *literary pattern* in the unfolding of the trumpets. The first four trumpets are separated from the last three (which are called "woes"; 8:13; 9:12; 11:14) and are generally reminiscent of the plagues in Exodus. Although John refers in 15:3 to the Song of Moses (Exod. 15:1–18), he does not work out the plague parallelism precisely, and the connections should not always be pressed.

Shofar trumpets (usually made of a ram's horn) were used in Jewish life as signaling instruments. They sounded alarms for war or danger as well as signals for peace and announced the new moon, the beginning of the Sabbath, or the death of a notable. Trumpets were also used to throw enemies into panic (Judg. 7:19–20). Their use as eschatological signals of the Day of the Lord or the return of Christ is well established in the Old and New Testaments (Isa. 27:13; Joel 2:1; Zeph. 1:16; Matt. 24:31; 1 Cor. 15:52; 1 Thess. 4:16). The Dead Sea community had an elaborate trumpet signal system patterned after Joshua 6.

The first trumpet (v. 7). Hail and fire are reminiscent of the fourth Egyptian plague of the Exodus (Exod. 9:23–26), with added intensity suggested by the words "mixed with blood" (cf. Ezek. 38:22). A "third" refers simply to a fraction of the total and should not be construed as a specific quantity (cf. Ezek. 5:2; Zech. 13:8–9).

The second trumpet (vv. 8–9). A huge blazing mass like a mountain is thrown into the sea and turns part of the sea into blood. This suggests the first plague, when the Nile was turned blood-red and the fish were destroyed (Exod. 7:20–21; cf. Zeph. 1:3). The destruction of ships shows the intense turbulence of the sea.

The third trumpet (vv. 10–11). John next sees a huge fiery star fall on the rivers and springs of water and turn a part of these fresh-water supplies into very bitter water. The star's name is "Wormwood," which refers to the bitter herb *Artemesia absinthium*, found in the Near East and mentioned elsewhere in the Bible (Jer. 9:15; 23:15; Lam. 3:15, 19; Amos 5:7). It is not clear whether John intended the star to be understood as an angel as in 1:20 and 9:1. This is the first plague that results in the loss of human life (cf. 9:15, 20). This plague, aimed at the fresh water, is a counterpart of the preceding one, which was aimed at the sea.

The fourth trumpet (v. 12). The heavens are struck with partial darkness, reminiscent of the ninth plague (Exod. 10:21–23). "A third of . . ." refers to a partial impairment of the ordinary light from these bodies. In the Old Testament, the darkening of the heavens is connected with God's appearing in judgment (cf. Isa. 13:10; Ezek. 32:7–8; Joel 2:10; 3:15; cf. Matt. 24:29). An unusual darkness also attended the crucifixion of Christ (Matt. 27:45).

Before the last three trumpets sound, John hears a flying eagle call out "Woe" three times (v. 13). His cry announces the especially grievous nature of the last three plagues, which kill a third part of the population of the earth (9:18). Two of the woes are identified with the fifth and sixth trumpets (9:12; 11:14). (See comments on 8:6, which argue that the third woe should be seen as the seven bowl judgments in 16:1ff.) The "inhabitants of the earth" are those who have rejected Christ, in contrast to the true, faithful followers of the Lamb (cf. comments on 3:10). The flying "eagle" must be taken symbolically. There are two other references to eagles in Revelation (4:7; 12:14); since 4:7 relates to the description of one of the four living beings, it may be that John intends the eagle mentioned here to have the same significance.

The fifth trumpet: The first woe. (9:1–11). John now focuses attention on the fifth and sixth trumpets (first and second woes) by giving more than twice as much space to their description as he gives the previous four trumpets together. John sees a "star" that has fallen to the earth (v. 1). Since this star is given a key to open the Abyss, it is reasonable to understand it as being a symbolic reference to an angel. This is supported by verse 11, where "the angel of the Abyss" is mentioned and named "Abaddon," as well as 20:1, which also refers to "an angel coming down" (parallel to "a star falling") who has the key to the Abyss, where Satan is thrown.

The Abyss is also the place from which the beast arises (11:7; 17:8). The word "Abyss" refers to the underworld as (1) a prison for certain demons (Luke 8:31; cf. 2 Peter 2:4; Jude 6) and (2) the realm of the dead (Rom. 10:7). When the Abyss is opened, huge billows of smoke pour out, darken the sky, and release horselike locusts on the earth. For five months these locusts torment the inhabitants of the earth who do not have the seal of God.

The imagery of locusts, appearing like armies, advancing like a cloud, darkening the heavens, and sounding like the rattle of chariots, goes back to Joel's vision of the locust army that came on Israel as a judgment from God (Joel 1:6; 2:4–10). But the locusts of the Apocalypse inflict agony like that of scorpion stings (vv. 3, 5, 10). This, together with the fact that they do not eat grass (v. 4), shows that these locusts are something other than ordinary earthly insects. Indeed, they have the special task of inflicting a nonfatal injury only on the beast worshipers, who do not have the seal of God on their foreheads (v. 4; cf. comments on 7:3). This may imply that these locustlike creatures are not simply instruments of a physical plague, such as those in Moses' or Joel's day or under the first four trumpets, but are *demonic* forces out of the Abyss from whom the true people of God are protected (cf. John's use of frogs to represent demonic powers in 16:13). The "five months" of agony (vv. 5, 10) may refer to the life span of the locust (i.e., through spring and summer). So severe is the torment they inflict that their victims will seek death (v. 6; cf. Job 3:21; Jer. 8:3; Hos. 10:8).

John describes the locusts as an army of mounted troops ready for the attack (v. 7). The heads of the locusts resemble horses' heads. John does not say that the locusts had crowns of gold on their heads but that they wore "something like crowns of gold" on their heads; Charles suggests that this might refer to the yellow green of their breasts. This, combined with the resemblance to human faces, suggests something unnatural, hence demonic. The comparison of their "hair" with that of women may refer (as in other ancient texts) to the locusts' long antennae, while their "breastplates of iron" refer to their scales, which appear as a cuirass of metal plates across the chest and as long flexible bonds of steel over the shoulders. Their sound was like the rushing of war chariots into battle (v. 9: cf. Joel 2:5).

This description creates an image of the fearful onslaught of demonic forces in the last days. Their leader is called "Abaddon" in Hebrew and "Apollyon" in Greek (v. 11). The term Abaddon means "destruction" or "ruin" (Job 26:6 mg.; Prov. 27:20 mg.) and more often "the place of ruin" in Sheol (Job 26:6 mg.; Prov. 15:11 mg.; 27:20 mg.), or "death" (Job 28:22 mg.), or "the grave" (Ps. 88:11 mg.). In late Jewish nonbiblical apocalyptic texts and the Qumran literature, it refers to the personification of death.

The term Apollyon means "exterminator" or "destroyer" and does not occur eleswhere in the Bible, though it can be readily understood as the Greek equivalent of what is personified in the Hebrew word Abaddon. Some understand Apollyon to be a separate angel entrusted with authority over the Abyss. The creature, his name, and his responsibility seem to be original with the author of the Apocalypse.

Why John names the king of the Abyss in both Hebrew and Greek is not clear. Perhaps his readers' background in Hebrew, the language on which John's names and thoughts seem to turn (cf. 16:16), was so slender that an additional help here and there was necessary. This stylistic trait of giving information in bilingual terms is peculiar to Revelation and the fourth gospel (John 6:1; 19:13, 17, 20; 20:16). It may also reveal a mind steeped in the Targum tradition of the ancient synagogue, where it was customary to read Scripture in Hebrew and then in either Aramaic or Greek for those who did not understand Hebrew.

Verse 12 seems to be a transitional verse, indicating that the "first woe" (fifth trumpet) is finished and two woes are yet to come (presumably the sixth and seventh trumpets; cf. 8:13 with 11:14). This verse may again be spoken by the eagle (cf. 8:13).

The sixth trumpet: The second woe (vv. 13–19). Here we find a description of disasters that result in the death of a third of mankind (vv. 15, 18; cf. 8:7). "Four angels," the instruments of God's judgment, are held at the river Euphrates, from where in the past the enemies of God's ancient people often advanced on the land of Israel (Jer. 2:18 mg.; 13:4f. mg.; 51:63; Rev. 16:12) and which was recognized as the eastern extremity of the Promised Land (Gen. 15:18). John here makes use of the ancient geographical terms to depict the fearful character of the coming judgment of God on a rebellious world. While the language is drawn from historical-political events of the Old Testament, it describes realities that far transcend a local event. God's dealings are not accidental but planned and precise in time, down to the year, month, day, and hour (v. 15). The reference to the "golden altar" of incense connects the release of these angels again with the prayers of God's saints for vindication (6:9; 8:3).

Verse 16 rather abruptly introduces a mounted army of some 200 million horses and riders. While some argue for a literal, human army here, several factors point to their identity as *demonic* forces. First, the horsemen are not in themselves important, but they wear brightly colored breastplates of fiery red, dark blue, and sulfurous yellow, more suggestive of supernatural than natural riders. More important are the horses, which have heads resembling those of lions; they, rather than their riders, are the instruments of death by the plagues of fire, smoke, and sulfur that come from their mouths. Furthermore, these horses have tails like snakes that are able to kill (vv. 17–19), unlike the locusts' scorpionlike tails that do not inflict death but only injury (v. 5). Finally, according to General William K. Harrison (an expert in military logistics), an army of 200 million could not be conscripted, supported, and moved to the Middle East without totally disrupting all societal needs and capabilities; God has made men with certain limitations and the actual raising and transporting of an army of the size spoken of in verse 16 completely transcends human capability. All the Allied and Axis forces at their peak in World War II numbered only about 70 million.

Thus it seems better to understand the vast numbers and the description of the horses as indicating demonic hordes. Elesewhere in Scripture such large numbers do occasionally indicate angelic hosts (Ps. 68:17; Rev. 5:11; cf. 2 Kings 2:11–12; 6:17). This would not eliminate the possibility of human armies of manageable size also being involved. But the emphasis here (vv. 16–19) is on their wholly demonic character—utterly cruel and determined, showing no mercy to man, woman, or child. These demons, besides constituting an army, might also manifest themselves in pestilences, epidemic diseases, or misfortunes; this would explain the use of "plagues" to describe these hordes (vv. 18, 20; cf. 11:6; 16:9, 21).

2. The Purpose of God's Judgment (9:20–21)

God's purpose behind the plagues is first of all a *judgment* on humanity for willfully choosing idolatry and the corrupt practices that go with it (v. 21). John had earlier called on the churches to "repent" of their faithless tendencies, lest they too should share in God's judgment (2:5, 16, 21–22; 3:19). In these verses we see the end result of refusing to turn to God. This stubbornness leads to worship of demons as well as worship of cultic objects made by human hands (of "gold, silver, bronze, stone, and wood"; cf. Pss. 115:4–7; 135:17; Jer. 10:1–16; Dan. 5:23). "Demons" may mean either pagan deities (Deut. 32:17; Ps. 106:37) or malign spirits (1 Cor. 10:20–21; 1 Tim. 4:1). But since John here distinguishes the cultic objects from the demons, he no doubt shared Paul's concept of demons as evil spirits (Rev. 16:14; 18:2). Hence, there is a twofold evil in idol worship: it robs the true God of His glory (Rom. 1:23) and it leads to consorting with evil spirits that corrupt man.

This demonic corruption is manifest in the inhuman acts of those who have given up God for idols—acts of murder, sexual immorality, and thefts (cf. Rom. 1:24, 28–31). In general, these are violations of the ten commandments. "Magic arts" means "a practice of sorceries" or "witchcraft" (Exod. 7:11; 9:11; Gal. 5:20; Rev. 21:8; 22:15).

The second purpose of God revealed in the agonizing plagues described in chapters 8 and 9 is to bring societies to *repentance* (cf. 16:9, 11). God is not willing that any person should suffer His judgment but that all should repent and turn to Him (Luke 13:3, 5; 2 Peter 3:9). But when God's works and words are persistently rejected, only judgment remains (Eph. 5:6; Heb. 10:26–31).

C. Second Interlude: The Little Book and the Two Witnesses (10:1–11:14)

The sequence of the sixth and seventh trumpets, like that of the sixth and seventh seals, is interrupted to provide additional information bearing on the previous events and to prepare the reader for further developments.

1. *The little book* (10:1–11)

The author sees a mighty angel (possibly Michael, "the great prince"; Dan. 12:1 whom he describes in such dazzling terms (cloud, rainbow, sun, fiery pillars) that some have identified him with Christ. But angels are always angels in the Apocalypse, as well as in the rest of the New Testament, and should not be identified with Christ. The voice that speaks in verses 4 and 8 could, however, be that of Jesus.

The angel has in his hand a small scroll (v. 2). This scroll should not be confused with the Lamb's scroll of chapters 5–7, but should be connected with the symbolic scroll of Ezekiel (Ezek. 2:9–3:3; cf. Jer. 15:15–17). Ezekiel was told to "eat" the scroll just as John is told to eat the scroll given him (vv. 9–10), an action symbolizing the reception of the Word of God into the innermost being as a necessary prerequisite to proclaim it with confidence. John could see the words on the scroll because it "lay open" in the angel's hand. The angel standing on both land and sea symbolizes that the prophetic message is for the whole world.

When the angel shouts (v. 3), seven thunders speak, and John proceeds to write down their words. But he is interrupted and is commanded, "Seal up what the seven thunders have said and do not write it down" (v. 4). Conceivably, this might have been another series of seven. Either the seven thunders were intended for John's own illumination and were not essential to the main vision of the seven trumpets, or the reference is designed to strike a note of mystery with reference to God's revelatory activities (cf. 2 Cor. 12:4). As the visible portion of an iceberg is only a small part of it, so God's disclosures reveal only part of His total being and purposes.

The angel's raising his right hand to heaven doubtless alludes to the Jewish oath-swearing procedure (Deut. 32:40; Dan. 12:7). He swears that "there will be no more delay" (v. 6). Clearly there is some type of progression in the seals, trumpets, and bowls that nears its conclusion as the seventh trumpet is about to sound (v. 7). When the seventh trumpet is finally sounded, there is an announcement that "the kingdom of the world has become the kingdom of our Lord and of his Christ" and that the time has come to judge the dead, to reward the saints, and to destroy those who destroy the earth (11:15, 18). These events are recorded in the remaining chapters of the book, which include the seven bowl judgments and the new heavens and the new earth.

In 10:7 it is announced that "the mystery of God" (His purposes for man and the world as revealed to both the Old Testament and New Testament prophets) will be accomplished. The NIV translation of verse 7 suggests that this consummation comes before the blowing of the seventh trumpet: "when the seventh angel is about to sound his trumpet. . . ." While this is grammatically possible, it is also possible to render the expression "about to sound" as "when he shall sound." Thus understood, the meaning is that "in the days of" (i.e., during the period of) the sounding of the seventh trumpet the final purposes of God will be completed. This rendering clarifies the statement in 11:14, made just before the seventh trumpet sounds, "The second woe has passed: the third woe is coming soon." The seventh trumpet will therefore reveal the final judgments of the bowls and the final establishment of God's rule on the earth.

John, like Ezekiel, is now commanded to take the prophetic scroll and eat it (v. 9). The scroll tasted "as sweet as honey" but was bitter to the stomach (v. 10). Receiving the Word of God is a great joy; but since the Word is an oracle of judgment, it results in the unpleasant experience of proclaiming a message of wrath and woe (cf. Jer. 15:16, 19). Some argue that the content of the scroll is more specifically

> a message for the believing church and is to be found in the following verses (11:1–13). . . . It is *after* the eating of the book that John is told he must prophesy again, this time concerning many peoples, nations, tongues, and kings (Rev. 10:11). This begins with chapter 12. The sweet scroll which turns the stomach bitter is a message for the church. Before the final triumph believers are going to pass through a formidable ordeal . . . . So the little scroll unveils the lot of the faithful in those last days of Satanic opposition (Mounce).

In any case, the sweetness should not be taken to refer to the joy of proclaiming a message of wrath, for to all God's prophets this was a sorrowful, bitter task (Jer. 9:1).

The chief import of chapter 10 seems to be a confirmation of John's prophetic call, as verse 11 indicates: "You must prophesy again about many peoples, nations, languages and kings." This prophesying should not be understood as merely a recapitulation in greater detail of the previous visions but as a further progression of the events connected with the end. Notice in verse 11 the use of the word "kings" instead of "tribes" (as in 5:9; 7:9; 13:7; 14:6). This may anticipate the emphasis on the kings of the earth in 17:9–12 and elsewhere.

2. The temple and the two prophets (11:1–14)

Some have considered this chapter one of the most difficult to interpret in the Book of Revelation. In it, John refers to the temple, the Holy City, and the two prophets who are killed by the beast and after three and one-half days are resurrected and ascend to heaven. Does John intend all this to be understood literally—viz., the literal temple in Jerusalem; two people prophesying for 1,260 days, who are killed by the Antichrist, raised from the dead, and ascend to heaven; a great earthquake that kills seven thousand people, while the survivors glorify God? Or does he intend all or part of these as symbols? Furthermore, how does this section (11:1–13) relate to the total context (10:1–11:19)?

As in chapter 7, John's references to particular Jewish entities create the chief source of the problem. Does he use these references in a plain, one-to-one sense, or does he use them representatively or symbolically? While details of interpretation vary, there are but two main approaches to the chapter: (1) the temple, altar, worshipers, and Holy City have to do with the Jewish people and their place in the plan of God; or (2) John here refers to the Christian church.

While both views will be discussed in the following verses, at the outset it may be helpful to state why the Jewish view is less preferable. One school of commentators, generally dispensational, understands the "temple" and the "city" to refer to a rebuilt Jewish temple in Jerusalem. While in this view some elements in the description may be symbolic, the main import of the passage is seen as depicting a future protection of the nation of Israel prior to her spiritual regeneration. The Antichrist (beast) will permit the rebuilding of the temple in Jerusalem as well as the restoration of Jewish worship for three-and-a-half years; but then he will break his covenant and trample down a part of the temple and the Holy City until Christ returns to deliver the Jewish people (cf. Dan. 9:27).

The Jewish view suffers from its inability to relate this chapter to the context of chapter 10, to the parallelism with the seal interlude (ch. 7), to the ministry and significance of the two witnesses, and to the further chapters in Revelation (esp. chs. 12–13). Therefore, it is better to understand chapter 11 as referring to the whole Christian community.

a) *The measuring of the temple* (11:1–2a)

John is given a "reed," or "cane," long and straight like a "rod," and thus suitable for measuring a large building or area. (The measuring rod referred to in Ezek. 40:5 was about ten feet long.) The purpose of the reed is to "measure the temple of God and the altar." Most agree that the principal Old Testament passage in John's mind was Ezekiel's lengthy description of the measuring of the future kingdom temple (Ezek. 40:3–48:35). Since interpreters are confused about what Ezekiel's vision means, the ambiguity extends also to John's description. In the ancient world, measuring of shorter lengths was accomplished with the reed cane (Ezek. 40:2ff.) or, of longer distances, with a rope line (1 Kings 7:23; Isa. 44:13). "Measuring" may refer to the promise of restoration and rebuilding, with emphasis on extension or enlargement (Jer. 31:39; Zech. 1:16), or also the marking of something for destruction (2 Sam. 8:2; 2 Kings 21:13; Isa. 28:17; Lam. 2:8; Amos 7:7–9). In Ezekiel 40:2ff., this latter sense would be inappropriate. But what does John's measuring mean?

Since John is told in verse 2 not to measure the outer court but to leave it for the nations to overrun, it may be that here in chapter 11 the measuring means that the temple of God, the altar, and the worshipers are to be secured for blessing and preserved from spiritual harm or defilement. In 21:15–17, John similarly depicts the angel's measuring of the heavenly city (with a golden rod), apparently to mark off the city and its inhabitants from harm and defilement (21:24, 27). As a parallel to the sealing of 7:1–8, the measuring does not symbolize preservation from physical harm but the prophetic guarantee that none of the faithful worshipers of Jesus as the Messiah will perish, even though they suffer physical destruction at the hand of the beast (13:7).

In Ezekiel 43:10, the prophet is told to "describe the temple to the people of Israel, that they may be ashamed of their sins." The purpose of the elaborate description and temple measurement in Ezekiel is to indicate the glory and holiness of God in Israel's midst and to convict them of their defilement of His sanctuary (43:12). Likewise, John's prophetic ministry calls for a clear separation between those who are holy and those who have defiled themselves with the idolatry of the beast.

John is to measure "the temple of God." Does John mean the heavenly temple often mentioned in Revelation (cf. 11:19; 15:5, 8; 16:17), or does he refer to the Christian community as in 3:12: "Him who overcomes I will make a pillar in the temple of my God"? In the postapostolic Epistle of Barnabas (16:1ff.), the temple is the individual Christian or alternately the community of Christians, as it is in Paul (1 Cor. 3:16; 6:19; 2 Cor. 6:16). Since John refers to the "outer court" in verse 2, which is trampled by the nations, it is likely that he has in mind not the heavenly temple of God but an earthly one—either the (rebuilt?) temple in Jerusalem or, symbolically, the covenant people.

In the Gospels, "temple" always refers to the temple in Jerusalem, with the single exception of John's gospel, where it refers to Jesus' own body (John 2:19–21; cf. Rev. 21:22). Outside the Gospels it refers either to pagan shrines (Acts 17:24; 19:24) or, in Paul's letters, metaphorically to the physical bodies of Christians or to the church of God (1 Cor. 3:16; 6:19; 2 Cor. 6:16; Eph. 2:21). In only one case is it debatable whether Paul means the literal Jerusalem temple or the church (2 Thess. 2:4). It seems therefore best (although this view is not without problems) to take the temple in this verse (11:1) as representing the church in the Great Tribulation, the messianic community of both Jews and Gentiles, comparable to the symbol of the woman in chapter 12 (q.v.).

The "altar," which literally refers to the huge stone altar of sacrifice in the court of the priests, and the "worshipers," which would most naturally indicate the priests and others in the three inner courts (the court of the priests, the court of Israel, the court of the women), then represent symbolically the true servants of God, while the measuring symbolizes their recognition and acceptance by God in the same manner as the numbering in chapter 7. The writer of Hebrews likewise speaks of an "altar" from which Christians eat, but from which the Jewish priests who serve in the temple are not qualified to eat (Heb. 13:10)—referring to the once-for-all sacrifice of Christ on the cross, utilizing images derived from the temple.

As the "outer court" (v. 2) of the Jerusalem temple was frequented by a mixed group including Gentiles and unbelievers, so in John's mind there may be a part of the earthly temple or community of God where those who are impure or unfaithful will be (21:8, 22:15). It may be argued on the one hand that the effect of not measuring this part of the temple is to exclude it and those in it from spiritual security and God's blessing, in contrast to the way the measuring secured these things for the true community. Thus, when measuring the temple, Ezekiel is instructed to exclude from the sanctuary "the foreigners uncircumcised in heart and flesh" (Ezek. 44:5–9)—i.e., pagans who do not worship the true God and whose presence would desecrate the sanctuary. Previously, John has shown concern over those who were associated with the local churches but were not true worshipers of Christ (cf. 2:14–16, 20–25; 3:1–5, 16). When the great test comes, they will join the ranks of the beast and reveal their true colors.

On the other hand, it may be better to understand the desecration of the outer court as a symbolic reference to the victory of the beast over the saints which is described in verse 7. Thus, by using two slightly different images, that of the temple, altar, and worshipers and that of the outer court and Holy City, John is viewing the church under different aspects. Though the Gentiles (pagans) are permitted to touch the "outer court" and to trample on the "Holy City" for a limited time ("42 months"), they are not able to destroy the church because the "inner sanctuary" is measured or protected in keeping with Christ's earlier words: "and the gates of Hades will not overcome it" (Matt. 16:18).

Since John says that the outer court will be "given to the Gentiles," it is important to establish the best translation of "Gentiles." The word may have, in the New Testament, the more general sense of "nations," describing the various ethnic or national groups among mankind (e.g., Matt. 24:9, 14; Luke 24:47; Rom. 1:5; 15:11). In other contexts, it may be used as a narrower technical term to denote "Gentiles" in contrast to the Jewish people (e.g., Matt. 4:15; 10:5; Luke 2:32; Acts 10:45; Rom. 11:11). In many cases the broader sense may shade off into the narrower, producing ambiguity. Furthermore, just as the Jews referred to all other peoples outside the covenant as "Gentiles," so there gradually developed a similar Christian usage of the term that saw all peoples who were outside of Christ as "Gentiles," including unbelieving Jews (1 Cor. 5:1; 12:2; 1 Thess. 4:5; 1 Peter 2:12; 3 John 7). Our word "heathen" may parallel this usage of the word.

However, when the sixteen cases of the plural form in Revelation are examined, not once is the sense "Gentiles" appropriate. Throughout Revelation, the word refers to the peoples of the earth, either in rebellion against God (11:18; 14:8; 19:15; 20:3) or redeemed and under the rule of Christ (2:26; 21:24, 26; 22:2). There is no good reason why John would not intend the same sense in 11:2. Nevertheless, the versions reflect the uncertainty of the translators: "Gentiles" (KJV, KNOX, NEB, NIV) or "nations" (RSV, NASB, PHILLIPS).

To sum up, John's words "given to the Gentiles" refer to the defiling agencies that will trample down the outer court of the church, leading either to defection from Christ or physical destruction, though the inner sanctuary of the true believers will not be defiled by idolatry. This spiritual preservation of the true believers will be accomplished by John's prophetic ministry, which will separate true loyalty to Christ from the deception of the beast.

b) *The trampling of the Holy City* (11:2b)

The nations will "trample on the holy city for 42 months." Opinion varies as to the literal or the symbolic significance of the term "the holy city." The more literal viewpoint sees "the holy city" as the earthly city of Jerusalem. Support for this is found in (1) the Old Testament's use (Neh. 11:1; Isa. 48:2; 52:1; Dan. 9:24) and Matthew's use of "holy city" for Jerusalem (Matt. 4:5; 27:53); (2) the proximity of the term "the holy city" to the temple reference (v. 1); and (3) the mention in verse 8 of the "great city . . . where also their Lord was crucified."

Since Jerusalem was destroyed in A.D. 70, and since Revelation was presumably written about A.D. 95 (cf. Introduction), the more literalistic interpreters hold two views about the meaning of this reference to the city. Some believe it to refer to the rebuilt city and temple during the future Tribulation period. Others see the city as merely a representative or symbolic reference to the Jewish people, without any special implication of a literal city or temple. But if John does in fact differentiate here between believing Jews (inner court) and the nation as a whole (outer court), this would be the only place in the book where he does so. Furthermore, such a reference at this point in the context of chapters 10 and 11 would be abrupt and unconnected with the main themes in these chapters, the subject of which is the nature of the prophetic ministry and the great trial awaiting Christians.

Far more in keeping with the emphasis of the whole book and of these chapters in particular is the view that in the mind of John "the holy city," like the temple, refers to the church; the expression "holy city" consistently means the community of those faithful to Jesus Christ, composed of believing Jews and Gentiles (21:2, 10; 22:19; cf. 3:12; 20:9). It should also be noted that the name Jerusalem is not used in chapter 11 and that the circumlocution for it in verse 8, "where also their Lord was crucified," is prefaced with the word "figuratively." While the vision of the future Holy City (chs. 21–22) describes the condition of the city when she has completed her great ordeal and is finally delivered from the great deceiver, the present reference is to the people as they must first endure the trampling of the pagan nations for "42 months."

Does the trampling indicate defilement and apostasy, or does it instead mean persecution? The word "trample" can metaphorically mean either of these, but two factors favor the latter sense. The time of the trampling is "42 months," which is the exact time John attributes to the reign of the beast (13:5–7). Furthermore, in Daniel's prophecy the "trampling" of the sanctuary and of the host of God's people by Antiochus Epiphanes (Dan. 8:10, 13; 2 Macc. 8:2) is clearly a persecution of the people of God.

The expression "42 months" occurs in the Bible only here and in 13:5. Mention is also made of a period of 1,260 days (i.e., 42 months of 30 days each) in 11:3 and 12:6. In 12:14 a similar length of time is referred to as "a time, times [i.e., two times] and half a time." All these expressions equal a three-and-one-half-year period.

The term "42 months" refers to the period of oppression of the Holy City and the time of the authority of the beast (11:2; 13:5). The "1,260 days" is the period the two witnesses prophesy and the time the woman is protected from the dragon's reach (11:3; 12:6). "Time, times and half a time" seems to be used synonymously for the 1,260 days during which the woman will be protected in the desert (12:14). We cannot assume that because these periods are equal they are identical. On the other hand, the three different expressions may well be literary variations for the same period. Daniel is generally taken to be the source of the terms.

Daniel 9:27 speaks of a "week" ("seven," NIV), and the context makes it clear that this is a week of years, i.e., seven years. This "week" is divided in half—i.e., three years and a half for each division. Daniel 7:25 refers to these half weeks of years as "a time, times and half a time." Early Jewish and general patristic interpretation, followed by the early Protestant commentators, referred this to the period of the reign of the Antichrist.

In Daniel 12:7 the identical expression refers to the period "when the power of the holy people has been finally broken"; in 12:11 the same period refers to the time of the "abomination" and defilement of the temple.[2] Whether or not these references relate to the activities of Antiochus Epiphanes in the second century B.C. must be left to the exegetes of Daniel; but it is known that the Jews and later the Christians believed that these events at least foreshadow, if not predict, the last years of world history under the Antichrist. Thus John would have a ready tool to use in this imagery for setting forth his revelation of the last days.

Some, following certain early church fathers, suggest that the first three-and-a-half years is the period of the preaching of the two witnesses, while the second half of the week is the time of bitter trial when Antichrist reigns supreme. Others believe that the expressions are synchronous and thus refer to the identical period. With some reservations, the first view may be followed. The 1,260-day period of protected prophesying by the two witnesses (11:3-6) coincides with the period of the woman in the desert (12:6, 14). After the death of the witnesses (11:7) follows the forty-two-month murderous reign of the beast (13:5, 7, 15), which coincides with the trampling down of the Holy City (11:2). This twofold division seems also to be supported by Jesus' Olivet Discourse, where He speaks of the "beginning of birth pains" (Matt. 24:8) and then of the period of "great distress" shortly before His Parousia (coming) (Matt. 24:21).

Finally, are the two periods of three-and-a-half years symbolic or do they indicate calendar years? Not all will agree, but a symbolic sense that involves a real period yet understands the numbers to describe the *kind* of period rather than its length is in keeping with John's use of numbers elsewhere (cf. 2:10; 4:4; 7:4). Hence, if we tentatively follow the twofold division of Daniel's seventieth week of seven years, the preaching of the two witnesses occupies the first half, while the second half is the time of bitter trial when the beast reigns supreme and the fearful events of chapters 13-19 take place.

c) *The two prophets* (11:3-14)

Perhaps more diversity of interpretation surrounds these two personages than even the temple in the previous verses. They are called "two

---

[2]In Daniel 12:11 the length of the period is given as 1,290 rather than 1,260 days; the context, however, makes it clear that verse 7 and verse 11 both refer to the same three-and-a-half-year period.

witnesses" (v. 3), "two prophets" (v. 10), and figuratively "the two olive trees and the two lampstands who stand before the Lord of the earth" (v. 4). Identifications range all the way from two historic figures raised to life to two principles, such as the law and the prophets. Jewish tradition taught that Moses and Elijah would return, and this view is followed by a number of Christian interpreters. Some believe that they are two prophets of the future who will perform the functions of Moses and Elijah. Others understand the figures to represent the church. "The witness of the church, borne by her martyrs and confessors, her saints and doctors, and by the words and lives of all in whom Christ lives and speaks, is one continual prophecy" (Swete). More recently, an interpreter has identified them with the Christian prophets Peter and Paul. Another sees them as representatives of the Jewish and Gentile believers in the church. Still another understands the two to represent all the prophets.

Since opinion varies so greatly on this point, it may be wise not to be dogmatic about any one view. Our suggestion is that the two witnesses represent those in the church who are specially called, like John, to bear prophetic witness to Christ during the whole age of the church. They also represent those prophets who will be martyred by the beast.[3] They are "clothed in sackcloth" because they are prophets (cf. Isa. 20:2; Zech. 13:4) who call for repentance and humility (Jer. 6:26; 49:3; Matt. 11:21); it was the most suitable garb for times of distress, grief, danger, crisis, and humility. That God Himself will appoint them ("give power" to them) would encourage the church to persevere even in the face of strong opposition.

The reference to the "two olive trees and the two lampstands" is an allusion to Joshua and Zerubbabel in Zechariah's vision, who were also said "to serve the LORD of all the earth" (Zech. 4:1–6a, 10b–14). The whole import of Zechariah's vision was to strengthen the two leaders by reminding them of God's resources and to vindicate them in the eyes of the community as they pursued their God-given tasks. Thus John's message would be that the witnesses to Christ, who cause the church to fulfill her mission to burn as bright lights to the world, will not be quenched (cf. Rev. 1:20; 2:5).

Why there should be *two* olive trees and *two* lampstands has been variously answered. Some suggest that "two" is the number of required legal witnesses (Num. 35:30; Deut. 19:15; cf. Matt. 18:16; Luke 10:1–24);

---

[3]Indications that they are representative of *many* individuals and not just two are that (1) they are never seen as individuals but do everything together—they prophesy together, suffer together, are killed together, are raised together, and ascend together—which stresses their collective aspect; (2) the beast (lit.) "makes war on them" (v. 7), which is strange if they are merely two individuals; (3) people throughout the whole world view their ignominious deaths (v. 9)—something impossible if only two individuals are involved; (4) they are described as two "lamps" (v. 4), a figure applied in chapters 1 and 2 to local churches comprised of many individuals.

two witnesses are world-wide in scope (vv. 9–10), we may infer that earthquake is also symbolic of a world-wide event. Verse 13 shows it even in the midst of judgment, God is active in the world to save those who repent. If there is such hope in the terrible time of final judgment, how much more now! God has not abandoned the human race, regardless of the recurring waves of unbelief. Neither should we!

In verse 14 we are reminded that all the events from 9:13 to 11:14 fall under the sixth trumpet and are called the second "woe" (see comments on 8:13 and 9:12). Since there are further judgments (woes) mentioned in this chapter, it is natural to see the third woe as taking place at the sounding of the seventh trumpet (vv. 15–19). Its nature is described in the bowl judgments (16:11ff.). Apparently the third woe will come without further delay. Indeed, the seventh trumpet (v. 15) brings us to the final scenes of God's unfolding mystery (10:7).

For Further Study

1. Review the two basic views of the relationship between the seals, trumpets, and bowls. Write out your understanding of the best view.

2. How do you feel about the relationship between the symbolical and literal in the wording used in the trumpet judgments (e.g., "fire mingled with blood," 8:7)?

3. If John received a revelation from Christ, why does this commentary talk so much about Old Testament sources (such as the Exodus plagues) for John's language?

4. Which of the trumpet plagues actually affect mankind in a deadly sense?

5. Why does God send judgment on the world (9:20–21)? Are there other reasons as well?

6. Explain the significance of the "little book" that was sweet and bitter to John (10:9–11). Relate this to Christian witness today.

7. Following the Jewish interpretation of the temple and the two witnesses in chapter 11, what application could be brought to the contemporary church? Following the alternate interpretation?

others suggest that "two" represents the priestly and kingly aspects of the church, or the Jewish and Gentile components, etc. Perhaps the dualism was suggested to John by the two olive trees from Zechariah and the two great prophets of the Old Testament who were connected with the coming of the Messiah in Jewish thought, i.e., Moses and Elijah (v. 6; cf. Matt. 17:3–4). What Joshua (the high priest) and Zerubbabel (the prince) were to the older community and temple, Jesus Christ is to the new community. He is both anointed Priest and King, and His church reflects this character especially in its Christian prophets (1:6; 5:10; 20:6).

In verse 5 the prophets' divine protection from their enemies is described in terms reminiscent of the former prophets' protection by God (2 Kings 1:10; Jer. 5:14). Fire is understood symbolically as judgment from God; and since it proceeds from the witnesses' mouths, we understand that their message of judgment will eventually be fulfilled by God's power (Gen. 19:23f.; 2 Sam. 22:9; Ps. 97:3). Their Lord gives them immunity from destruction until they complete their affirmation of God's saving deed in Christ. This assures the people of God that no matter how many of its chosen saints are oppressed and killed, God's witness to Christ will continue until His purposes are fulfilled.

The words "power to shut up the sky . . . and power to turn the waters into blood" (v. 6) clearly allude to the ministries of the prophets Elijah and Moses (1 Kings 17:1; Exod. 7:17–21). There is, however, no need for the literal reappearing of these two if it is understood that the two witnesses come in the same spirit and with the same function as their predecessors (cf. Luke's interpretation of the significance of John the Baptist as a ministry in the "spirit and power of Elijah"; Luke 1:17). According to Luke 4:25 and James 5:17, Elijah's prophecy shut up the heaven for "three and a half years," a curious foreshadowing, perhaps, of the span of time that these prophets witness (i.e., 1,260 days; v. 3).

When they have finished their testimony, the witnesses are killed by the beast from the Abyss (v. 7). This is the first reference to the "beast" in the book. The abruptness with which it is introduced seems not only to presuppose some knowledge of the beast but also to anticipate what is said of him in chapters 13 and 17. Only here and in 17:8 is the beast described as coming "up from the Abyss" (cf. 9:1), showing his demonic origin. He attacks the prophets (lit., "makes war with them"; cf. 9:7; 12:7, 17; 13:7; 16:14; 19:19; 20:8); this may reflect Daniel 7:21: "As I watched, this horn was waging war against the saints and defeating them." This attack is again described in 12:17: "Then the dragon was enraged at the woman and went off to make war against the rest of her offspring" and in 13:7: "[The beast] was given power to make war against the saints and to conquer them." This is the second and final phase of the dragon's persecution of the Christian prophets and saints.

In verse 8 we have the place of the attack on the witnesses and the place of their death: "The street of the great city, which is figuratively called Sodom and Egypt, where also their Lord was crucified." At first glance, it seems apparent that in verse 8 John refers to the actual city of Jerusalem where Christ died. Yet John's terminology implies more than this. The city is called the "great city," a designation that refers to Babylon throughout the rest of the book (16:19; 17:18; 18:10, 16, 18–19, 21). Moreover, John's use of the word "city," from its first occurrence in 3:12, is symbolic. In fact, there are really only two cities in the book, the city of God and the city of Satan, which is later referred to as Babylon. A city may be a metaphor for the total life of a community of people (Heb. 11:10; 12:22; 13:14).

Here the "great city" is clearly more than merely Jerusalem, for John says it is "figuratively called Sodom and Egypt." "Figuratively" means "spiritually, in a spiritual manner, full of the divine Spirit." Elsewhere in the New Testament, the word characterizes that which pertains to the Spirit in contrast to the flesh (1 Cor. 2:14–15; Eph 1:3; 5:19; Col. 3:16; 1 Peter 2:5, etc.).[4] The spiritually discerning will catch the significance of the threefold designation of this city. It is called "Sodom," which connotes rebellion against God, rejection of God's servants, moral degradation, and the awfulness of divine judgment (Cf. Ezek. 16:49). In Isaiah's day the rebellious rulers of Jerusalem were called the rulers of Sodom (Isa. 1:10; cf. Ezek. 16:46). The second designation is "Egypt." Egypt, however, is a country, not a city; but it is virtually certain that by John's time "Egypt" had become a symbolic name for antitheocratic world kingdoms that enslaved Israel. The third designation is "the great city, . . . where also their Lord was crucified" (cf. Matt. 23:28–31, 37–38; Luke 13:33ff.; 21:20–24).

If, as most commentators believe, John also has Rome in mind when speaking of the "great city," then there are at least five places John sees as one—Babylon, Sodom, Egypt, Jerusalem, and Rome. This one city represents, to the spiritually discerning, all places opposed to God and to the witness of his servants—Sodom, Tyre, Egypt, Babylon, Nineveh, Rome, etc. Wherever God is opposed and His servants harassed and killed, there is the "great city," the transhistorical city of Satan, the great mother of prostitutes (cf. 17:1ff.). What can happen to God's witnesses in any place is what has already happened to their Lord in Jerusalem. Bunyan's city, called "Vanity Fair," approaches this idea, though not precisely, since John uses actual historical places where this great transhistorical city found its manifestation. "The great city in which the martyred church lies dead is the world under the wicked and oppressive sway of Antichrist" (Mounce).

---

[4]The RSV and NEB translate it "allegorically," which is questionable; the NASB has "mystically." Closer may be Knox's rendering "in the language of prophecy," or Minear's "prophetically," or Phillips' "is called by those with spiritual understanding."

People from every nation—Jews and Gentiles—will [...] corpses and refuse them the dignity of burial (vv. 9–[...] humiliation a person could suffer from his enemies was to [...] body lie in view of all (Ps. 79:3–4; Tobit 1:18ff.). Furthermo[...] world will celebrate the destruction of the witnesses and the[...] them by exchanging gifts, a common custom in the Near East [...] 12; Esth. 9:19, 22). Thus the beast will silence the witness of the[...] the glee of the beast-worshiping world. The time of their sile[...] sponds in days to the time of their witness in years: it will be on[...] time of triumph for the beast.

The witnesses now experience a resurrection and an ascen[...] heaven following their three-and-one-half-day-long death (vv. 11–[...] is generally held that Ezekiel's vision of the restoration of the dry [...] was in John's mind here (Ezek. 37:5, 10–12). Just as interpretation[...] Ezekiel's vision vary, so interpretations of Revelation 11:11–12 also va[...] Some hold that the vision of the dry bones refers to the spiritual quicke[...] ing of the nation of Israel. Others, following rabbinic interpretation an[...] certain church fathers, understand the descriptions to refer to the physi[...] cal resurrection of the dead. If the two witnesses represent the witness of[...] the church, then physical resurrection and ascension could be in view. The summons "Come up here" followed by "they went up to heaven in a cloud" perhaps points to the Rapture (cf. 1 Thess. 4:16–17.)

On the other hand, John may be using the figure of physical resurrection to represent the church's victory over the death blow delivered by the beast (cf. Rom. 11:15, where Paul uses the figure of resurrection symbolically to depict a great spiritual revival among the Jews in a future day). The "cloud" (v. 12) depicts the divine power, presence, and glory; this is the only instance in the book where strictly human figures are associated with a cloud. The two witnesses share in Christ's resurrection and the cloud is a sign of heaven's acceptance of their earthly career. Even their enemies see them, as they will see Christ when He returns with the clouds (1:7). The events of Christ's return and the ascension of the witnesses seem to be simultaneous. Thus, in the two witnesses John has symbolized the model of all true prophets, taking as a central clue the story of Jesus' appearance in Jerusalem and describing the common vocation of appearing in the Holy City (or temple) in such a way that reaction to their work would separate the worshipers of God from the unbelievers, in language drawn from the stories of many prophets. (Minear).

The earthquake (v. 13) is God's further sign of the vindication of His servants (cf. 6:12). But unlike the earthquake under the sixth seal, this one produces what appears to be repentance: "The survivors . . . gave glory to the God of heaven." The opposite response in 16:9, "they refused to repent and glorify him," seems to confirm that 11:13 speaks of genuine repentance (cf. 14:7; 15:4). Since the death, resurrection, and ascension of

Chapter 6

The Seventh Trumpet
(Revelation 11:15-14:20)

A. The Sounding of the Seventh Trumpet (11:15-19)

The seventh trumpet sounds, and in heaven loud voices proclaim the final triumph of God and Christ over the world. The theme is the kingdom of God and Christ—a dual kingdom, eternal in its duration. The kingdom is certainly a main theme of the Book of Revelation (1:6, 9; 5:10; 11:17; 12:10; 19:6; 20:4; 22:5); it involves the millennial kingdom and its blending into the eternal kingdom (chs. 20-22). The image suggests the transference of the world empire that, once dominated by a usurping power, has now at length passed into the hands of its true Owner and King. The present rulers are Satan, the beast, and the false prophet. The announcement of the reign of the King is made here, but the final breaking of the enemies' hold over the world does not occur till the return of Christ (19:11ff.).

Verses 15-18 are reminiscent of Psalm 2. The opening portion of this psalm describes the pagan nations and kings set in opposition to God and His Messiah (Anointed One), followed by the establishment of the Son in Zion as the Sovereign of the world and an appeal to the world rulers to put their trust in the Son before His wrath burns. John does not distinguish between the millennial kingdom of Christ and the eternal kingdom of the Father (but cf. 3:21) as Paul does (1 Cor. 15:24-28). This should be viewed as a difference merely of detail and emphasis, not of basic theology. Furthermore, in John's view this world becomes the arena for the manifestation of God's kingdom. While at this point the emphasis is on the future, visible establishment of God's kingdom, in John's mind that same kingdom is in a real sense present now, and he is participating in it (1:9).

As the other features in verses 16-17 are anticipatory, so the expression "have begun to reign" looks forward to the millennial reign depicted in chapter 20. Significantly, the title of God found earlier in the book, "who is, and who was, and who is to come" (1:8; 4:8), now is "who is and who was"—He has now *come*! God has taken the power of the world from Satan (Luke 4:6).

Verse 18 contains a synopsis of the remaining chapters of Revelation. The nations opposed to God and incited by the fury of the dragon (12:12) have brought wrath on God's people (Ps. 2:1–3). For this, God has brought His wrath upon the nations (14:7; 16:1ff.; 18:20; 19:19b; 20:11–15). The time ("season") has now come for three further events: the judgment of the dead (20:11–15); the final rewarding of the righteous (21:1–4; 22:3–5); and the final destruction of the destroyers of the earth (Babylon, the beast, the false prophet, and the dragon; 19:2, 20; 20:10).

In Revelation there are three groups of persons who receive rewards: (1) God's "servants the prophets" (cf. 18:20; 22:9); (2) the "saints" (perhaps the martyrs, cf. 5:8; 8:3–4; 13:7, 10; 16:6; 18:20, 24; or simply believers in every age, cf. 19:8; 20:9); and (3) "those who reverence God's name" (cf. 14:7; 15:4). It is important to note that in Revelation the prophets are specially singled out (16:6; 18:20, 24; 22:6, 9).

In the heavenly temple John sees the ark of God's covenant (v. 19). In the Old Testament the ark of the covenant was the chest that God directed Moses to have made and placed in the Most Holy Place in the tabernacle (Exod. 25:10–22). Moses was to put in the ark the two stone tablets of the Decalogue—the documentary basis of God's redemptive covenant with Israel (Exod. 34:28–29). It is presumed that the ark was destroyed when Nebuchadnezzar burned the temple in 586 B.C.; there was no ark in the second temple.

A Jewish legend reported in 2 Maccabees 2:4–8 indicates that Jeremiah hid the ark in a cave on Mount Sinai until the final restoration of Israel. There is no reason, however, to believe that John is alluding in verse 19 to this Jewish tradition, since he is clearly referring to a heavenly temple and ark, symbolic of the new covenant established by the death of Christ. While under the old covenant the way into the holiest was barred to all except the high priest, now full and immediate access for all, as well as a perfect redemption, has been secured by Christ's death (Heb. 9:11–12; 10:19–22).

In verse 19 the kingdom of God is seen retrospectively as having fully come, although its coming will be elaborated in chapters 20–22. Prospectively, this sight of the ark of the covenant also prepares us for the following chapters, which concern the faithfulness of God to His covenant people. As the ark of the covenant was the sign to Israel of God's loyal love throughout their wilderness journeys and battles, so this sign of the new covenant will assure the followers of Christ of His loyal love through their severe trial and the attack by the beast. "Flashes of lightning, rumblings, peals of thunder" call our attention to God's presence and vindication of His people (cf. comments on 6:12; 8:5).

At the sounding of the seventh trumpet, loud voices in heaven proclaimed that the "kingdom of the world" had become "the kingdom of our Lord and his Christ" (11:15). In chapters 12–14, which are interposed others suggest that "two" represents the priestly and kingly aspects of the church, or the Jewish and Gentile components, etc. Perhaps the dualism was suggested to John by the two olive trees from Zechariah and the two great prophets of the Old Testament who were connected with the coming of the Messiah in Jewish thought, i.e., Moses and Elijah (v. 6; cf. Matt. 17:3–4). What Joshua (the high priest) and Zerubbabel (the prince) were to the older community and temple, Jesus Christ is to the new community. He is both anointed Priest and King, and His church reflects this character especially in its Christian prophets (1:6; 5:10; 20:6).

In verse 5 the prophets' divine protection from their enemies is described in terms reminiscent of the former prophets' protection by God (2 Kings 1:10; Jer. 5:14). Fire is understood symbolically as judgment from God; and since it proceeds from the witnesses' mouths, we understand that their message of judgment will eventually be fulfilled by God's power (Gen. 19:23f.; 2 Sam. 22:9; Ps. 97:3). Their Lord gives them immunity from destruction until they complete their affirmation of God's saving deed in Christ. This assures the people of God that no matter how many of its chosen saints are oppressed and killed, God's witness to Christ will continue until His purposes are fulfilled.

The words "power to shut up the sky . . . and power to turn the waters into blood" (v. 6) clearly allude to the ministries of the prophets Elijah and Moses (1 Kings 17:1; Exod. 7:17–21). There is, however, no need for the literal reappearing of these two if it is understood that the two witnesses come in the same spirit and with the same function as their predecessors (cf. Luke's interpretation of the significance of John the Baptist as a ministry in the "spirit and power of Elijah"; Luke 1:17). According to Luke 4:25 and James 5:17, Elijah's prophecy shut up the heaven for "three and a half years," a curious foreshadowing, perhaps, of the span of time that these prophets witness (i.e., 1,260 days; v. 3).

When they have finished their testimony, the witnesses are killed by the beast from the Abyss (v. 7). This is the first reference to the "beast" in the book. The abruptness with which it is introduced seems not only to presuppose some knowledge of the beast but also to anticipate what is said of him in chapters 13 and 17. Only here and in 17:8 is the beast described as coming "up from the Abyss" (cf. 9:1), showing his demonic origin. He attacks the prophets (lit., "makes war with them"; cf. 9:7; 12:7, 17; 13:7; 16:14; 19:19; 20:8); this may reflect Daniel 7:21: "As I watched, this horn was waging war against the saints and defeating them." This attack is again described in 12:17: "Then the dragon was enraged at the woman and went off to make war against the rest of her offspring" and in 13:7: "[The beast] was given power to make war against the saints and to conquer them." This is the second and final phase of the dragon's persecution of the Christian prophets and saints.

In verse 8 we have the place of the attack on the witnesses and the place of their death: "The street of the great city, which is figuratively called Sodom and Egypt, where also their Lord was crucified." At first glance, it seems apparent that in verse 8 John refers to the actual city of Jerusalem where Christ died. Yet John's terminology implies more than this. The city is called the "great city," a designation that refers to Babylon throughout the rest of the book (16:19; 17:18; 18:10, 16, 18–19, 21). Moreover, John's use of the word "city," from its first occurrence in 3:12, is symbolic. In fact, there are really only two cities in the book, the city of God and the city of Satan, which is later referred to as Babylon. A city may be a metaphor for the total life of a community of people (Heb. 11:10; 12:22; 13:14).

Here the "great city" is clearly more than merely Jerusalem, for John says it is "figuratively called Sodom and Egypt." "Figuratively" means "spiritually, in a spiritual manner, full of the divine Spirit." Elsewhere in the New Testament, the word characterizes that which pertains to the Spirit in contrast to the flesh (1 Cor. 2:14–15; Eph 1:3; 5:19; Col. 3:16; 1 Peter 2:5, etc.).[4] The spiritually discerning will catch the significance of the threefold designation of this city. It is called "Sodom," which connotes rebellion against God, rejection of God's servants, moral degradation, and the awfulness of divine judgment (Cf. Ezek. 16:49). In Isaiah's day the rebellious rulers of Jerusalem were called the rulers of Sodom (Isa. 1:10; cf. Ezek. 16:46). The second designation is "Egypt." Egypt, however, is a country, not a city; but it is virtually certain that by John's time "Egypt" had become a symbolic name for antitheocratic world kingdoms that enslaved Israel. The third designation is "the great city, . . . where also their Lord was crucified" (cf. Matt. 23:28–31, 37–38; Luke 13:33ff.; 21:20–24).

If, as most commentators believe, John also has Rome in mind when speaking of the "great city," then there are at least five places John sees as one—Babylon, Sodom, Egypt, Jerusalem, and Rome. This one city represents, to the spiritually discerning, all places opposed to God and to the witness of his servants—Sodom, Tyre, Egypt, Babylon, Nineveh, Rome, etc. Wherever God is opposed and His servants harassed and killed, there is the "great city," the transhistorical city of Satan, the great mother of prostitutes (cf. 17:1ff.). What can happen to God's witnesses in any place is what has already happened to their Lord in Jerusalem. Bunyan's city, called "Vanity Fair," approaches this idea, though not precisely, since John uses actual historical places where this great transhistorical city found its manifestation. "The great city in which the martyred church lies dead is the world under the wicked and oppressive sway of Antichrist" (Mounce).

---

[4]The RSV and NEB translate it "allegorically," which is questionable; the NASB has "mystically." Closer may be Knox's rendering "in the language of prophecy," or Minear's "prophetically," or Phillips' "is called by those with spiritual understanding."

People from every nation—Jews and Gentiles—will "gloat over" their corpses and refuse them the dignity of burial (vv. 9–10). The worst humiliation a person could suffer from his enemies was to have his dead body lie in view of all (Ps. 79:3–4; Tobit 1:18ff.). Furthermore, the pagan world will celebrate the destruction of the witnesses and the victory over them by exchanging gifts, a common custom in the Near East (Neh. 8:10, 12; Esth. 9:19, 22). Thus the beast will silence the witness of the church to the glee of the beast-worshiping world. The time of their silence corresponds in days to the time of their witness in years: it will be only a brief time of triumph for the beast.

The witnesses now experience a resurrection and an ascension to heaven following their three-and-one-half-day-long death (vv. 11–12). It is generally held that Ezekiel's vision of the restoration of the dry bones was in John's mind here (Ezek. 37:5, 10–12). Just as interpretations of Ezekiel's vision vary, so interpretations of Revelation 11:11–12 also vary. Some hold that the vision of the dry bones refers to the spiritual quickening of the nation of Israel. Others, following rabbinic interpretation and certain church fathers, understand the descriptions to refer to the physical resurrection of the dead. If the two witnesses represent the witness of the church, then physical resurrection and ascension could be in view. The summons "Come up here" followed by "they went up to heaven in a cloud" perhaps points to the Rapture (cf. 1 Thess. 4:16–17.)

On the other hand, John may be using the figure of physical resurrection to represent the church's victory over the death blow delivered by the beast (cf. Rom. 11:15, where Paul uses the figure of resurrection symbolically to depict a great spiritual revival among the Jews in a future day). The "cloud" (v. 12) depicts the divine power, presence, and glory; this is the only instance in the book where strictly human figures are associated with a cloud. The two witnesses share in Christ's resurrection and the cloud is a sign of heaven's acceptance of their earthly career. Even their enemies see them, as they will see Christ when He returns with the clouds (1:7). The events of Christ's return and the ascension of the witnesses seem to be simultaneous. Thus, in the two witnesses John has symbolized the model of all true prophets, taking as a central clue the story of Jesus' appearance in Jerusalem and describing the common vocation of appearing in the Holy City (or temple) in such a way that reaction to their work would separate the worshipers of God from the unbelievers, in language drawn from the stories of many prophets. (Minear).

The earthquake (v. 13) is God's further sign of the vindication of His servants (cf. 6:12). But unlike the earthquake under the sixth seal, this one produces what appears to be repentance: "The survivors . . . gave glory to the God of heaven." The opposite response in 16:9, "they refused to repent and glorify him," seems to confirm that 11:13 speaks of genuine repentance (cf. 14:7; 15:4). Since the death, resurrection, and ascension of the two witnesses are world-wide in scope (vv. 9–10), we may infer that the earthquake is also symbolic of a world-wide event. Verse 13 shows that even in the midst of judgment, God is active in the world to save those who repent. If there is such hope in the terrible time of final judgment, how much more now! God has not abandoned the human race, regardless of the recurring waves of unbelief. Neither should we!

In verse 14 we are reminded that all the events from 9:13 to 11:14 fall under the sixth trumpet and are called the second "woe" (see comments on 8:13 and 9:12). Since there are further judgments (woes) mentioned in this chapter, it is natural to see the third woe as taking place at the sounding of the seventh trumpet (vv. 15–19). Its nature is described in the bowl judgments (16:11ff.). Apparently the third woe will come without further delay. Indeed, the seventh trumpet (v. 15) brings us to the final scenes of God's unfolding mystery (10:7).

For Further Study

1. Review the two basic views of the relationship between the seals, trumpets, and bowls. Write out your understanding of the best view.

2. How do you feel about the relationship between the symbolical and literal in the wording used in the trumpet judgments (e.g., "fire mingled with blood," 8:7)?

3. If John received a revelation from Christ, why does this commentary talk so much about Old Testament sources (such as the Exodus plagues) for John's language?

4. Which of the trumpet plagues actually affect mankind in a deadly sense?

5. Why does God send judgment on the world (9:20–21)? Are there other reasons as well?

6. Explain the significance of the "little book" that was sweet and bitter to John (10:9–11). Relate this to Christian witness today.

7. Following the Jewish interpretation of the temple and the two witnesses in chapter 11, what application could be brought to the contemporary church? Following the alternate interpretation?

Chapter 6

The Seventh Trumpet
(Revelation 11:15–14:20)

A. The Sounding of the Seventh Trumpet (11:15–19)

The seventh trumpet sounds, and in heaven loud voices proclaim the final triumph of God and Christ over the world. The theme is the kingdom of God and Christ—a dual kingdom, eternal in its duration. The kingdom is certainly a main theme of the Book of Revelation (1:6, 9; 5:10; 11:17; 12:10; 19:6; 20:4; 22:5); it involves the millennial kingdom and its blending into the eternal kingdom (chs. 20–22). The image suggests the transference of the world empire that, once dominated by a usurping power, has now at length passed into the hands of its true Owner and King. The present rulers are Satan, the beast, and the false prophet. The announcement of the reign of the King is made here, but the final breaking of the enemies' hold over the world does not occur till the return of Christ (19:11ff.).

Verses 15–18 are reminiscent of Psalm 2. The opening portion of this psalm describes the pagan nations and kings set in opposition to God and His Messiah (Anointed One), followed by the establishment of the Son in Zion as the Sovereign of the world and an appeal to the world rulers to put their trust in the Son before His wrath burns. John does not distinguish between the millennial kingdom of Christ and the eternal kingdom of the Father (but cf. 3:21) as Paul does (1 Cor. 15:24–28). This should be viewed as a difference merely of detail and emphasis, not of basic theology. Furthermore, in John's view this world becomes the arena for the manifestation of God's kingdom. While at this point the emphasis is on the future, visible establishment of God's kingdom, in John's mind that same kingdom is in a real sense present now, and he is participating in it (1:9).

As the other features in verses 16–17 are anticipatory, so the expression "have begun to reign" looks forward to the millennial reign depicted in chapter 20. Significantly, the title of God found earlier in the book, "who is, and who was, and who is to come" (1:8; 4:8), now is "who is and who was"—He has now *come*! God has taken the power of the world from Satan (Luke 4:6).

Verse 18 contains a synopsis of the remaining chapters of Revelation. The nations opposed to God and incited by the fury of the dragon (12:12) have brought wrath on God's people (Ps. 2:1–3). For this, God has brought His wrath upon the nations (14:7; 16:1ff.; 18:20; 19:19b; 20:11–15). The time ("season") has now come for three further events: the judgment of the dead (20:11–15); the final rewarding of the righteous (21:1–4; 22:3–5); and the final destruction of the destroyers of the earth (Babylon, the beast, the false prophet, and the dragon; 19:2, 20; 20:10).

In Revelation there are three groups of persons who receive rewards: (1) God's "servants the prophets" (cf. 18:20; 22:9); (2) the "saints" (perhaps the martyrs, cf. 5:8; 8:3–4; 13:7, 10; 16:6; 18:20, 24; or simply believers in every age, cf. 19:8; 20:9); and (3) "those who reverence God's name" (cf. 14:7; 15:4). It is important to note that in Revelation the prophets are specially singled out (16:6; 18:20, 24; 22:6, 9).

In the heavenly temple John sees the ark of God's covenant (v. 19). In the Old Testament the ark of the covenant was the chest that God directed Moses to have made and placed in the Most Holy Place in the tabernacle (Exod. 25:10–22). Moses was to put in the ark the two stone tablets of the Decalogue—the documentary basis of God's redemptive covenant with Israel (Exod. 34:28–29). It is presumed that the ark was destroyed when Nebuchadnezzar burned the temple in 586 B.C.; there was no ark in the second temple.

A Jewish legend reported in 2 Maccabees 2:4–8 indicates that Jeremiah hid the ark in a cave on Mount Sinai until the final restoration of Israel. There is no reason, however, to believe that John is alluding in verse 19 to this Jewish tradition, since he is clearly referring to a heavenly temple and ark, symbolic of the new covenant established by the death of Christ. While under the old covenant the way into the holiest was barred to all except the high priest, now full and immediate access for all, as well as a perfect redemption, has been secured by Christ's death (Heb. 9:11–12; 10:19–22).

In verse 19 the kingdom of God is seen retrospectively as having fully come, although its coming will be elaborated in chapters 20–22. Prospectively, this sight of the ark of the covenant also prepares us for the following chapters, which concern the faithfulness of God to His covenant people. As the ark of the covenant was the sign to Israel of God's loyal love throughout their wilderness journeys and battles, so this sign of the new covenant will assure the followers of Christ of His loyal love through their severe trial and the attack by the beast. "Flashes of lightning, rumblings, peals of thunder" call our attention to God's presence and vindication of His people (cf. comments on 6:12; 8:5).

At the sounding of the seventh trumpet, loud voices in heaven proclaimed that the "kingdom of the world" had become "the kingdom of our Lord and his Christ" (11:15). In chapters 12–14, which are interposed between the seventh trumpet and the final bowl judgments (15:1–19:10), John describes the efforts of the deposed ruler, Satan, to destroy the subjects of the new King. He picks up and further develops the theme of the persecution of God's people (cf. 3:10; 6:9–11; 7:14; 11:7–10). Chapter 12 gives us a glimpse into the dynamics of the persecution of God's people under the symbolism of the dragon who wages war on the woman and her children (v. 17). Chapter 13 continues the same theme by telling of the persecution of the saints by the two dragon-energized beasts. Finally, the section closes with the scene of the redeemed 144,000 on Mount Zion who are triumphant over the beast (14:1–5) and the final hour of judgment on the beast worshipers (14:6–20).

B. The Woman and the Dragon (12:1–17)

In this chapter there are three main figures: the woman, the child, and the dragon. There are also three scenes: the birth of the child (vv. 1–6), the expulsion of the dragon (vv. 7–12), and the dragon's attack on the woman and her children (vv. 13–17).

1. The birth of the child (12:1–6)

Background. John sees a dazzling sight—a pregnant woman, "clothed with the sun, with the moon under her feet," wearing a victor's crown (cf. 2:10; 3:11; 4:4, 10; 6:2; 9:7; 14:14) of twelve stars (v. 1). John calls the sight a "great sign." This shows that the woman is more than a mere woman—she signifies something. John generally uses "sign" to refer to a miraculous event or object (John 2:11, 18, et al.; Rev. 12:1, 3; 13:13–14; 15:1; 16:14; 19:20).

The basic plot of the story was a familiar one in the myths of the ancient world. A usurper doomed to be killed by a yet unborn prince plots to succeed to the throne by killing the royal seed at birth. The prince is miraculously snatched from his clutches and hidden away, until he is old enough to kill the usurper and claim his kingdom.[1] While it is easy to point to parallels between these earlier myths and Revelation 12, the differences are striking enough to eliminate the possibility that John merely borrowed pagan myths.

Did he, then, draw more directly on Old Testament parallels? Some cite Genesis 37:9–11, where the sun, moon, and eleven stars appear together in Joseph's vision. Joseph's father, Jacob, and his mother,

---

[1]In the Greek myth of the birth of Apollo, when the child's mother, the goddess Leto, reached the time of her delivery, she was pursued by the dragon Python who sought to kill both her and her unborn child. Only the tiny island of Delos welcomed the mother, where she gave birth to the god Apollo. Four days after his birth, Apollo found Python at Parnassus and killed him in his Delphic cave. In Egypt it is Set the red dragon who pursues Isis, the pregnant mother of Horus. When the child is grown, he too kills the dragon. These stories were living myths in the first century and were probably know to both John and his Asian readers.

Rachel, (the sun and the moon), together with his eleven brothers (the stars), bow down before Joseph. Yet while the sun, moon, and twelve stars are parallel in both accounts, the other details are quite different. For example, the woman and the child who are central in John's account are totally absent from Joseph's dream. It thus seems highly unlikely that John intended his readers to interpret this chapter on the basis of the Genesis material.

Others see a more conscious parallelism between this story and the activities of the emperor Domitian around A.D. 83. After the death of his ten-year-old son, Domitian immediately proclaimed the boy a god and his mother, Domitia, the mother of God. Coinage of this period shows Domitia as the mother of the gods (Cerea, Demeter, Cybele) or enthroned on the divine throne or standing with the scepter and diadem of the queen of heaven with the inscription "Mother of the Divine Caesar."

Whereas the coinage of Domitian glorifies the son of Domitia as the lord of heaven and savior of the world, Revelation 12 presents Jesus Christ, the Lord of heaven and earth, who will rule all nations with a rod of iron (v. 5). John thus demythologizes the contemporary Domitian myth by presenting Christ as the true and ascended Lord of heaven, the coming Ruler and Savior of the world.

Another approach is to compare the chapter with a passage in the Dead Sea Scrolls. The Hymn scroll contains a passage describing a woman who is pregnant with a man-child who is called "Marvelous Counselor" and "firstborn," perhaps a reference to the Messiah based on Isaiah 9:5–6. The woman symbolizes the "congregation of the just, the Church of the Saints, victim of the persecution of the wicked," and is also associated with the redeeming work of the Messiah.

Old Testament references to the birth of the Messiah through the messianic community (Isa. 9:6–7; Mic. 5:2) and to the travailing messianic community (Isa. 26:17; 66:7) should also be noted. In the Old Testament, the image of a woman is frequently associated with Israel, Zion, or Jerusalem (Isa. 54:1–6; Jer. 3:20; Ezek. 16:8–14; Hos. 2:19–20). This background seems to provide a much closer link to the intended significance of chapter 12 than the other proposed parallels. In any case, there seems to be in chapter 12 a blending of elements from Old Testament concepts, Jewish materials, ancient mythical stories, and possibly the Domitian child myth. Regardless of the sources or allusions, John reinterprets the older stories and presents a distinctively Christian view of history in the imagery of the woman and her child.

Who is the woman? While it is not impossible that she is an actual woman (e.g., Mary), the evidence clearly shows that she, like the woman in chapter 17, has symbolic significance. At the center of chapter 12 is the persecution of the woman by the dragon, who is identified as Satan (v. 9). This central theme, as well as the reference to the persecution of the "rest of her offspring" (v. 17), renders it virtually certain that the woman does not refer to a single individual.

Some identify the woman exclusively with the Jewish people, the nation of Israel. This view seems to be supported by the reference to the woman giving birth to the Messiah or "male child" (v. 5); the twelve stars then refer to the twelve tribes (Gen. 37:9–11; the twelve signs of the zodiac were thought by the Jews to represent the twelve tribes; their tribal standards corresponded to the zodiacal names). While these factors must be taken seriously, this view has internal problems. The dragon's persecution of the woman after the Messiah's birth can hardly refer to the devil's attack on the nation as a whole but could apply only to the believing part of the people. The whole intent of the passage is to explain the persecution of the believing community, not the persecution of the nation of Israel as a whole.

Since the context indicates that the woman under attack represents a continuous entity from the birth of Christ until at least John's day or later, her identity in the author's mind must be the believing covenant-messianic community. This group would include the early messianic community, which under John the Baptist's ministry was separated from the larger Jewish community to be the people prepared for the Lord (Mark 1:2–3). Later this group merged into the new community of Christ's disciples called the church, or, less appropriately, the new Israel, composed of both Jews and Gentiles. John does not at this point seem to distinguish between the earlier, almost totally Jewish community and the one present in his day. Their continuity in identity is so strong that whatever ethnic or other differences there may be between them do not affect his single image representing one entity.

The woman's dazzling appearance like the sun (v. 1) relates her to the glory and brilliance of her Lord (Rev. 1:16) as well as to her own light-bearing quality (1:20). With the moon under her feet signifying her permanence (Pss. 72:5; 89:37; cf. Matt. 16:18) and the crown of twelve stars on her head indicating her elect identity (cf. comments on 7:4ff.), she appears in her true heavenly and glorious character despite her seemingly fragile and uncertain earthly history (vv. 13–16). An allusion to her priestly nature may be suggested by the cosmic imagery of stars, sun, and moon, figures that the early Jewish historian Josephus uses in describing the high priestly vestments (cf. Rev. 1:6; 5:10). Peter likewise refers to the priestly function of the church (1 Peter 2:5, 9). The church viewed as a woman is found elsewhere in the New Testament as well as in early Christian literature (2 Cor. 11:2; Eph. 5:25–27, 32; cf. 2 John 1, 5, with 3 John 9).

Who is the child? The woman is in the throes of childbirth (v. 2). The emphasis is on her pain and suffering, both physical and spiritual. The meaning of her anguish is that the faithful messianic community has been suffering as a prelude to the coming of the *Messiah* Himself and of the new age (Isa. 26:17; 66:7–8; Mic. 4:10; 5:3). The "birth" itself does not necessarily refer to the actual physical birth of Christ but denotes the travail of the community from which the Messiah has arisen (cf. the use of the same verb in Heb. 6:7—"produces"—and James 1:15).

Who is the dragon? The second "sign" (v. 3) introduces the ultimate antagonist of the woman. The dragon is clearly identified with the "ancient serpent called the devil or Satan" (v. 9; cf. 20:2–3). The description of him as an "enormous red dragon" symbolically suggests his fierce power and murderous nature. He is further described as having "seven heads and ten horns and seven crowns on his heads." With some variations, the same description is used for the beast from the sea in chapter 13 and the beast in chapter 17. There is no way of understanding how the horns fit on the heads. While some have tried to find a specific meaning for each of the heads and horns, John probably intends to give no more than a symbolic impression of the whole rather than of its parts. It is a picture of the fullness of evil in all its hideous strength. (Compare here the Old Testament references to Rahab and Leviathan: Ps. 74:13–14; Isa. 27:1; 51:9–10; Dan. 7:7; 8:10. There is more than a coincidental similarity in these descriptions and John's image.) The diadem crowns on the heads may indicate fullness of royal power (13:1; 19:12).

So great is the dragon's power that his tail can even sweep away a large number of the stars and cast them down to the ground (v. 4; for "a third," see comments on 8:7). This should probably be understood simply as a figure representing the dragon's power and not as a reference to Satan's victory over some of the angels. In any event, the stars cast down would, after the analogy of Daniel 8:10, 24, refer to the saints of God who were trampled by Satan and not to fallen angels. Satan has placed himself before the woman, expecting certain victory over the messianic child. It is through this image that the church shows her awareness that Satan is always threatening the purposes of God within history. Although the attack of Herod against the children of Bethlehem and many incidents during the life of Jesus—such as the attempt of the crowd at Nazareth to throw Him over the cliff (Luke 4:28–39)—must also be included, the greatest attempt to devour the child must certainly be the crucifixion.

Verse 5 records the final element of the story. The messianic child comes, finishes His mission, is delivered from the dragon, and is enthroned in heaven. John again refers to the destiny of the child by once more alluding to Psalm 2:9: "Who will rule all the nations with an iron scepter" (Rev. 2:27; 19:15). It is not clear whether John also intends a collective identity in the birth of the male child. Daniel 7:13–14, 27 seems to fuse the individual "son of man" with the people of God. Likewise in Revelation John seems to alternate between the rule of Christ (1:5; 11:15) and the rule of the saints (1:6; 2:26–27). It is, however, difficult to see how both the child and the woman could be a group of believers. Nevertheless, many early interpreters understood the male child to be simultaneously Christ and the members of Christ; and a few even saw in the child a reference only to the church. Through Christ's resurrection and ascension, the dragon's attempt to destroy God's purposes by destroying the Messiah has been decisively defeated.

What is the desert? Is the flight into the desert symbolic or an actual historical event (v. 6)? Among those who take it literally, some have understood it to refer to the flight of the early Jerusalem Christians to Pella (modern Tabaqat Fahil, about twenty miles south of the Sea of Galilee) in A.D. 66 to escape the Roman destruction of Jerusalem. Others place the event in the future, when a portion of the Jewish people will be preserved through the Tribulation to await the return of Christ.

Most commentators, however, understand the wilderness symbolically as the place of safety, discipline, and testing. This view is preferable because of the highly symbolic nature of the whole chapter, the symbolic use of "desert" in 17:3 (q.v.), and the parallelism with the Exodus, in which the children of Israel fled from Pharaoh. All are agreed that the flight of the woman in verse 7 anticipates verses 13ff, while the intervening verses (vv. 7–12) show why the dragon is persecuting the woman. (For a discussion of the 1,260 days, see comments on 11:2.)

2. *The dragon thrown out of heaven* (12:7–12)

All agree that this section, which describes the battle in heaven between Michael and the dragon, provides the explanation of why the dragon has turned on the woman and caused her to flee into the desert for protection (vv. 6, 13ff.). The account has two parts: (1) the battle in heaven between Michael and his angels and the dragon and his angels, which results in the ejection of Satan from heaven to the earth (vv. 7–9), and (2) the heavenly hymn of victory (vv. 10–12).

a) *The battle between Michael and the dragon* (12:7–9)

As elsewhere in the book, the narrative material can be interpreted only in the light of the hymns. This principle is especially important in verses 7–9, where a victory in heaven is the result of Michael's defeat of the dragon. Were this the only thing told us about the "war in heaven," it might be concluded that the dragon's defeat was unrelated to Jesus Christ. But the interpretative hymn (vv. 10–12) says that it was in fact the blood of Christ that dealt the actual death blow to the dragon and enabled the saints to triumph (v. 8; cf. 5:9). This suggests that the redeeming work of Christ is here depicted by the cosmic battle of Michael and the dragon as it is elsewhere seen as a loosing from sin (1:5), as a washing of our garments (7:14), and as a purchasing to God (5:9). The time of the dragon's defeat and ejection from heaven must therefore be connected with the incarnation, ministry, death, and resurrection of Jesus (v. 13; Luke 10:18; John 12:31). Christ has appeared in order that He may destroy the works of the devil (Matt. 12:28–29; Acts 10:38; 2 Tim. 1:10; 1 John 3:8).

Early Jewish belief held that Michael would cast Satan from heaven in the first of the end-time struggles to establish the kingdom of God on earth. John, by contrast, sees this event as already having taken place through Jesus Christ's appearance and work. Only the final, permanent ejection of Satan from earth remains (Rev. 20:10). The fact that the battle first took place in heaven between Michael, the guardian of God's people (Dan. 10:13, 21; 12:1; Jude 9), and the dragon shows that evil is cosmic (not limited merely to this world) and also that events on earth are first decided in heaven. The single intent of the passage is to assure those who meet satanic evil on earth that it is really a defeated power, however contrary this might seem to human experience.

The triumph of the archangel results in the ejection of the dragon and his angels from heaven to earth (vv. 8–9). Apparently, prior to this event Satan had access to the heavens and continually assailed the loyalty of the saints (Job 1:9–11; Zech. 3:1), but now, together with his angels, he has been cast out (cf. Luke 10:18). Whatever appears to be the earthly situation of God's people now, the victory has already been won. When the battle grows fiercer and darker for the church, it is but the sign of the last futile attempt of the dragon to exercise his power before the kingdom of Christ comes (v. 12). The "ancient serpent" who tempted Eve with lies about God (Gen. 3:1ff.) is in John's mind the same individual as the "devil" and "Satan." Satan is also the one who "leads the whole world astray." His power lies in deception, and by his lies the whole world is deceived about God (2:20; 13:14; 18:23; 19:20; 20:3, 8, 10; 2 John 7; cf. Rom. 1:25).

b) A hymn of victory (12:10–12)

This anonymous hymn, which interprets the great battle of the preceding verses, has three stanzas: the first (v. 10) focuses on the victorious inauguration of God's kingdom and Christ's kingly authority; the second (v. 11) calls attention to the earthly victory of the saints as they confirm the victory of Christ by their own identification with Jesus in His witness and death; the third (v. 12) announces the martyrs' victory and the final woe to the earth because of the devil's ejection and impending demise.

In the first stanza (v. 10) the triumph of Christ is described as the arrival of three divine realities in history: God's "salvation" or victory (7:10; 19:1), God's "power," and God's "kingdom." This latter reality is further identified as Christ's assumption of His "authority." The historic event of Christ's life, death, and resurrection has challenged the dominion of Satan and provoked the crisis of history. At the time of Christ's death on earth, Satan was being defeated in heaven by Michael. "Michael

. . . is not the field officer who does the actual fighting, but the staff officer in the heavenly room, who is able to remove Satan's flag from the heavenly map because the real victory has been won at Calvary" (Caird).

In times past, Satan's chief role as adversary involved accusing God's people of disobedience to God. The justice of these accusations was recognized by God, and therefore Satan's presence in heaven was tolerated. But now the crucified Savior in God's presence provides the required satisfaction of God's justice with reference to our sins (1 John 2:1–2; 4:10). Therefore, Satan's accusations are no longer valid and he is cast out. What strong consolation this provides for God's faltering people!

The stanza in verse 11 is both a statement and an appeal. It announces that the followers of the Lamb also become victors over the dragon because they participate in the "blood of the Lamb," the weapon that defeated Satan, and because they have confirmed their loyalty to the Lamb by their witness even to death. The blood of the martyrs, rather than signaling the triumph of Satan, shows instead that they have gained the victory over the dragon by their acceptance of Jesus' Cross and their obedient suffering with Him. This is one of John's chief themes (1:9; 6:9; 14:12; 20:4).

Verses 12 and 17 lead to the conclusion that only a portion of the martyrs are in view (cf. 6:11). Thus this hymn of victory also becomes an appeal to the rest of the saints to do likewise and confirm their testimony to Christ even if doing so means death. This seems to suggest that in some mysterious sense the sufferings of the people of God are linked to the sufferings of Jesus in His triumph over Satan and evil (John 12:31; Rom. 16:20; Col. 1:24). Since the martyrs have gained the victory over the dragon because of the Cross of Jesus (i.e., they can no longer be accused of damning sin, since Jesus has paid sin's penalty; 1:5b), they are now free even to give up their lives in loyalty to their Redeemer (John 12:25; Rev. 15:2).

Satan has failed. Therefore, the heavens and all who are in them should be glad (v. 12). But Satan does not accept defeat without a bitter struggle. His final death throes are directed exclusively toward "the earth and the sea." Therefore their inhabitants will mourn, for the Devil will now redouble his wrathful effort in one last futile attempt to make the most of an opportunity he knows will be brief (three and one-half years; cf. vv. 6, 14).

3. *The dragon's attack* (12:13–17)

In verse 13 the narrative that was interrupted after the flight of the woman into the wilderness (v. 6) is resumed: she is now under attack from the defeated but still vicious dragon (vv. 7–12). No longer able to attack the male child who is in heaven or to accuse the saints because of the victory of Jesus on the cross, the Devil, banned from heaven, now pursues the woman, who flees into the desert. The word "pursue" was no doubt carefully chosen by John because it is also the New Testament word for "persecute" (Matt. 5:10; et al.). Since the woman has already given birth to the child, the time of the pursuit by the dragon follows the earthly career of Jesus.

The reference to eagle's wings (v. 14) once again introduces imagery borrowed from the Exodus account in which Israel was pursued by the dragon in the person of Pharaoh: "You yourselves have seen what I did to Egypt, and how I carried you on eagles' wings and brought you to myself" (Exod. 19:4). As God's people were delivered from the enemy by their journey into the Sinai desert, so God's present people will be preserved miraculously from destruction (cf. Deut. 32:10–12; Isa. 40:31).

Next, the serpent spews a floodlike river of water out of his mouth to engulf and drown the woman (vv. 15–16). The water imagery symbolizes destruction by an enemy (Pss. 32:6; 69:1–2; 124:2–5; Nah. 1:8) or calamity (Ps. 18:4). As the desert soil absorbs the flash torrent, so the covenant people will be helped by God and preserved from utter destruction (Isa. 26:20; 42:15; 43:2; 50:2). The dragon-inspired Egyptians of old were swallowed by the earth: "You stretched out your right hand and the earth swallowed them" (Exod. 15:12). In similar fashion, the messianic community will be delivered by God's power. Whatever specific events were happening to Christians in Asia in John's day would not exhaust the continuing significance of the passage.

This attack of Satan against "the rest" of the woman's offspring (v. 17) seems to be the final attempt to destroy the messianic people of God. Having failed in previous attempts to eliminate them as a whole, the dragon now strikes at individuals who "obey God's commandments and hold to the testimony of Jesus." To "make war" is the identical expression used of the beast's attack on the two witnesses in 11:7 and on the saints in 13:7. Could this possibly correlate the three groups and indicate their common identity under different figures?

Those attacked are called "the rest of her [the woman's] offspring." Some identify this group as Gentile Christians as distinct from the Jewish mother church. Others identify the mother as the nation of Israel and see the "rest" as the believing remnant in the Jewish nation who turn to Christ. Still others have suggested that the woman represents the believing community as a whole, the universal or ideal church composed of both Jews and Gentiles, whereas the "offspring" of the woman represent *individuals* of the community (Jews and Gentiles) who suffer presecution and martyrdom for the dragon in the pattern of Christ. This close identification of the seed of the woman as first of all Jesus and then also those who have become His brethren through faith agrees with other New Testament teaching (Matt. 25:40; Heb. 2:11–12). While Satan cannot prevail against the Christian community itself, he can wage war on certain of its members who are called on to witness to their Lord by obedience even unto death, i.e., "those who obey God's commandment and hold to the testimony of Jesus" (Matt. 16:18; Rev. 11:7; 13:7, 15). The church, then, is paradoxically both invulnerable (the woman) and vulnerable (her children) (cf. Luke 21:16–18).

C. The Two Beasts (13:1–18)

This chapter continues the theme of the persecution of God's people that John began to develop in chapter 12. Turning from the inner dynamics of the struggle, chapter 13 shifts to the actual earthly instruments of this assault—viz., the two dragon-energized beasts. In accord with the discussion in chapter 12, we may assume that the activities of the two beasts constitute the way the dragon carries out his final attempts to wage war on the seed of the woman (12:17).

The dragon and the first beast enter into a conspiracy to seduce the whole world into worshiping the beast. The partnership is successful—except for the failure to seduce the followers of the Lamb. The conspirators summon yet a third figure to their aid—the beast from the earth, who must be sufficiently similar to the Lamb to entice even the followers of Jesus. He must be able to perform miraculous signs much as the two witnesses did (vv. 11ff.; cf. 13:13 with 11:5). As the battle progresses, the dragon's deception becomes more and more subtle. Thus the readers are called on to discern the criteria that will enable them to separate the lamblike beast from the Lamb Himself (cf. 13:11 with 14:1).

1. The beast from the sea (13:1–10)

This chapter has been the source of endless speculations. Yet it is a key to the interpretation of the whole book. Two basic interpretative problems confront the reader, which have led students of the book to different understandings of this chapter: (1) The identification of the beast and his associate—are they persons or some other entities? (2) The time of the beast's rule—is it past, continuous, or still future? In seeking satisfactory answers to these questions, it may be helpful to first set forth the facts about the beast. He (1) rises from the sea (v. 1); (2) resembles the dragon (v. 1); (3) has composite animal features (v. 2); (4) is dragon empowered (v. 2); (5) has one head wounded to death but healed (vv. 3–4, 7b–8); (6) blasphemes God and God's people for forty-two months (vv. 5–6); (7) makes war against the saints and kills them (vv. 7a, 15); and (8) gives through the second beast to those who follow him his "mark," which is either his name or his number, 666 (vv. 16–18).

In addition, there are no fewer than ten further references in Revelation to the beast (11:7; 14:9, 11; 15:2; 16:2, 10, 13; 19:19–20; 20:4, 10), excluding the nine references to the scarlet-colored beast in chapter 17, which should probably be included. These further references contain no new information, except that the beast rises from the Abyss (11:7), that he makes a coalition with the "kings of the earth" (19:19), and his final end in the lake of fire (19:20).

The history of the interpretation of chapter 13 is far too extensive for this commentary to cover. As early as the second century, two different understandings of the Antichrist appeared. Some early interpreters take the position that the Antichrist will be a person, a world deceiver who will reign for the last half of Daniel's seventieth week (Dan. 7:25).[2] In its favor is the more literal reading of 2 Thessalonians 2:1–10 and the natural understanding of the Antichrist as being the personal counterpart to the personal Christ.

On the other hand, from the earliest times some interpreters have understood the Antichrist as a present threat of heresy, depending more on the concept found in the Johannine Epistles (1 John 2:18, 22; 4:3; 2 John 7). Luther, Calvin, and other Reformers who adopted this general view identified the beast with the papacy of the Roman Catholic Church. A number of modern commentators likewise adopt the theological heresy interpretation of the Antichrist without singling out the Roman Catholic Church as the enemy. In its favor are the interpretations of the Antichrist in the Johannine Epistles and the advantage of seeing the beast as a present threat to the church and not merely as an eschatological figure of the end time. This view also argues that 2 Thessalonians 2:1–10 need not be understood as referring to a single future individual. The issue is difficult to settle with any finality. However, I will develop chapter 13 more in accord with the theological heresy view, while recognizing at the same time that a future archdeceiver may also come. (See also comments on v. 11.)

In modern interpretation there is almost complete agreement that the "wounded head" (v. 3) refers to the Nero redivivus legend. After the death of Nero, the myth emerged that he would revive from the dead and lead a huge army against all his enemies. This Neronic interpretation presupposes an identification in John's mind between the sea beast and the Roman Empire (a view espoused in our day by both preterist and not a few preterist-futurist interpreters of Revelation; see Introduction) and usually assumes that Revelation 17 identifies the seven heads of the beast as the successive emperors of the Roman Empire. However, the Nero redivivus view will fit neither the facts of history nor the text of Revelation 13 and 17 (see comments on 17:8–9).[3] Furthermore, since the beast of Revelation 13 is a composite that unites all the features of the four beasts of Daniel 7, it cannot be identified with Rome. An attempt will be made in this exposition to demonstrate that the Rome hypothesis is untenable.

---

[2]For references and documentation on these views, see Johnson, EBC, 12, pp. 521–2.

[3]For a more detailed argument against the Neronic view, see Johnson, EBC, 12, p. 523.

This leaves the question open as to whether John sees the Antichrist (or beast) as a person or some more encompassing entity.

John emphasizes three things about the first beast: he shows (1) the conspiracy of the dragon with the beast (vv. 3–4); (2) the universal success of this partnership in deceiving the whole world to worship them (vv. 3–4, 8); and (3) that the partnership will succeed in temporarily defeating the saints of God, thus accomplishing the greatest blasphemy of God (vv. 6–7a).

a) *Description and identification* (13:1–2)[4]

The beast ("wild beast") has already been described in 11:7 as rising from the "Abyss" (cf. 17:8). Thus the sea may symbolize the Abyss, the source of demonic powers that are opposed to God (cf. 9:1; 20:1–3). This view agrees with the Old Testament images of the sea as the origin of the satanic sea monsters—the dragon (Tannin), Leviathan ("Coiled One"), and Rahab ("Rager") (Job 26:12–13; Pss. 74:13–14; 87:4; 89:10; Isa. 27:1; 51:9; cf. also Ezek. 32:6–8). The ancient Hebrews demythologized the sea-monster myths to depict the victory of the Lord of Israel over the demonic forces of evil that in various manifestations had sought to destroy the people of God. Thus John later foresees the final day of Christ's victory when there will "no longer [be] any sea" or source of demonic opposition to God and His people (21:1).

John describes the beast in words similar to those he used in 12:3 of the dragon: "He had ten horns and seven heads, with ten crowns on his horns." As previously indicated (cf. comments on 12:3), any attempt to identify the heads or horns as separate kings, kingdoms, etc., should be resisted. The image of the seven-headed monster is well attested in ancient Sumerian, Babylonian, and Egyptian texts.

It may be argued that John's beast from the sea is to be connected with Leviathan in the Old Testament (see Ps. 74:14, where the "heads" of the monster are specifically mentioned: "It was you who crushed the heads of Leviathan"). It is true that Leviathan, Rahab, and the dragon (serpent) in the cited Old Testament texts refer to political powers, such as Egypt and Assyria, that were threatening Israel. In the minds of the Old Testament writers, however, the national entities were inseparably identified with the archetypal reality of the satanic, idolatrous systems represented by the seven-headed monster (Leviathan, Rahab, and the dragon), so that the beast represented not the political power as such, but the system of

---

[4]The NIV and most other modern translations include verse 1a as the concluding verse of chapter 12 because a variant Greek reading changes the KJV text "I stood" to "he stood" (i.e., the dragon). The latter reading is favored by a majority of textual scholars. If "he stood" is the correct reading, the sense would be that the dragon, who has now turned his rage on the children of the woman (12:17), stands on the seashore to summon his next instrument, the beast from the sea. But if the text reads "I stood," the sense is that John receives a new vision (cf. 10:1) as he gazes out over the sea in the same manner as Daniel (7:2).

evil that found expression in the political entity. The reason this point is so important is that it helps us see that the beast is not to be identified with any one historical form of its expression or with any one institutional aspect of its manifestation. In other words, the beast may appear as Sodom, Egypt, Rome, or even Jerusalem and may manifest itself as a political power, an economic power, a religious power, or a heresy (1 John 2:18, 22; 4:3).

In John's mind, the chief enemy is diabolical deception; his description therefore has theological overtones, not political ones. This interpretation does not exclude the possibility that there will be a final climactic appearance of the beast in history in a person, in a political, religious, or economic system, or in a final totalitarian culture combining all these. The point is that the beast cannot be limited to either the past or the future.

John further states that this beast had "on each head a blasphemous name." This prominent feature is repeated in 17:3 (cf. 13:5–6). Arrogance and blasphemy also characterize the "little horn" of Daniel's fourth beast (7:8, 11, 20, 25) and the willful king of Daniel 11:36. John alludes to the vision of Daniel but completely transforms it.

The blasphemies of the beast are directed against God: "to blaspheme God, by blaspheming his name, his temple, those who dwell in heaven" (13:6, my translation). Thus the beast challenges the sovereignty and majesty of God by denying the first commandment: "You shall have no other gods before me" (Exod. 20:3).

Therefore, whatever person or system—whether political, social, economic, or religious—cooperates with Satan by exalting itself against God's sovereignty and by setting itself up to destroy the followers of Jesus, or by enticing them to become followers of Satan through deception, idolatry, blasphemy, and spiritual adultery, embodies the beast of Revelation 13.

The description John gives of the beast from the sea does not describe a mere human political entity such as Rome. Rather, it describes in archetypal language the hideous, Satan-backed system of deception and idolatry that may at any time express itself in human systems of various kinds. Yet at the same time John also seems to be saying that this blasphemous, blaspheming, and blasphemy-producing reality will have a final, intense, and, for the saints, utterly devastating manifestation.

b) *The wounded head.* (13:3–4)

The beast has a fatal wound, but the wound is healed (v. 3). This results in great world-wide influence, acceptance, and worship of both the beast and the dragon (v. 4). Verse 3 is important and requires careful exegesis, since a number of features of John's description are inconsistent with both the Nero redivivus and the Roman Empire interpretations.

1. The wounded "head" of verse 3 is elsewhere in the chapter a wound of the *whole* beast (vv. 12, 14).

2. Everywhere in Revelation, the Greek word for "wound" means "plague," a divinely inflicted judgment (9:18, 20; 11:6; 15:1ff.; 16:9, 21; 18:4, 8; 21:9; 22:18). In 13:14 we find that the beast has the plague of the "sword." Elsewhere in Revelation, the "sword" (1) symbolically refers to the divine judgment of the Messiah (1:16; 2:12, 16; 19:15, 21); (2) is the sword of the rider on the red horse and equals divine judgment (6:4, 8); and (3) is a sword used as a weapon against the saints of God (13:10). We are, then, nearer to John's mind if we see the sword, not as referring to an emperor's death, but as the symbol of God's wrath, which has struck a death blow to the authority of the beast (and the dragon), a death blow that has been deceptively covered up or restored (for a probable antecedent, see Isa. 27:1).

3. Everywhere in the book the only sufficient conqueror of the beast and the dragon is the slain Lamb, together with His faithful saints (12:11; 19:19–21). Furthermore, it is the event of the life and especially the crucifixion, resurrection, and exaltation of Jesus that dealt this death blow to the dragon and the beast (1:5; 5:9; 12:11). This same thought is paralleled by other New Testament teaching (Luke 10:17–24; 11:14–22; John 12:31–33; Col. 2:15). Irenaeus suggests that the wound, so central in the Apocalypse, must be understood as an appeal to Genesis 3:13ff.

4. The same paradox found in chapter 12 also appears here in chapter 13. While the dragon (ch. 12) is, on the one hand, defeated and cast out of heaven, on the other hand he still has time and ability to wage a relentless war against the people of God. Likewise, the beast (ch. 13) has been dealt a fatal blow by the cross of Christ and yet still has time and the ability to wage war against the saints. He appears to be alive and in full command of the scene; his blasphemies increase. What the sea beast cannot accomplish, he commissions the earth beast to do (vv. 11ff.). All three—the dragon, the sea beast, and the earth beast—though distinguishable, are nevertheless in collusion to effect the same end: the deception that leads the world to worship the dragon and the sea beast and the destruction of all who oppose them.

It is this description that leads to the fourth reason why identifying the beast exclusively with any one historical personage or empire is probably incorrect. In John's description of the beast there are numerous parallels with *Jesus* that should alert the reader to the fact that John is seeking to establish, not a historical identification, but a theological characterization (although in this there is no implication against the historicity of Jesus): Both wield swords; both have followers on whose foreheads are inscribed their names (13:16–14:1); both have horns (5:6; 13:1); both were slain, the same Greek word being used to describe their deaths (vv. 3, 8); both have arisen to new life and authority; and both are given (by different authorities) power over every nation, tribe, people, and tongue as well as over the kings of the earth (1:5; 7:9; and 13:7; 17:12). The beast described here is the great theological counterpart to all that Christ represents, not the Roman Empire or any of its emperors.

While the references in the Johannine literature may be taken as supporting the view that the Antichrist is manifested in multiple persons and was a reality present in John's day (1 John 2:18, 22; 4:3; 2 John 7), Paul's description in personal terms of the coming "man of lawlessness" (2 Thess. 2:3–4, 8–9) has led the majority of ancient and modern interpreters to adopt the viewpoint that it is a personal Antichrist. Some believe that the solution to the conflict between Paul and John lies in seeing John as describing the forerunners (anti-Christian powers in history), while Paul talks about the day when these powers will be embodied in one king(dom) of the world, the epitome of apostasy. John, however, says that in the false teachers "the antichrist" was actually present (2 John 7).

But the question must remain open as to whether John in the Apocalypse points to a *single* archenemy of the church—whether past or future—or to a transhistorical reality with many human manifestations in history (the imagery would function similarly with regard to the woman of ch. 12 or the harlot of ch. 17). The latter view would prevent us from limiting the imagery merely to the Roman Empire or to any other single future political entity.

Finally, the goal of the dragon and the beast in their conspiracy is to promote the idolatrous worship of themselves (v. 4). This perversion is further enhanced by the earth beast (vv. 12, 15). The means of deception vary, because not all mankind is deceived in the same way. People follow and worship the beast because he is apparently invincible: "Who can make war against him?" His only real enemy seems to be the saints of Jesus, whom he effectively destroys (2:10, 13; 12:11; 13:15). But little does he realize that in the death of the saints the triumph of God appears. As they die, they do so in identification with the slain Lamb who through the Cross has decisively conquered the dragon by inflicting on him a truly fatal wound. "Who is like the beast?" echoes in parody similar references to God Himself (Exod. 15:11; Mic. 7:18).

c) *The career of the beast* (13:5–10)

The period of the beast's authority is given as "forty-two months," the same period already referred to in 11:2–3; 12:6, 13 (see comments on 11:2).

To "make war" (v. 7), as elsewhere in the Apocalypse, does not mean to wage a military campaign but refers to hostility to and destruction of the people of God in whatever manner and by whatever means the beast may choose (study carefully 2:16; 11:7; 12:7, 17; 16:14; 17:14; 19:11, 19; 20:8; 2 Cor. 10:4). "To conquer them" refers not to the subversion of their faith but to the destruction of their physical lives (cf. Matt. 10:28). As in T.S.

Eliot's *Murder in the Cathedral*, their apparent defeat by the beast and his victory turn out to be in reality the victory of the saints and the defeat of the beast (15:2). Messiahlike universal dominion was given the beast by the dragon (Luke 4:4–7; 1 John 5:19).

In verse 8 John further identifies the worshipers of the beast as "all whose names have not been written in the book of life belonging to the Lamb" (concerning the "book of life," see comments on 3:5; also 17:8; 20:12, 15; 21:27). This contrast further emphasizes the theological nature of the description of the beast. The beast from the earth represents the idolatrous system of worship instigated by the dragon to deceive mankind into breaking the first commandment.

It has been debated whether the words "from the creation of the world" (see also 17:8) belong grammatically with "have not been written" or with "that was slain." In other words, is it the Lamb who was slain from the creation of the world, or were the names not recorded in the book of life from the creation of the world? In the former instance, the emphasis would rest on the decree in eternity to elect the Son as the Agent for mankind's salvation (13:8; 1 Peter 1:20); in the latter, stress lies on God's eternal foreknowledge of a company of people who would participate in the elect Son's redeeming work (17:8). Either interpretation is grammatically acceptable. But comparison with 17:8 shows that the Greek word order (not the grammar) favors the latter view and suggests that John is deliberately providing a complementary thought to 17:8. In any event, the words "from the creation of the world" cannot be pressed to prove eternal individual election to salvation or damnation, since 3:5 implies that failure of appropriate human response may remove one's name from the book of life. This verse strikes a sharp note of distinction between the followers of the beast and those of the slain Lamb. It also calls for faithful commitment and clear discernment of error on the part of the Lamb's people.

Verses 9–10 are both important and difficult. This is the only occurrence in Revelation of the words "he who has an ear, let him hear" outside the messages to the seven churches (chs. 2–3). Here they call special attention to the need for obedience to the exhortation in verse 10b. Some feel that verse 10 is the focal point of the whole chapter as it calls on the Christian to display faith and patience in the face of the divinely permitted predominance of evil. Most agree that the language of verse 10 alludes to Jeremiah 15:2 and 43:11, where the prophet describes the certainty of divine judgment that will come upon the rebels in Israel—they will suffer captivity, famine, disease, and death from the sword. Yet it is difficult to see how Jeremiah's words are appropriate here in the context of an exhortation for believers to be faithful. John's meaning must be different—viz., that as the rebels in Jeremiah's day would certainly encounter the divine judgment, so the faithful to Christ are assured that their captivity and martyrdom are in God's will.

No completely satisfying resolution of the problems in verse 10 is available. Since the difficult part (v. 10a) is both preceded and followed by appeals to obedience and loyalty, it seems best to stay with the sense of obedient faithfulness and follow the textual readings that support it. It may be put this way: "The day of persecution is at hand: the Christians must suffer captivity, exile or death: in calmly facing and undergoing this final tribulation they are to manifest their endurance and faithfulness" (Charles). Paul's statement is similar: "Without being frightened in any way by those who oppose you. This is a sign to them that they will be destroyed, but that you will be saved—and that by God" (Phil. 1:28). While the Dead Sea Scrolls reveal that the Essenes held to an active, violent participation in the final eschatological battle for the elect, and while the then current holy-war doctrine of the Zealots advocated violent revolution, John seems to call believers here to passive resistance against their enemies. Yet this resistance, which may result in captivity and even martyrdom, seems to contribute to the eventual defeat of evil.

2. The beast from the land (13:11–18)

John sees another ("one of a similar kind") beast rising from the earth (v. 11). This second beast completes the triumvirate of evil—the dragon, the sea beast, and the land beast. The land beast is subservient to the beast from the sea and seems utterly dedicated to promoting not himself but the wounded beast from the sea. Elsewhere the land beast is called the "false prophet" (16:13; 19:20; 20:10). As with the first beast, identification is a problem. That this beast comes from the land rather than the sea may simply indicate his diversity from the first, while other references stress their collusion.

A survey of the history of interpretation reveals, as in the case of the first beast, two main lines: the beast either represents a power or a movement, or describes a human being allied with the Antichrist at the close of the age.

Calvin and Luther, as well as other Reformers, drawing on earlier traditions, identified this beast with the papacy or specific popes. While the Reformers may have been mistaken in their specific identification, they were right in seeing the beast as a present threat and not some entity awaiting a yet future manifestation. Most modern commentators, following the Nero redivivus view of the first beast, identify this beast as the priesthood of the imperial cultus of Rome. While recognizing that no view is without problems, the following discussion takes the position that the land beast is John's way of describing the false prophets of the Olivet Discourse (Matt. 24:24; Mark 13:22). This identification is consistent with the previously stated view of the sea beast as describing not just a specific political reality but the world-wide anti-God system of Satan and its manifestation in periodic, historical human antichrists. The land beast is the antithesis to the true prophets of Christ symbolized by the two witnesses in chapter 11. If the thought of a nonpersonal antichrist and false prophet seems to contradict the verse that describes them as being cast alive into the lake of fire (19:20), consider that "death" and "Hades," both nonpersonal and nonconcrete entities, are also thrown into the lake of fire (20:14); since John reifies, if not personifies the latter two, it is not illogical to assume that he also personifies the former two.

a) The character of the second beast (13:11)

The reference to the "two horns like a lamb" (v. 11) can be understood as highlighting the beast's imitative role with respect to the true Lamb in the rest of the book (e.g., 5:6ff.; 13:8; 14:1). Could the two horns be in contrast to the two witnesses in chapter 11? Since one of the primary characteristics of this second beast is his deceptive activity (v. 14; 19:20), his appearance as a lamb would contribute to the confusion over the beast's true identity. If the land beast represents satanic false teaching and false prophets, their evil is intensified because of its deceptive similarity to the truth. Even though the beast is like the Lamb, in reality he is evil because "he [speaks] like a dragon," i.e., he teaches heresy. Jesus gave such a twofold description of false prophets in the Sermon on the Mount: "Watch out for false prophets. They come to you in sheep's clothing, but inwardly they are ferocious wolves" (Matt. 7:15). On the other hand, the lamblikeness may simply be a reference to the beast's gentle outward manner in contrast to his true identity as a fierce dragon.

b) The career of the second beast (13:12–17)

The activity of the land beast is repeatedly described as that of promoting the first beast's worship (vv. 12, 15). Could this be the same kind of activity as that of the false prophets in Pergamum and Thyatira who seduced the servants of God to idolatry (2:14–15, 20, 24)? The NIV misses a nuance by the rendering "in behalf of," as if the second beast exercised all the authority of the first beast merely as the latter's representative. The same preposition occurs no fewer than thirty-four times in Revelation and in every instance means "in the presence of" or "before." The same word is used of the two witnesses in 11:4: "These are the two olive trees and the two lampstands that stand before the Lord of the earth." As the antithesis to the two witnesses, the false prophets derive their authority and ministry from the first beast.

Miracles (vv. 13–14a). One of the strategies the land beast uses to deceive people into following the first beast is the performance of "miraculous signs." The ability of the Satan-inspired prophets to perform deceiving miracles is attested elsewhere in Revelation and in other parts of the Bible (16:14; 19:20; Deut. 13:1–5; Matt. 7:22; 24:24; Mark 13:22;

2 Thess. 2:9). Distinguishing between the true and false prophets has always been difficult—the followers of Jesus must be constantly alert to discern the spirits (1 John 4:1–3).

"Fire . . . from heaven" may refer to the fire that the prophet Elijah called down from heaven (1 Kings 18:38) or to the fire coming out of the mouths of the two witnesses (Rev. 11:5). John may intend a deliberate contrast between the true witnesses' use of fire and its use by the false prophets (11:5; cf. Luke 9:54). Some connect the fire of God with the true Word of God and the Holy Spirit's witness (as at Pentecost; Acts 2:3). The false fire would then be a reference to pseudocharismatic gifts that create a counterfeit church community whose allegiance is to the Antichrist. In any case, the reference to fire from heaven indicates that no mighty deed is too hard for these false prophets, because they derive their power from the Antichrist and the dragon. Christ's true servants are not to be deceived even by any spectacular miracles the false prophets may perform. Such miracles in themselves are no evidence of the Holy Spirit.

The quality of the miracles deceives those who follow the beast—viz., "the inhabitants of the earth" (v. 14a). "Deceive" is John's term for the activity of false teachers who lead people to worship gods other than the true and living God (2:20; 12:9; 18:23; 19:20; 20:3, 8, 10; cf. 1 John 2:26; 3:7; 4:6; also Matt. 24:11, 24).

Image (vv. 14b–15). The second beast orders the setting up of an "image" of the first beast. Elsewhere, the worship of the first beast, his "image," and his "mark" are inseparable (14:9, 11; 15:2; 16:2; 19:20; 20:4). The image of something is not a mere copy but partakes in its reality and in fact constitutes its reality. Most interpreters, following the Roman-emperor exegesis, readily identify the image with the statue of Caesar and attribute the "breath" and speaking of the image to the magic and ventriloquism of the imperial priests. But as has been argued earlier (see introductory comments and v. 11), John's language is much more theologically descriptive than the Roman hypothesis allows. This is not to deny that the imperial cult could be one form the worship of the beast might take; but the reality described transcends the mere worship of a bust of Caesar. In every age the beast kills those who will not worship his image. In terms reminiscent of the great golden image Nebuchadnezzar made, in which every person was commanded to worship under the threat of death (Dan. 3:1–11), John describes the world-wide system of idolatry represented by the first beast and the false prophet who promotes it. John describes this reality as a blasphemous and idolatrous system that produces a breach of the first two commandments (Exod. 20:3–5).

In speaking about giving "breath" to the image, John implies the activity of the false prophets in reviving idolatrous worship, giving it the appearance of vitality, reality, and power. Curiously, the two witnesses were also said to receive "breath" (11:11). The idolatrous satanic system has the power of death over those who worship the true God and the Lamb. The same "image" tried to kill Daniel and his friends, killed many of the prophets of God, crucified the Lord Jesus, put to death Stephen (Acts 7:60), James the apostle (Acts 12:1–2), and Antipas (Rev. 2:13). Thus he demonstrated to his followers the apparent healing of the wounded head of the first beast. To limit the image to the bust of Caesar or to some future statue or ventriloquistic device restricts John's deeper meaning and eliminates the present significance of his language.[5]

The mark of the beast (vv. 16–17). The immediate effect of the worship of the beast involves receiving a mark on the right hand or forehead. By comparing the other passages where the image, mark, and name of the beast are mentioned, it seems clear that the "mark" is an expression equivalent to the "name of the beast" (13:17; 14:11; also 14:9; 15:2; 16:2; 19:20; 20:4), which is also the "number of his name" (13:17; 15:2).

In Greek "mark" may refer to a work of art such as a carved image of a god (Acts 17:29), to any written inscription or document, to the "bite" of a snake, to a red "seal" (impress) of the emperor and other official attestors of documents, or to a "brand" on camels indicating ownership. No evidence, however, can be cited from the ancient world where a "mark" is placed on a *person*, let alone on the "right hand" or on the "forehead." As the servants of God receive on their foreheads the impress of the divine seal (7:3; 14:1), so the servants of the beast are marked with the stamp of the beast. In other words, the mark is not a literal impress seal, certificate, or similar mark of identification, but it is John's way of symbolically describing authentic ownership and loyalty. Those who worship the beast have his mark or brand of ownership on them, as the followers of Jesus have the brand of God's possession on them. John may also have in mind here the Jewish practice of wearing phylacteries or tefillin, black leather boxes containing Scripture passages that are bound on the left hand and forehead with leather straps. This practice is based on Exodus 13:9, 16; Deuteronomy 6:8; 11:18 (cf. also Matt. 23:5).

Those having the "mark" can "buy or sell," those without it cannot. (v. 17). This statement apparently refers to some sort of socio-economic sanctions that would, of course, affect the condition of Christians in the world. Earlier, John alluded to certain such conditions: Smyrna was a greatly persecuted church and was "poor" (2:9); Philadelphia was of "little strength" (3:8); those faithful to Christ in the Great Tribulation are seen in heaven as never again hungering (7:16), while the great harlot grows rich

---

[5]The contemporary phenomenon of the Korean religious leader Sun Myung Moon and his official interpreter and prophetess, Young Oon Kim, embody what seems to be a clear example of John's teaching about antichrists and false prophets. Moon is being heralded as the "Lord of the Second Advent" by Kim and others. His whole stance clearly embodies heresy and blasphemy and many are being deceived into following him and his teaching. Moon's idolatrous image receives continual breath by worship from his followers.

and wallows in luxury (18:3). Other New Testament writers also apparently refer to socio-economic sanctions practiced against Christians (Rom. 15:26; Heb. 10:34). Such sanctions were more social than political, imposed not by the government but by the communities. When governmental Rome took official notice of an illegal religion, it was always by criminal charges in the courts, not by economic sanctions (Caird).

The number of the beast: 666 (v. 18). In verse 17 John indicated that the "mark" is "the name of the beast or number of his name." He now reveals the number of the beast: "His number is 666." The list of conjectures concerning the meaning of the number is almost as long as the list of commentators on the book. Taking their cue from the words "let him calculate the number of the beast," most of these interpreters have tried to play the ancient Hebrew game of gematria or its Greek equivalent. Ancient languages, including Hebrew and Greek, used standard letters from their alphabets as numerical signs. A series of letters could form a word and at the same time indicate a number. Gematria took many forms and consisted in trying to guess the word from the number or trying to connect one word with another that had the same numerical value.[6]

Thus it is not difficult to understand why most commentators have understood John's words "Let him calculate the number . . . His number is 666" to be an invitation to the reader to play gematria and discover the identity of the beast. This approach is not new. Irenaeus (second century) mentions that many names of contemporary persons and entities were being offered in his day as solutions to this number mystery. Yet he cautioned against the practice and believed that the name of the Antichrist was deliberately concealed because he did not exist in John's day. The name would be secret till the time of his future appearance in the world. Irenaeus expressly refutes the attempt of many to identify the name with any of the Roman emperors. He feels, however, that the gematria approach is John's intended meaning but warns the church against endless speculations. Irenaeus' fear was not misplaced. Endless speculation is just what has happened in the history of the interpretation of verse 18. The sheer disagreement and confusion created through the years by the gematria method should have long ago warned the church that it was on the wrong track. If John was seeking to illumine believers so that they could penetrate the deception of the beast as well as to contrast the beast and his followers with the Lamb and His followers (14:1ff.), he has clearly failed—that is, if he intends for us to play the gematria game.

Nowhere does John use gematria as a method. Everywhere, however, he gives symbolic significance to numbers (e.g., seven churches, seals, trumpets, bowls; twenty-four elders; 144,000 sealed, etc.). Furthermore,

---

[6]For a number of specific examples from both Greek and Hebrew sources see Johnson, EBC, 12, 533.

in 15:2 the victors have triumphed over three enemies: the beast, his image, and *the number of his name,* which suggests a symbolic significance connected with idolatry and blasphemy rather than victory over a mere puzzle of correctly identifying someone's name.

John seeks to give "wisdom" and "insight" to believers as to the true identity of their enemy (v. 18). A similar use of "insight" and "wisdom" occurs in 17:9, where John calls attention to the identity of the beast ridden by the harlot. What John seems to be asking for in both cases is divine discernment and not mathematical ingenuity! Believers need to penetrate the deception of the beast and John's reference to his number will help them to recognize his true character and identity.

The statement "it is man's number" further identifies the kind of number the beast represents. It alerts the reader to some hidden meaning in 666. From this it may be concluded that the number of the beast is linked to humanity. Why would it be necessary for John to emphasize this relationship unless he assumed that his readers might have understood the beast to be otherworldly without any connection to humanity? Might it be, then, that the statement signifies that the satanic beast, which is the great enemy of the church, manifests itself in human form?

Finally, how are we to understand the number 666 itself? Irenaeus proposed (while still holding to a personal Antichrist) that the number indicates that the beast is the sum of "all apostate power," a concentrate of six thousand years of unrighteousness, wickedness, deception, and false prophecy. He states that "the digit six, being adhered to throughout, indicates the recapitulations of that prophecy, taken in its full extent, which occurred at the beginning, during the intermediate periods, and which shall take place at the end." Irenaeus also held that the wound of the beast has reference to Genesis 3:13ff. The Messiah has freed men by wounding Satan.

The significance of the name of the beast is abundantly clear in Revelation (12:3; 13:1–6; 14:11; 17:3ff.). Wherever there is blasphemy, there the beast's name is found. The number 666 is the heaping up of the number 6. "Because of its contrast with 7 we may be content with an interpretation which sees in 666 an allusion to incompleteness, to the demonic parody of the perfection of 7, to the deceptiveness of the almost-perfect, to the idolatrous blasphemy exemplified by false worshipers" (Minear). This interpretation of 666 as a symbolic number referring to the unholy trinity of evil or to the human, imperfect imitation of God rather than a cipher of a name is not restricted to Minear. It has been held by a long line of conservative commentators.

D. The Harvest of the Earth (14:1–20)

The two previous chapters have prepared Christians for the reality that, as the end draws near, they will be harassed and sacrificed like sheep.

This section shows that their sacrifice is not meaningless. A glance back at chapter 7 reminds us that there the 144,000 were merely sealed; here, however, they are seen as already delivered. When the floods have passed, Mount Zion appears high above the waters; the Lamb is on the throne of glory, surrounded by the triumphant songs of His own; the gracious presence of God fills the universe (Lilje).

Chapter 14 briefly answers two pressing questions: What becomes of those who refuse to receive the mark of the beast and are killed (vv. 1–5)? What happens to the beast and his servants (vv. 6–20)?

1. *The Lamb and the 144,000* (14:1–5)

The Lamb standing on Mount Zion (v. 1) is contrasted with the dragon standing on the shifting sands of the seashore (13:1). Although the mood of rapid movement of the previous chapters gives way to one of victorious rest (vv. 1–5, 13), activity continues because the battle between the dragon and the woman (cf. 12:11) is still going on.

Chapter 14 advances the drama a step further than chapter 7. While the members of the multitude are the same, the circumstances in which they are seen have altered. In chapter 7, the whole company of God's people are sealed (7:1–8), readied for the satanic onslaught, and then a company (a martyred portion?) are seen in heaven serving before the throne of God (7:9ff.); but in chapter 14, the whole body of the redeemed is seen (resurrected?) with the Lamb in the earthly eschatological kingdom.

The background of verses 1–5 may reflect John's reinterpretation of Psalm 2, to which he has alluded elsewhere and which described the battle between the rebellious nations and God, with God suppressing the revolt by enthroning His Son on Mount Zion (Caird). John, however, does not see the warrior-king the writer of Psalm 2 hoped for, but the Lamb and those who repeated His victory over the enemy by their submission (His name on their forehead). Psalm 76, where Zion is the symbol of the defeat of God's enemies and the salvation of His people, may also be part of the background.

The problem of the *location* of this group of 144,000 is more complex. "Mount Zion" may refer to the hilly area in southeast Jerusalem, the temple mount, the whole city of Jerusalem, or, as in postexilic days, the whole land of Judah and the whole Israelite nation. In the prophetic tradition, Zion came to symbolize the place where the Messiah would gather to Himself a great company of the redeemed (Ps. 48:1ff.; Isa. 24:23; Joel 2:32; Obad. 17, 21; Mic. 4:1, 7; Zech. 14:10). Zion may here symbolize the strength and security that belong to the people of God.

In the seven New Testament references to Zion, five occur in Old Testament quotations. Of the other two, one is here in Revelation and the remaining reference (Heb. 12:22–23) implies a connection between Mount Zion and the church: "But you have come to Mount Zion, to the heavenly Jerusalem, the city of the living God . . . to the church of the firstborn." Some, connecting the reference in Hebrews to the one here in Revelation 14:1, have argued for the *heavenly* location of the 144,000. According to others, Mount Zion refers to the *earthly* seat of the messianic or millennial kingdom. Whether the locale of this Mount Zion has any connection with the ancient and historical Zion, John does not say.

The 144,000 have on their foreheads the names of the Father and the Lamb, showing that they belong to God, not the beast. In 7:3ff., the elect group of 144,000 has the seal of God on their foreheads, linking them to this group in chapter 14, while the further description that "they follow the Lamb" (v. 4) may show their connection with the second group in 7:9ff., the "great multitude" (see esp. 7:17: "lead them"). One of the most beautiful and assuring promises in the whole book is that God's servants will have His name on their foreheads (cf. 3:12; 22:4).

The "sound" John hears (v. 2) is probably a "voice" as in 1:15. It is important to recognize that this voice is not that of the redeemed; it is a loud angelic chorus (cf. 5:11), sounding like "the roar of rushing waters," like "a loud peal of thunder," and like "harpists playing their harps" (1:15; 5:8; 6:1; 19:1, 6; cf. comments on 5:8).

This "new song" in verse 3 should be related to the "new song" in 5:9 (q.v.), also sung by the angelic choirs. It is the song of redemption and vindication. What was seen in chapter 5 as secured for the redeemed by Christ's death (viz., that "they will reign on the earth," 5:10) has now been realized on Mount Zion. In the one further reference to a song in Revelation, the redeemed "victors" sing "the song of Moses . . . and the song of the Lamb" (15:3), which may also relate to the new song of chapters 5 and 14 (see comments on 15:3). This heavenly example of worship may help us understand and appreciate Paul's references to songs inspired by the Spirit and sung in the first-century congregations (Eph. 5:19; Col. 3:16). Also instructive are the Old Testament references to a "new song" (Pss. 33:3; 40:3; 96:1; 144:9; 149:1; Isa. 42:10). A "new song," in consequence of some mighty deed of God, comes from a fresh impulse of gratitude and joy in the heart. We are reminded again of the Passover motif (Exod. 15:1ff.).

While the angels sing, only the 144,000 can "learn" the new song, for they alone of earth's inhabitants have experienced God's mighty victory over the beast through their ordeal of suffering and death. Possibly, the word "learn" in this context may mean to "hear deeply."

The 144,000 who were "redeemed" or "purchased" "from the earth" or "from among men" (v. 4) must be the same as those "purchased" from all the earth's peoples in 5:9 and those sealed in 7:4–8, who have washed their garments in the blood of the Lamb (7:14ff.).

John's most difficult statement about this group is that they did "not defile themselves with women" (v. 4). Does he mean that this group consists only of men who had never married? Or should it be understood as referring to spiritual apostasy or cult prostitution? It is unlikely that "defiled" refers merely to sexual intercourse, since nowhere in Scripture does intercourse within marriage constitute sinful defilement (cf. Heb. 13:4). Therefore, the words can refer only to adultery or fornication; and this fact, in turn, establishes "pure" as the meaning of "virgins" in this context (the NIV is paraphrastic here, but accurately so).

Some think the reference is to actual celibacy, which alone could make a man fit to be a sacrificial lamb for God. Others connect the reference to purity with holy-war regulations for soldiers who were ceremonially unclean for sexual reasons (Deut. 23:9–10; 1 Sam. 21:5; 2 Sam. 11:11). Each of these views founders because of the assumption that "uncleanness" is the equivalent of "defile," which not only fails on linguistic grounds but involves us in a scriptural contradiction, i.e., that the marriage bed is defiling and sinful. It is better, then, to see the reference to purity as contrasting with the defilement of idolatry. In fact, John seems to use "defile" in this way elsewhere of cult prostitution (3:4; cf. 2:14, 20, 22).

The group as a whole has remained faithful to Christ; "they follow the Lamb wherever he goes" in obedient discipleship. They are purchased by Christ's blood and offered to God as a holy and pure sacrifice of firstfruits. Surely this symbolically implies that the bride of Christ must be pure from idolatry. Paul likewise uses this figure: "I promised you to one husband, to Christ, so that I might present you as a pure virgin to him" (2 Cor. 11:2–3).

Those spoken of in verse 3 are "firstfruits" (v. 4) presented to God. The word can have two meanings. It may designate the initial ingathering of the farmer, after which the rest of the harvest comes. So it may mean a pledge or downpayment with more to follow. Although it is difficult to find this sense of the word in the Old Testament, it seems to be its meaning in several New Testament references (Rom. 8:23; 11:16; cf. 1 Cor. 15:20; 16:15). On the other hand, in the usual Old Testament sense and alternate New Testament usage, "firstfruits" means simply an *offering* to God in the sense of being separated to Him and sanctified (wholly consecrated), without any later addition, because the firstfruits constitutes the whole (Num. 5:9 [NIV, "sacred contributions"]; Deut. 18:4; 26:2; Jer. 2:3; James 1:18). That this is John's intended sense is evident from the expression "offered as firstfruits to God."

The "lie" that would bring "blame" (v. 5) refers to the blasphemy of the beast worshipers who deny the Father and the Son and ascribe vitality to the beast by believing his heresies and worshiping his image (21:27; 22:15; cf. John 8:44–45; Rom. 1:25; 2 Thess. 2:9–11; 1 John 2:4, 21–22, 27).

2. The harvest of the earth (14:6–20)

This section forms a transition from the scene of the saints' final triumph (14:1–5) to the seven bowls (16:1ff.), which depict the final judgments on the enemies of the Lamb. As such, it forms a consoling counterpart to the earlier vision as it assures the 144,000 that God will judge the beast, his followers, and his world-wide system—Babylon.

a) Preparatory: The three angels (14:6–13)

The eternal Gospel (vv. 6–7). The first angel announces that there is still hope, for even at this crucial moment in history God is seeking to reclaim the followers of the beast by issuing a message appealing to the people of the world to "fear God . . . and worship him." That this appeal is called a "gospel" has raised a question. How can it be good news? Yet is not the intent of the gospel message that men should fear God and worship Him? Is it not the "eternal" gospel because it announces eternal life (John 3:16)? Could this be John's way of showing the final fulfillment of Mark 13:10? Let us not fail to see how in the New Testament the announcement of divine judgment is never separated from the proclamation of God's mercy.

The reference to the coming of the hour of judgment (v. 7) supports the view that there is chronological progression in Revelation and that not everything described by John is simultaneous (see comments on 15:1). This is the first reference in the book to the "judgment of God" (16:7; 18:10; 19:2), though the "wrath" of God, which appears to be a synonymous term (v. 19), has been mentioned earlier (6:16–17; 11:18; 14:8, 10; 15:1; cf. 16:1, 19; 18:3; 19:15).

The Fall of Babylon (v. 8). In anticipation of a more extended description in chapters 17 and 18, the fall of Babylon, the great anti-God system of idolatry, is announced, although the actual fall does not occur until the final bowl judgment (16:19). There may be a previous allusion to Babylon as the "great city" in 11:8 (cf. 17:18).

The final end of the worshipers of the beast (vv. 9–12). The explicit reference to the certain judgment of the beast worshipers ties this section to chapter 13. John describes God's judgment inflicted on those who refused His truth and worshiped a lie (Rom. 1:18, 25) by means of Old Testament figures of eschatological judgment: unmixed wine (not diluted with water) in the cup of God's wrath (Ps. 75:8; Jer. 25:15) and burning sulfur (Isa. 30:33; 34:8–10; cf. Gen. 19:24; Rev. 19:20; 20:10; 21:8). To those who drink Babylon's cup (v. 8), the Lord will give His own cup of wrath.

The reference to "torment" (v. 10; cf. 9:5; 11:10; 12:2; 20:10) has troubled some commentators since the torment takes place "in the presence . . . of the Lamb." While the view that some recalcitrant individuals will suffer eternal deprivation seems repugnant to Christian sensitivity, it is clear that it is not only John's understanding but that of Jesus and of other

New Testament writers as well (Matt. 25:46; Rom. 2:3–9; 2 Thess. 1:6–9).

John's imagery conveys a sense of finality and sober reality. It is not clear whether the imagery points only to the permanency and irreversibility of God's punitive justice or whether it also includes the consciousness of eternal deprivation (cf. Rev. 20:10; John 5:28–29). Preaching about hell should never be used as a terror tactic by the church but should always be presented in such a way as to show that God's mercy is the final goal. C.S. Lewis acknowledges that hell is a detestable doctrine that he would willingly remove from Christianity if it were in his power. But, as he goes on to point out, the question is not whether it is detestable but whether it is true. We must recognize that the reality of hell has the full support of Scripture and of our Lord's own teaching. Indeed, it has always been held by Christians and has the support of reason (*The Problem of Pain,* ch. 8).

The worshipers of the beast will be unable to rest day or night. Notice the constrast with the saints who will "rest" from their labor (v. 13). The beast worshipers have their time of rest while the saints are persecuted and martyred, but in the final time of judgment God will reverse their roles (7:15ff.; cf. 2 Thess. 1:6–7).

The great test for Christians is whether through patient endurance they will remain loyal to Jesus and not fall prey to the deception of the beasts (v. 12; see comments on 13:10). They do this by their serious attention to God's Word and their faithfulness to Christ Jesus (1:3; 2:26; 3:8, 10; 22:7, 9; cf. Phil. 1:28–30).

A fourth voice comes from heaven (an angel's or Christ's?), pronounces a beatitude, and evokes the Spirit's response (v. 13). This is the second beatitude in Revelation (cf. comments on 1:3). Its general import is clear: John expects the imminent intensification of persecution associated with the beast, and the beatitude indicates that those who remain loyal to Jesus when this occurs will be blessed indeed.

Apart from 22:17, this is the only place in Revelation where the Spirit speaks directly (cf. Acts 13:2; Heb. 3:7; 10:15). The beatitude is no doubt intended to emphasize the reality of the martyrs' future. Their blessedness consists in "rest" from the onslaught of the dragon and his beasts and in the assurance that their toil (cf. 2:2) for Christ's name will not be in vain but will be remembered by the Lord Himself after their death (Heb. 6:10; cf. 1 Tim. 5:24–25).

b) *The divine judgment of the world* (14:14–20)

The grain harvest (vv. 14–16). After the brief pause to encourage the faithfulness of the saints, John returns to the theme of divine judgment on the world. He does this by first describing the judgment in terms of a *harvest* (14:14–20) and then by presenting the seven *bowl plagues* (chs. 15–16).

John sees a white cloud and seated on it one resembling a human being ("like a son of man"). He has a crown of gold and a sharp sickle, the main instrument of harvest. John clearly wishes to highlight this exalted human figure and his role in the eschatological judgment. The question of the identity of the "son of man" is not unlike the problem of the identity of the rider of the white horse (6:1). The same words "like a son of man" (also without the definite article) are used of Jesus in 1:13. Some have noted the close association of the one "seated on the cloud" with the words "another angel" in verse 15 and the statement in verse 17 that another angel "too" had a sharp sickle, implying that the former figure with the sickle was likewise an angel. Furthermore, if the figure on the cloud is Jesus, how can we account for an angel giving a command to Him to reap the earth (v. 15)?

Although there are difficulties, there can be no question as to the identity of the divine figure seated on the cloud. It is quite appropriate for John to use the term Son of Man, since in the Gospels that term is most frequently associated with the Messiah's suffering and the glory of the Second Advent as well as with His right to judge the world (Matt. 26:64; John 5:27). The imagery of Daniel 7, frequently used in the Apocalypse, links the suffering people of God ("the saints") to the Son of Man who sits in judgment on the kingdoms of the world. It should, of course, be remembered that this is a highly symbolic description of the final judgment.

The harvest is an Old Testament figure used for divine judgment (Hos. 6:11; Joel 3:13), especially on Babylon (Jer. 51:33). Jesus also likens the final judgment to the harvest of the earth (Matt. 13:30, 39). He may use the instrumentality of angels or men, but it is His prerogative to put in the sickle. While this first reaping may be the gathering of His elect from the earth (so Caird), the context favors taking the harvest to be a reference not to salvation but to judgment.

The grape harvest (vv. 17–20). The divine eschatological judgment is presented in a threefold imagery: the unmixed wine in the cup (v. 10), the grain harvest (vv. 14–16), and the grape harvest (vv. 17–20). These are best understood as three metaphors describing different views of the same reality, i.e., the divine judgment. Again the Old Testament provides the background for this imagery (Isa. 63:1–6; Lam. 1:15; Joel 3:13; cf. Rev. 19:13, 15).

The final verse (v. 20) is gruesome: blood flows up to the horses' bridles for a distance of about two hundred miles (sixteen hundred stadia). Again the source of the imagery is Isaiah 63:1–6, heightened by John's hyperbole. The judgment is not the task of human vengeance but belongs exclusively to the Son of Man and His angelic reapers (cf. Rom.

12:19–21). The symbolism is that of a head-on battle, a great defeat of the enemy, a sea of spilled blood. To go beyond this and attempt to find a symbolic meaning in the sixteen hundred stadia or to link the scene to some geographic location (cf. 16:4–6) is pure speculation.

The term "outside the city" requires explanation. It may refer merely to ancient warfare when a besieging army was slaughtered at the city walls and the blood flowed outside the city. Some think John may have had an actual city in mind and have suggested Jerusalem because of the Old Testament predictions of a final battle to be fought near the city (Dan. 11:45; Joel. 3:12; Zech. 14:4; but cf. Rev. 16:16—"Armageddon" is not near Jerusalem). On the other hand, John's symbolic use of "city" in every other reference favors taking the word symbolically in this verse also. In Revelation there are only two cities (the cities of the seven churches in Rev. 2–3 are not called "cities"): the "city of God," which is the camp of the saints, and the "city of Satan," Babylon, which is made up of the followers of the beast. There is no way to be really sure of the identity of the city, nor is its identity important. It is sufficient to take it as the same city that was "trampled" by the pagans in 11:2 and is seen again in 20:9, i.e., the community of the saints.

For Further Study

1. Compare and contrast the woman in chapter 12 with the woman in chapter 17. How, then, may we understand our calling as believers?

2. In what sense are Christians involved in a cosmic struggle with evil (12:10–12)? Why should we believe that we will eventually win the battle?

3. Study the references to the 1,260 days, the time, times, and half a time, and the 42 months in chapters 11–13. Are they alternate ways of describing the same time? Is this symbolic or literal?

4. Summarize the inner dynamics of the struggle and the various means that Satan uses against God's people found in chapters 12–13.

5. Do you see the beast (Antichrist) as a present threat to the church or only future? If present, where is the greatest manifestation or danger?

6. Using at least three different commentaries from three different schools of interpretation (see bibliography), study their interpretations of the beast (ch. 13) and identify agreements and differences among them. Which view do you favor? Why?

7. Has the game of gematria over the number 666 been successful? Do you favor this approach or another?

8. What does John mean when he refers to the 144,000 as "virgins"?

9. Do you believe that 14:10–11 indicates that hell will be conscious and eternal? Why?

Chapter 7

The Seven Bowls
(Revelation 15:1–19:10)

It is difficult to know where the divisions should fall in these further visions. Since this last series of seven in Revelation includes the fall of Babylon under the seventh bowl (16:19), it has seemed appropriate to include the extensive description of the city's fall under the bowl series.

Chapter 15, a kind of celestial interlude before the final judgment, is preparatory to the execution of the bowl series described in chapter 16, while chapter 17 and 18 elaborate the fall of Babylon. What has already been anticipated under the preceding figures of the divine eschatological judgment—the cup of wine (14:10), the harvest of the earth (14:14–16), and the grape harvest (14:17–20)—is now further described under the symbolism of the seven bowls. In typical Hebrew fashion, each cycle repeats in new ways the former events and also adds fresh details not in the former series.

It is clear that in these final judgments only the unbelieving world is involved; therefore, they are punitive plagues (16:2). Yet even in these last plagues God is concerned with effecting repentance, though none abandon their idolatry (16:9, 11). But are the faithful still on earth? Verse 2 of chapter 15 locates the whole company of conquerors not on earth but before the throne. So intense are these final judgments that the third-century church commentator Victorinus argues: "For the wrath of God always strikes the obstinate people with seven plagues, that is, perfectly, as it is said in Leviticus; and these shall be in the last time, when the church shall have gone out of the midst." It is difficult to support or refute such a view.

My position is that the inclusive series of bowl judgments constitutes the "third woe," announced in 11:14 as "coming soon" (see comments on 11:14). Since the first two woes occur under the fifth and sixth trumpets, it is reasonable to see the third woe, which involved seven plagues, as unfolding during the sounding of the seventh trumpet, when the mystery of God will be finished (10:7). The actual events of the third woe were delayed until John could give important background material concerning not only the inhabitants of the earth but also the church herself, her glory and shame, her faithfulness and apostasy (12:1–14:20). These last plagues take place "immediately after the distress of those days" referred to by Jesus in the Olivet Discourse and may well be the fulfillment of His apocalyptic words: "The sun will be darkened, and the moon will not give its light; the stars will fall from the sky, and the heavenly bodies will be shaken" (Matt. 24:29). Significantly, the event that follows this judgment in Matthew, the coming of the Son of Man in the clouds, is the same event John describes following the bowl judgments (19:11).

A. Preparation: The Seven Angels With the Seven Last Plagues (15:1–8)

Chapter 15 is tied closely to chapter 16. Both deal with the seven last plagues of God's wrath. One is preparatory and interpretative, the other descriptive. Chapter 15 is related to the Old Testament account of the Exodus and is strongly suggestive of the liturgical tradition of the ancient synagogue. The chapter has two main visions: the first portrays the victors who have emerged triumphant from the great ordeal (vv. 2–4); the second relates the emergence from the heavenly temple of the seven angels clothed in white and gold who hold the seven bowls of the last plagues (vv. 5–8).

1. A marvelous sign (15:1)

Verse 1 forms a superscription to chapters 15 and 16. The final manifestation of the wrath of God takes the form of seven angels of judgment and is called a "sign." This is the third explicitly identified heavenly "sign" (cf. the woman and dragon, 12:1, 3). The qualifying adjective "marvelous" apparently is added because John understood the seven angels to represent the completion of God's wrath, viz., the last plagues. They are awesome as well as final in character. As has already been argued, the first reference to the eschatological judgments is found in 6:17: "For the great day of their wrath has come, and who can stand?" After the interlude of the sealing of the saints from spiritual harm (ch. 7), the seven trumpets are sounded (8:1ff.). The sixth one involves three plagues that kill a third of mankind (9:18). The third woe (11:14) includes the bowl judgments that are called the "last" plagues. From this we may conclude that the eschatological wrath of God begins with the trumpets and ends with the seven bowls.

2. The victors (15:2)

As in 14:1ff., John again focuses His attention on a scene that contrasts sharply with the coming judgment, an indication of His pastoral concern. He sees before the throne the likeness of a sea of glass shot through with fire (cf. 4:6). It is a scene of worship, and its imagery is suitable for depicting the majesty and brilliance of God, which the sea of glass is reflecting in a virtual symphony of color. No further symbolic significance than this needs to be sought here. Firmly planted on (or "beside," NIV) the sea are those who were "victorious over the beast." They are the same ones who are seen throughout Revelation as having won out over the idolatrous beasts through their faithful testimony to Christ, even to the extent of martyrdom (e.g., 2:7, 11, 26; 12:11; 21:7; cf. 3:21; 5:5). They are the 144,000 elect of God (7:4; 14:1), the completed company of martyrs (6:11). Note the absence of "received his mark," since the equivalent expression "the number of his name" is used (see comments on 13:17). Suddenly in this dazzling scene the sound of harps and singing is heard.

3. The song of Moses and the Lamb (15:3-4)

The song sung by the redeemed is the "song of Moses, the servant of God and the song of the Lamb"—a single song as verses 3-4 show. The Song of Moses is found in Exodus 15:1-18; it celebrates the victory of the Lord over the Egyptians at the Red Sea. In the ancient synagogue it was sung each Sabbath in the afternoon service to celebrate God's sovereign rule over the universe, which is also the emphasis in the liturgical collection of psalms and prophets John quotes in verses 3-4 (e.g., "King of the ages"). As the deliverance from Egypt, with its divine plagues of judgment on Israel's enemies, became for the Jew a signpost of God's just rule over the world, so God's eschatological judgment and the deliverance of the followers of the Lamb bring forth from the victors over the beast exuberant songs of praise to God for His righteous acts in history.

Each line in verses 3-4 picks up phrases from the Psalms and Prophets. Compare the following Old Testament words with verses 3-4: "Then Moses and the Israelites sang this song" (Exod. 15:1); "your works are wonderful" (Ps. 139:14); "LORD God Almighty" (Amos. 4:13); "all his ways are just. A faithful God . . . upright and just is he" (Deut. 32:4); "who shall not revere you, O King of the nations" (Jer. 10:7); "they will bring glory to your name" (Ps. 86:9); etc. While John may or may not have heard the victors over the beast singing these actual words, it was revealed to him that they were praising God for His mighty deliverance and judgment on their enemies. His rendering of the song may be drawn from the liturgy of the synagogue and no doubt from the early Christian church. In fact, it is precisely in connection with the ancient Easter liturgy that the church's dependence on the synagogue Passover liturgy is most easily recognizable. The Exodus background is quite obvious throughout chapters 15 and 16 (cf. 8:7ff. and see comments on 1:10).

4. The seven angels of the last plagues (15:5-8)

A second and still more impressive scene follows. The door to the temple in heaven is again opened (cf. 11:19), and the seven angels dressed in white and gold come out of the temple. One of the living creatures solemnly gives a "bowl" to each of the seven messengers. In Hebrew, a "bowl" could refer to a large banquet bowl for wine (Amos 6:6), but more often it was a ritual bowl used for collecting the blood of the sacrifices (Exod. 27:3). Golden bowls seem to be always associated with the temple (e.g., 1 Kings 7:50; 2 Kings 12:13; 25:15), especially for use in offerings or for incense (cf. 5:8).

The "smoke" that filled the temple refers to the shekinah cloud, first associated with the tabernacle and later with the temple. It symbolizes God's special presence: He is the source of the judgments (Exod. 40:34ff.; 1 Kings 8:10–11; Ezek. 11:23; 44:4). His awesome presence in the temple until the plagues are finished (16:17) prohibits even angels from entering it (cf. Isa. 6:4; Hab. 2:20).

B. The Pouring Out of the Bowl Judgments (16:1–21)

This chapter describes the "third woe" (see introduction to ch. 15) in the form of the outpouring of seven bowl judgments. They occur in rapid succession with only a brief pause for a dialogue between the third angel and the altar, accentuating the justice of God's punishments (vv. 5–7). This rapid succession is probably due to John's desire to give a telescopic view of the first six bowls and to hasten then on to the seventh, where the far more interesting judgment on Babylon occurs, of which the author will give a detailed account. Again, seven symbolizes fullness, this time fullness of judgment (cf. Lev. 26:21). The striking parallelism between the order of these plagues and those of the trumpets (8:2–9:21), though clearly not identical in every detail, has led many to conclude that the two series are the same. The similarity, however, may be merely literary.

Each plague in both series (the trumpets and the bowls) is reminiscent of the plagues on Egypt before the Exodus. The first four in both series cover the traditional divisions of nature: earth, sea, rivers, sky. But in each of the bowls, unlike the trumpets, the plague on nature is related to the suffering of mankind. Furthermore, each bowl plague seems to be all-inclusive in its effect ("every living thing . . . died," v. 3), whereas under the trumpets only a part is affected ("a third of the living creatures . . . died," 8:9). Therefore, it seems better to understand the trumpets and bowls as separate judgments; yet both are described in language drawn from the pattern of God's judgment on Egypt under Moses (see comments on 8:7ff.). The final three plagues are social and spiritual in their effect and shift from nature to humanity.

While these descriptions should probably not be taken in a strictly literal sense, the important point is that they depict God's sure and righteous judgment that will one day be literally and actually executed in this world.

1. *The first bowl* (16:2)

The first bowl has no strict counterpart in the trumpets but recalls the sixth plague of boils under Moses (Exod. 9:10–11). As the antagonists of Moses were affected by the boils, so the enemies of Christ who worship the beast will be struck by this plague. Perhaps "painful" sore may be translated "malignant" sore.

2. *The second bowl* (16:3)

The second bowl turns the sea into polluted blood (see comments on 8:8). Genesis 1:21 is reversed: all marine life dies (cf. Exod. 7:17–21).

3. *The third bowl* (16:4–7)

The third bowl affects the fresh waters of the earth, which are essential to human life. They too become blood (cf. Exod. 7:17–21).

The reference to blood calls forth the dialogue between the angel and the altar concerning the logic of the plagues. The blood that sinners now drink is just requital for their shedding of the blood of the saints (15:1–4) and prophets (11:3–13; cf. 17:6; 18:20). With blood, God vindicates the blood of the martyrs of Jesus. God's wrath is exercised in recognition of their love. People must choose whether to drink the blood of saints or to wear robes dipped in the blood of the Lamb (Minear).

4. *The fourth bowl* (16:8–9)

The fourth bowl increases the intensity of the sun's heat; it is the opposite of the fourth trumpet, which produced a plague of darkness (cf. 8:12). Instead of repenting of their deeds and acknowledging the Creator, the only act that could even now turn away God's wrath, the earth's inhabitants curse ("slander," "blaspheme") God for sending them agonizing pain (vv. 11, 21). Yet their problem goes beyond the awful physical pain and is moral and spiritual (cf. Isa. 52:5; Rom. 1:25, 2:24).

5. *The fifth bowl* (16:10–11)

The fifth bowl plunges the kingdom of the beast into darkness. This is not a reference to the fall of the Roman Empire or Caesar worship, although John's words would include this level of meaning. In 2:13, John used the word "throne" to designate the stronghold of Satan at Pergamum. Thus "the throne of the beast" symbolizes the seat of the worldwide dominion of the great satanic system of idolatry (the Abyss? cf. 20:1). This system is plunged into spiritual darkness or disruption, bringing chaos on all who sought life and meaning in it. Charles seeks to connect this darkness with the darkness and pain caused by the demon-locusts of the fifth trumpet (9:1ff.). But in the trumpet plague the locust-demons are the direct cause of the pain, while the darkness is incidental. This bowl plague, however, though similar to the fifth trumpet, strikes at the very seat of satanic authority over the world; the darkness is probably moral and spiritual rather than physical (cf. 21:25; 22:5; John 8:12; 12:35–36, 46; 1 John 1:5–7; 2:8–10; Wisd. of Sol. 17:21). Again the terrible refrain is repeated: "But they refused to repent of what they had done."

6. *The sixth bowl* (16:12–16)

The sixth bowl is specifically aimed at drying up the Euphrates River and so will allow the demonically inspired kings from the East to gather at Armageddon where God Himself will enter into battle with them. The reference to the Euphrates in the sixth trumpet is a striking parallel to the sixth bowl plague (9:14), a reason why many identify the two series as different aspects of the same plagues. But while the sixth trumpet releases demonic hordes to inflict death on the earth's inhabitants, the sixth bowl effects the assembling of the rulers (kings) from the East to meet the Lord God Almighty in battle.

a) *The Euphrates and the kings from the East* (16:12–14)

The Euphrates was not only the location of Babylon, the great anti-God throne, but the place from which the evil hordes would invade Israel (see comments on 9:14). Thus, by mentioning the Euphrates by name, John is suggesting that the unseen rulers of this world are being prepared to enter into a final and fatal battle with the Sovereign of the universe. It is a warfare that can be conceived only in terms that describe realities of a primordial and eschatological order. Thus John does not, in my opinion, describe the invasion of the Parthian hordes advancing on Rome or any future military invasion of Israel. How could such political groups be involved in the battle of the great day of God Almighty? Instead, in terms reminiscent of the ancient battles of Israel, John describes the eschatological defeat of the forces of evil, the "kings from the East."

Further confirmation that these kings represent the combined forces of evil in the world is John's reference to the three froglike evil ("unclean") spirits that proceed out of the mouths of the dragon, the beast, and the false prophet. Frogs were considered unclean animals by the Jews (Lev. 11:10, 41). The background for this figure is not clear but probably relates more to pagan metaphors for evil than to any specific Old Testament references. To the Persian, the frog was the double of Ahriman, god of evil and agent of plagues. To the Egyptian, the frog was not loathsome, as some suggest, but the symbol of Heqt, a goddess of resurrection and fertility. But to a Jewish mind, such gods were demons (v. 14), Satan's emissaries, and inseparable from idolatry (9:20; 18:2; 1 Cor. 10:20–21). These demons produce miraculous signs like the false prophet (13:13–14), and this connects their activity with the deception of the earth's kings. Since these demons come from the "mouths" of the figures, lying and deceptive words are implied (cf. the sword from Christ's mouth that is equal to His word of truth). These kings are summoned to the battle of the great day of God Almighty. It is not necessary to limit John's language to the emperor cult or to the Nero redivivus myth (see introduction to ch. 13). Under the sixth bowl, the kings are only gathered. Not until the seventh bowl do the confrontation and defeat actually occur (19:19–21).

b) *An exhortation to vigilance* (16:15)

Somewhat abruptly, but not inappropriately so, a warning is issued. The Parousia (coming) of Christ is here connected with the judgment of Armageddon and the fall of Babylon. After John has described the latter in more detail (chs. 17–18), he describes the vision of the return of Jesus (19:11–16). In verse 15 the third of the seven beatitudes is pronounced (cf. 1:3; 14:13; 19:9; 20:6; 22:7, 14).

Similar to the exhortation given to those in the churches at Sardis (3:2–4) and Laodicea (3:18), the warning about Jesus' coming "like a thief" implies a need for alertness to the deception of idolatry and disloyalty to Jesus (cf. Matt. 24:43ff; 1 Thess. 5:2, 4). Like a guard who watches by night, the true Christian will remain steadfast and prepared. It is not necessary to relate this warning only to the end time as in the context, since the appeal for the steadfast loyalty of Christians is relevant at any time. Such appeals, however, are associated in the Gospels with the return of Christ (Mark 13:32–37).

c) *Armageddon* (16:16)

Many modern interpreters identify Armageddon with the fortified Galilean city of Megiddo and believe that a literal military battle will be fought in that vicinity in the latter days.[1] While this sense is not impossible, it is better to understand the term symbolically (cf. 9:11, where "in Hebrew" alerts us to the symbolic significance of the name of the angel of the Abyss) and not as referring to any geographical location we can now identify, whether in Palestine or elsewhere; but it describes the eschatological confrontation in which God will meet the forces of evil in their final defeat.

> Har-Magedon is symbolic of the final overthrow of all the forces of evil by the might and power of God. The great conflict between God and Satan, Christ and Antichrist, good and evil, which lies behind the perplexing course of history will in the end issue in a final struggle in which God will emerge victorious and take with him all who placed their faith in him. This is Har-Magedon (Mounce).

Nevertheless, it refers to a real point in history and to real persons and powers who will encounter God's just sentence.

---

[1] For a discussion and evaluation of other suggestions of the name's meaning, see Johnson, EBC, 12, p. 552.

7. *The seventh bowl* (16:17–21)

The seventh bowl is poured out into the air. Nothing further is said about the "air"; rather, John is concerned with the loud voice that cries out, "It is done," or, "It has come to pass." With this seventh bowl, the eschatological wrath of God is completed (cf. 6:17; 21:6; John 19:30). Flashes of lightning, peals of thunder, and a severe earthquake occur (cf. 4:5; 8:5; 11:19). These eschatological signs symbolize the destruction of the anti-God forces throughout the world (cf. Heb. 12:27). So great is the earthquake of God's judgment that it reaches the strongholds of organized evil represented by the cities of the pagans ("nations"). Even the great city Babylon, which seduced all the earth's kings and inhabitants (17:2), now comes under final sentence (see comments on 11:8).

The judgment on Babylon will occupy John's attention in chapters 17 and 18. While the catastrophe continues to be described in geophysical terms (islands and mountains disappearing, huge hailstones accompanying a gigantic storm), there is a question as to whether John intends this destruction to be merely of natural or even politico-historical entities, or of the unseen powers of evil. In any event, like the Egyptian plague of hail that further hardened Pharaoh's heart, this plague of hail falls on the unrepentant to no avail; they curse God for sending His judgment on them (cf. Exod. 9:24). Thus John describes the rising pitch of God's wrath on the rebellious powers of the earth. His words should not be politicized as if he spoke merely of Rome or of some impending historical crisis for the church. He is speaking of the great realities of the end, when God has put down all His enemies.

C. The Prostitute and the Beast (17:1–18)

In a sense, the interpretation of this chapter controls the interpretation of the whole Book of Revelation. To a majority of modern exegetes, Babylon represents the city of Rome. The beast stands for the Roman Empire as a whole, including its subject provinces and peoples. The seven hills (v. 9) are the seven dynasties of Roman emperors from Augustus to Domitian. The ten kings are heads of lesser and restless states, eager to escape their enslavement to the colonizing power. John's prediction of the fall of Babylon is then the announcement of the impending dissolution of the Roman Empire in all its aspects. There is considerable evidence for this view: Babylon was a term used by both Jews and Christians for Rome, which was a great city (v. 18), a city set on seven hills (v. 9), and by the time of Domitian (A.D. 85) notorious for persecuting and killing the saints (v. 6). Many scholars of unquestioned competence have been fully convinced of these equations.

Yet there is evidence that casts doubt on this interpretation and impels us to look for a more adequate—if also a more subtle—understanding of

John's intention. It is simply not sufficient to identify Babylon with Rome. For that matter, Babylon cannot be confined to any one historical manifestation, past or future: it has multiple equivalents (cf. 11:8). The details of John's description do not neatly fit any past city, whether literal Babylon, Sodom, Egypt, Rome, or even Jerusalem. Babylon is found wherever there is satanic deception. It is defined more by dominant idolatries than geographic or temporal boundaries. Babylon is better understood here as the archetypal head of all entrenched worldly resistance to God. Babylon is a transhistorical reality that includes idolatrous kingdoms as diverse as Sodom, Egypt, Babylon, Tyre, Nineveh, and Rome. Babylon is an eschatological symbol of satanic deception and power; it is a divine mystery that can never be wholly reducible to empirical earthly institutions. It may be said that Babylon represents the total culture of the world apart from God, while the divine system is depicted by the New Jerusalem. Rome is simply one manifestation of the total system.

Chapters 17 and 18 form one continuous unit dealing with the judgment on Babylon. The woman is identified as the great city (17:18) whose fall is described in chapter 18. From internal evidence, the identity of Babylon the woman (ch. 17) with Babylon the great city (ch. 18) is so unmistakable that it would be inappropriate to make them different entities. These two chapters form an extended appendix to the seventh bowl, where the judgment on Babylon was mentioned (16:19). They also expand the earlier references to this city (11:8; 14:8) and look forward by way of contrast to the eternal Holy City (chs. 21–22).

Chapter 17 may be divided into the vision of the great harlot (vv. 1–6) and the interpretation of the vision (vv. 7–18). In suspenseful literary fashion, John first describes the nature of the harlot and the beast she rides (ch. 17); then he describes her momentous fall in terms drawn from the Old Testament descriptions of the fall of great cities (ch. 18).

1. The vision of the great prostitute (17:1–6)

"One of the seven angels" (v. 1) connects this vision with the preceding bowl judgments, showing that it is a further expansion of or appendix to the final bowl and not an additional event.

John sees a great prostitute established on many waters. The verse forms a superscription for the chapter. The relationship between prostitution and idolatry has already been discussed (see comments on 2:14, 20). The prevalence of cult prostitution throughout the ancient world makes this figure appropriate for idolatrous worship. The expressions "abominable things" (17:4) and "magic spell" (18:23) confirm this connection. In the Old Testament, the same figure of a harlot city is used of Nineveh (Nah. 3:4), of Tyre (Isa. 23:16–17), and frequently of idolatrous Jerusalem (Ezek. 16:15ff.). The best background for understanding the language of the chapter is not the history of the Roman Empire or parallels with a pagan god but the description of Jerusalem the harlot in Ezekiel 16 and 23 and Babylon the harlot in Jeremiah 51. A quick reading of these chapters will confirm the many parallels with John's language.

But the great prostitute, Babylon, that Revelation describes is not any mere historical city with its inhabitants, whether in John's past, present, or future. Rather, this city is the mother of all these historical prostitutes, the archetypal source of every idolatrous manifestation in time and space (v. 5).

All the harlot-city societies mentioned in Scripture have certain common characteristics that are also reflected in John's description of the great Babylon, in which he merges the descriptions of ancient Babylon and Jerusalem into one great composite. Royal dignity and splendor combined with prosperity, overabundance, and luxury (Jer. 51:13; Ezek. 16:13, 49; Nah. 2:9; cf. Rev. 18:3, 7, 16–17); self-trust or boastfulness (Isa. 14:12–14; Jer. 50:31; Ezek. 16:15, 50, 56; 27:3; 28:5; cf. Rev. 18:7); power and violence, especially against God's people (Jer. 51:35, 49; Ezek. 23:37; Nah. 3:1–3; cf. Rev. 18:10, 24); oppression and injustice (Isa. 14:4; Ezek. 16:49; 28:18; cf. Rev. 18:5, 20); and idolatry (Jer. 51:47; Ezek. 16:17, 36; 23:7, 30, 49; Nah. 1:14; cf. Rev. 17:4–5; 18:3; 19:2)—all are here. Wherever and whenever these characteristics have been manifested historically, *there* is the appearance of Babylon.

The great prostitute "sits on many waters." This goes back to Jeremiah's oracle against historical Babylon, situated along the waterways of the Euphrates, with many canals around the city, greatly multiplying its wealth by trade (Jer. 51:13). While the description alludes to ancient Babylon, it also has a deeper significance, explained in verse 15 as "peoples, multitudes, nations and languages"—figurative of the vast influence of the prostitute on the peoples of the world.

Earth's kings and inhabitants committed fornication with the prostitute (v. 2). This language goes back to references to the harlot cities of the past (e.g., Jer. 51:7) and means that the peoples of the world have become drunk with abundance, power, pride, violence, and especially false worship. "The kings of the earth" may simply describe the rulers in contrast to the hoi polloi.

John is carried in the Spirit (see comments on 1:10; cf. 4:2; 21:10) into a "desert" (v. 3). Again the allusion is to ancient Babylon (Isa. 14:23; 21:1; cf. Rev. 18:2; see comments on 12:6). It is in the desert that he sees the prostitute seated on "a scarlet beast"—scarlet, presumably, because the color symbolizes the beast's blasphemy in contrast to the white-horse rider and those dressed in white, who are faithful and true (19:8, 11, 14). Since this beast is a seven-headed monster, there is no cogent reason against identifying it with the first beast in chapter 13, which is also inseparable from the seven-headed dragon of chapter 12.

Dressed in queenly attire (Ezek. 16:13; cf. Rev. 18:7), the woman rides the beast, swinging in her hand a golden cup full of her idolatrous abominations and wickedness (v. 4). Note the contrast—beauty and gross wickedness. Her costly and attractive attire suggests the prostitute's outward beauty and attraction (Jer. 4:30). The golden cup filled with wine alludes to Jeremiah's description of Babylon's world-wide influence in idolatry (Jer. 51:7). Her cup is filled with "abominable things." The abominations are most frequently associated with idolatry, which was abhorrent to the Jew and likewise to the Christian (21:27). It is the same word Jesus used in referring to Daniel's "abomination that causes desolation" standing in the temple (Mark 13:14; cf. Dan. 9:27; 11:31; 12:11). Babylon is the archetype of all idolatrous obscenities in the earth (v. 5). "Filth" ("uncleannesses") is a word frequently associated in the New Testament with evil (unclean) spirits (e.g., Matt. 10:1; 12:43) and also with idolatry (2 Cor. 6:17) and perhaps cult prostitution (Eph. 5:5).

The woman has a *title* written on her forehead, showing that in spite of all her royal glamour she is nothing but a prostitute (v. 5). From the writings of Seneca and Juvenal, we know that it was the custom for Roman prostitutes to wear their names in the fillet that encircled their brow. The Old Testament also refers to the brow of the prostitute (Jer. 3:3, "a harlot's brow," NEB).

The first word in the woman's title is "MYSTERY" (cf. 1:20; 10:7; 17:7). Is this word part of her title ("MYSTERY BABYLON . . .") or part of the introductory statement ("She has a name written on her forehead, which is a mystery: BABYLON . . .")? Scholars disagree, but the latter explanation better fits John's use of mystery as a word denoting a divine secret or allegory that is now revealed.

No doubt the specific part of the title that is a divine mystery is that this prostitute is the *mother* of all earth's idolatrous prostitutes. She is the fountainhead, the reservoir, the womb that bears all the individual cases of historical resistance to God's will on earth; she is the unholy antithesis to the woman who weds the Lamb (19:7–8) and to the New Jerusalem (21:2–3). Therefore, she cannot be merely ancient Babylon, Rome, or Jerusalem, because these are only her children—*she* is the mother of them all. While from its beginning Babel was associated with resisting and defying God (Gen. 11:1–11), it is probably the epoch of the Babylonian captivity of Israel that indelibly etched the proud, idolatrous, and repressive nature of Babylon on the memory of God's people and thus provided for succeeding generations the symbolic image that could be applied to the further manifestations of the mother prostitute.

In verse 6 this mother prostitute is also described as the source of the shed blood of the followers of Jesus, the martyrs referred to throughout the book (6:9; 7:9ff.; 13:8; 18:24). The same mother harlot who had killed the saints of old throughout salvation history is now also responsible for the deaths of the Christians (cf. 2:13). Though there is no direct reference here to Rome or Jerusalem, early Christian readers would understand that whenever they were threatened with death by any temporal power—whether political, religious, or both—they were in reality facing the bloodthirsty mother prostitute whom God was about to judge and destroy once for all. To be drunk with blood was a familiar figure in the ancient world for the lust for violence.

2. The interpretation of the vision (17:7–18)

This section contains an extended interpretation of the vision that parallels the method used in apocalyptic sections in Old Testament prophecy (cf. Zech. 1:8ff., etc.; Rev. 7:9ff.). First the beast is described and identified (vv. 7–8), then the seven heads (vv. 9–11), the ten horns (vv. 12–14), the waters (v. 15), and finally the woman (v. 18). John's astonishment over the arresting figure of the woman on the beast is quickly subdued by the interpreting angel's announcement that John will be shown the explanation of the divine mystery of the symbolic imagery of woman and beast.

a) The beast (17:7–8)

Much difficulty in interpreting this section has resulted from incorrectly applying John's words either to the Roman emperors (the seven heads), to the Nero redivivus myth ("once was, now is not, and will come up out of the Abyss"; see introduction to ch. 13), or to a succession of world empires. None of these views is satisfactory for reasons stated below. John's description is theological, not political. He describes a reality behind the earth's sovereigns, rather than its successive manifestations in history.

The beast is the monster from the Abyss, i.e., the satanic incarnation of idolatrous power, mentioned in 11:7 and described in 13:1ff. (q.v.), whose destruction is seen in 19:19–20. John is told that the beast "once was, now is not, and will come up out of the Abyss" (v. 8). This seems clearly to be a paraphrase of the image in chapter 13 of the wounded beast who was healed (13:3, 14); the language is similar, the astonishment of the world's inhabitants identical, and the threefold emphasis on this spectacular feature is repeated in both contexts (13:3, 12, 13; 17:8, 11).

The play here on the tenses "was, . . . is not, . . . will come" refers to a three-stage history of the beast that requires a mind with wisdom to understand its mystery. Isaiah refers to the chaos monster as "Rahab the Do-Nothing," i.e., the monster thought to energize Egypt is in reality inactive, rendered impotent by the hand of the Lord (Isa. 30:7). That John's beast "is not" refers to his defeat by the Lamb on Calvary. To those who worship only the Father and the Son, all other gods are nothing or nonexistent (1 Cor. 8:4–6). Satan once had unchallenged power over the earth ("was," cf. Luke 4:6; Heb. 2:14–15). Now he is a defeated sovereign

("is not," cf. John 12:31–32); yet he is given a "little time" to oppose God
and His people (12:12c; 13:5; 20:3b) before his final sentencing to "destruction" (v. 11; cf. Matt. 7:13; John 17:12; Rom. 9:22; 2 Thess. 2:3). It is
this apparent revival of Satan's power and authority over the world after
his mortal wound (Gen. 3:15) that causes the deceived of the earth to
follow him.

Note the subtle change in perspective reflected in the wording of the
two references to the beast in verse 8: whereas the first instance refers to
his satanic origin ("out of the Abyss") and his final destruction, a divine
revelation to believers, the second simply states that he was, is not, and
yet comes, an unbeliever's view. This twofold viewpoint is paralleled in
verses 9–11, where one of the kings "is" (v. 10) and an eighth king "is"
(v. 11), yet the beast "is not" (v. 11). It seems that the author seeks to
identify theologically the nature of the power that supports the profligate
woman by means of intentional double-talk.

The use of the present tense for the beast's coming up out of the Abyss
(v. 8; cf. 11:7) may suggest a continuing aspect of his character, similar to
the use of the present tense to describe the New Jerusalem descending
from heaven (cf. 3:12; 21:2, 10). That the beast goes into perdition (present tense) may likewise indicate one of his continuing characteristics.
There is also a possible parallelism in the expression "once was, now is
not, and yet will come" with the divine attributes described in the phrase
"who is, and who was, and who is to come" (1:8). On the meaning of the
book of life, see comments on 3:5 (cf. 13:8).

b) *The seven heads* (17:9–11)

Verses 9–11 form the key of the Roman emperor view of the
Apocalypse. The woman not only sits on many waters (vv. 1, 15), and on
the beast (v. 3), but she also sits on seven hills (v. 9). As previously stated,
most scholars have no doubt that the seven hills refer to the seven hills of
Rome and the seven kings to seven successive emperors of that nation.

Yet there is good reason to doubt that this interpretation, or any variation thereof, is the meaning John intended. In the first place, the seven
hills belong to the monster, not the woman. It is the woman (i.e., the city,
v. 18) who sits upon (i.e., has mastery over) the seven heads (or seven
hills) of the monster. If the woman is the city of Rome, it is obvious that
she did not exercise mastery over seven successive Roman emperors who
are also the seven traditional hills of Rome. This introduces an unwar-
ranted twisting of the symbolism to fit a preconceived interpretation.
Also, how could the seven hills of Rome have any real importance to the
diabolical nature of the beast of the woman? Nor does it help to make the
prostitute the Roman Empire and the hills the city of Rome, since the
woman is explicitly identified in verse 18 not as the empire but as the city.

In fact, nowhere in the New Testament is Rome described as the enemy of the church.

If what is really important in the mention of the seven hills is the identification with Rome, how then does this require any special divine wisdom ("This calls for a mind with wisdom," v. 9)? Any Roman soldier who knew Greek could figure out that the seven hills referred to Rome. But whenever divine wisdom is called for, the description requires theological and symbolical discernment, not mere geographical or numerical insight (cf. comments on 13:18). Those who argue for a fusing of sources or images to explain the dual reference to the hills and kings simply evade the implications of the incongruity they have created.

In Revelation, the same word is always rendered "mountain" (6:14–16; 8:8; 14:1; 16:20; 21:10), except here in 17:9, where it is translated "hills." Is this a case where previous exegesis has influenced even the best translations (the KJV has "mountains")? On the other hand, mountains allegorically refer to world powers in the Prophets (Isa. 2:2; Jer. 51:25; Dan. 2:35; Zech. 4:7). It seems better, then, to interpret the seven mountains as a reference to the seven heads or kings, which describe not the city but the beast. The expression "they are also seven kings" (v. 9) seems to require strict identification of the seven mountains with seven kings rather than with a geographic location.

John's use of numbers elsewhere in the book also argues against the Roman Empire identification. He has already shown a strong affinity for their symbolic significance—e.g., seven churches, seals, trumpets, bowls, and thunders; twenty-four elders; 144,000 sealed, etc. By his use of seven, he indicates completeness or wholeness. The seven heads of the beast symbolize fullness of blasphemy and evil. It is much like our English idiom "the seven seas," i.e., all the seas of the world.

If the seven heads symbolically represent the complete or full source of evil power and blasphemy, why, then, does John in verse 10 talk about five fallen heads or kings, one existing head or king, and one yet to come? Does this not most readily fit the view of dynastic successions to the imperial throne? To be sure, there have been many attempts to fit the date of Revelation (the then contemporary king would be he who "is") into the emperor lists of the first century. But immediately there are problems. Where do we begin—with Julius Caesar or Caesar Augustus? Are we to count all the emperors or just those who fostered emperor worship? Are we to exclude Galba, Otho, and Vitellius who had short, rival reigns? If so, how can they be excluded except on a completely arbitrary basis? A careful examination of the historical materials yields no satisfactory solution. If Revelation were written under Nero, there would be too few emperors; if under Domitian, too many. The original readers would have had no more information on the succession of emperors than we do, and possibly even less. How many Americans can immediately name the last seven presidents? Furthermore, how could the eighth emperor who is identified as the beast also be one of the seven (v. 11)?

Recognizing these problems, others have sought different solutions to John's five-one-one succession of kings. Since the word "king" may also represent kingdoms, some have suggested an interpretation that takes the five-one-one to refer to successive world kingdoms that have oppressed the people of God: Egypt, Assyria, Babylon, Persia, Greece (five fallen), Rome (one is), and a future world kingdom. While this solves some of the emperor succession problems and fits nicely, it too must admit to arbitrary omissions, such as the devastating persecution of the people of God under the Seleucids of Syria, especially under Antiochus IV Epiphanes. Like the Roman emperor view, this view also suffers from not respecting the symbolic significance of John's use of "seven" throughout the book. Furthermore, how can these kings (or kingdoms) survive the destruction of the harlot and be pictured as mourning over her demise (18:9)? And what logical sense can be made of the fact that the seventh king (or kingdom), usually identified with Antichrist, is separate from the eighth king (or kingdom), which is clearly identified with the beast (vv. 10b–11)?

A convincing interpretation of the seven kings must do justice to three considerations: (1) Since the heads belong to the beast, the interpretation must relate their significance to this beast, not to Babylon; (2) Since the primary imagery of kingship in Revelation is a feature of the power conflict between the Lamb and the beast and between those who share the rule of these two enemies (cf. 17:14; 19:19), the kind of sovereignty expressed in 17:10 must be the true antithesis to the kind of sovereignty exercised by Christ and His followers; (3) Since the kings are closely related to the seven mountains and to the prostitute, the nature of the relationship between these must be clarified by the interpretation.

If we can see that the seven heads do not represent a quantitative measure but show qualitatively the fullness of evil power residing in the beast, then the "falling" of five heads conveys the message of significant victory over the beast. The image of a falling sovereignty relates better to God's judgment on a power than to a succession of kings or kingdoms (cf. Jer. 50:32; 51:8, 49; Rev. 14:8; 18:2).

The imagery of the seven heads presented in 12:3 and 13:1 must be restudied. The ancient seal showing the seven-headed chaos monster being slain (see comments on 13:1) well illustrates John's imagery here. In that ancient scene, the seven-headed monster is being slain by a progressive killing of its seven heads. Four of the heads are dead, killed apparently by the spear of a divine figure who is attacking the monster. Its defeat seems imminent, yet the chaos monster is still active because three heads still live. Similarly, John's message is that five of the monster's seven heads are already defeated by the power of the Lamb's death and by the identification of the martyrs of Jesus in that death (12:11). One head is now active, thus showing the reality of the beast's contemporary agents who afflict the saints; and one head remains, indicating that the battle will soon be over but not with the defeat of the contemporary evil agents. This last manifestation of the beast's blasphemous power will be short—"he must remain for a little while." This statement seems to go with the function of the ten horns (kings) who for "one hour" (v. 12) will rule with the beast. The seventh king (head) represents the final short display of satanic evil before the divine blow falls on the beast (cf. 12:12c; 20:3c).

Verse 11 presents all interpreters with a real difficulty. One of the common interpretations refers the language to the Nero redivivus myth (see introduction to ch. 13)—viz., a revived Nero will be the reincarnation of the evil genius of the whole Roman Empire. Furthermore, among futurist interpreters there is no agreement as to whether the seventh or eighth king is the Antichrist. It must be admitted that any hypothesis of a succession of kings or kingdoms founders on verse 11. On the other hand, if John has a qualitative rather than quantitative identification in mind, i.e., a theological rather than historical or political sense, the passage may yield further insight into the mystery of the beast.

First, we note the (to us) strange manner in which the sequence of seven kings gives way to the eighth, who is really the whole beast. This pattern was familiar to the early church and is a concept those raised in the great liturgical traditions can grasp. The eighth day was the day of the resurrection of Christ, Sunday. It was also the beginning of a new week. The seventh day, the Jewish Sabbath, is held over, to be replaced by the first of a new series, namely Sunday. The eighth day was the day of the Messiah, the day of the new age and the sign of the victory over the forces of evil. But does this provide a key to interpret the symbolism of the chaos monster?

Of the three stages of the beast—was, is not, will come—only the last is related to his coming "up out of the Abyss" (v. 8). These words appear to be the equivalent of the beast's healed wound (plague) mentioned in 13:3, 14. While, on the one hand, Christ has killed the monster by His death (Gen. 3:15; Rev. 12:7-9) and for believers he "is not" (has no power), yet, on the other hand, the beast still has life ("one is," v. 10) and will attempt one final battle against the Lamb and His followers ("the other has not yet come; . . . he must remain for a little while"). In order to recruit as many as possible for his side of the war, the beast will imitate the resurrection of Christ (he "is an eighth king," v. 11) and will give the appearance that he is alive and in control of the world (cf. Luke 4:5-7). But John quickly adds, for the pastoral comfort of God's people, that the beast belongs to the seven, i.e., qualitatively but not numerically (as if he were a former king revived); he is in reality not a new beginning of life but a part of the seven-headed monster that has been slain by Christ and, therefore, he goes "to his destruction." While this imagery may seem to us to be unnecessarily obscure, it reveals the true mystery of the beast in a fashion that exposes the dynamics of satanic deception so that every Christian may be forearmed.

c) The ten horns (17:12-14)

In this section John seems to allude to Daniel 7:7, 24. The ten horns are usually understood as either native rulers of Roman provinces, serving under the emperors, or native rulers of satellite states, or governors of Palestine. Others see in them a ten-nation confederacy of the future revived Roman Empire of which the European Common Market is a forerunner. There are good reasons for abandoning these explanations. In the first place, the number ten should—like most of John's numbers—be understood symbolically. "Ten" symbolizes a repeated number of times or an indefinite number. It is perhaps another number like seven, indicating fullness (Neh. 4:12; Dan. 1:12; Rev. 2:10). Thus the number should not be understood as referring specifically to ten kings (or kingdoms) but as indicating the multiplicity of sovereignties in confederacy that enhance the power of the beast.

Second, since these kings enter into a power conflict with the Lamb and His followers (v. 14), the kind of sovereignty they exercise must be the true antithesis to the kind of sovereignty the Lamb and His followers exercise. These rulers as well as the beast with which they will be allied can be no other than the principalities and powers, the rulers of the darkness of this world, the spiritual forces of evil in the heavenly realms that Paul describes as the true enemies of Jesus' followers (Eph. 6:12). To be sure, they use earthly instruments, but their reality is far greater than any specific historical manifestations. These "kings" embody the fullness of Satan's attack against the Lamb in the great eschatological showdown. They are the "kings from the East" (16:12-14, 16), and they are also the "kings of the earth" who ally themselves with the beast in the final confrontation with the Lamb (19:19-21).

Finally, there is a link between verse 12 and verse 11. The ten kings are said to receive authority for "one hour" along with the beast. This corresponds to the "little while" of the seventh king (v. 10). From the viewpoint of the saints, who will be greatly persecuted, this promise of brevity brings comfort. These kings have "one purpose": they agree to oppose the Lamb. But the Lamb will overcome them because He is Lord of Lords and King of Kings (cf. Deut. 10:17; Dan. 2:47; Rev. 19:16). He conquers by His death, and those who are with Him also aid in the defeat of the beast by their loyalty to the Lamb even to death (cf. 5:5, 9; 12:11)—a sobering thought.

d) *The prostitute and the ten horns* (17:15–17)

On first reading, verse 15 appears to be out of place. However, closer examination shows that verse 16 also refers to the prostitute and the horns. Verse 15 teaches that the influence of the idolatrous satanic system of Babylon is universal (cf. vv. 1–2) and embraces all peoples, from the humblest to the kings of the earth.

On verses 16–17 the Roman hypothesis (empire and city) breaks down, since in that view the emperors (the beast and its heads) will turn against the city or empire and destroy her. Some try to locate this event in Rome's history and argue that there is some supporting evidence for it, but the attempt is not convincing. Rather, the attack on the prostitute indicates that in the final judgment the kingdom of Satan, by divine purpose, will be divided against itself. The references to the prostitute being hated by her former lovers, stripped naked, and burned with fire are reminiscent of the Old Testament prophets' descriptions of the divine judgment falling on the harlot cities of Jerusalem and Tyre (e.g., Ezek. 16:39–40; 23:25–27; 28:18). The description of the punishment of convicted prostitutes who are priests' daughters (cf. Lev. 21:9; the burning with fire is explained as "a pouring of molten lead down their throats") is combined with the picture of judgment on rebellious cities (18:8). "The ravaging of the whore by the monster and its horns is John's most vivid symbol for the self-destroying power of evil" (Caird).

In the declaration "God has put it into their hearts to accomplish his purpose" (v. 17) lies another indication of God's use of the forces of evil as instruments of His own purposes of judgment (Jer. 25:9–14; cf. Luke 20:18). Nothing will distract them from their united effort to destroy the prostitute until God's purposes given through the prophets are fulfilled (cf. 10:7; 11:18).

e) *The prostitute is the great city* (17:18)

The "woman" and "the great city" are one. Yet this city is not just a historical one; it is the *great* city, the *mother* city, the archetype of every evil system opposed to God in history (see introduction to ch. 17). Her kingdom holds sway over the powers of the earth. John's concept of the city in Revelation entails much more than a historical city even in its political and sociological aspects. The two cities in Revelation are communities; they are the city of God, the New Jerusalem (3:12; 21:2, 10; 22:2ff.) and the city of Satan, Babylon the Great (11:8; 14:8; 16:19; 18:4, 20, etc.). The meaning cannot be confined to Sodom or Egypt or Jerusalem or Rome or any future city. Instead, John describes the real transhistorical system of satanic evil that infuses them all.

D. The Fall of Babylon the Great (18:1–24)

Chapter 18 contains the description of the previously announced "judgment," (NIV, "punishment") of the prostitute (17:1). It is important not to separate this chapter from the portrayal of the prostitute in chapter 17, since there is no warrant for making the prostitute in chapter 17 different from the city in chapter 18 (cf. 17:18). Under the imagery of the destruction of a great commercial city, John describes the final overthrow of the great prostitute, Babylon. However, he is not writing a literal description, even in poetic or figurative language, of the fall of an *earthly* city, such as Rome or Jerusalem; but in portraying the destruction of a city, he describes God's judgment on the great satanic *system* of evil that has corrupted the earth's history. Drawing especially from the Old Testament accounts of the destruction of the ancient harlot cities of Babylon (Isa. 13:21; 47:7–9; Jer. 50–51) and Tyre (Ezek. 26–27), John composes a great threnody that might well be the basis of a mighty oratorio. Here in chapters 17–18 is some of the most beautifully cadenced language in the whole book. John combines the song of triumph and the wailing strains of lamentation into a noble funeral dirge (cf. 2 Sam. 1:17–27; Isa. 14:4–21; Lam.).

First, there is a kind of prelude in which the whole judgment is proclaimed (vv. 1–3). Then follows a call to God's people to separate themselves from the city because the divine plagues are about to descend on her in recompense from her crimes (vv. 4–8). The main movement that expresses the laments for the city's fall is divided into three parts: (1) the lament of the kings of the earth (vv. 9–10); (2) the lament of the merchants who traded with her (vv. 11–17); and (3) the lament of the sea captains who became rich from the cargoes they took to the city (vv. 18–20). The finale sounds the death knell for the life of the city because she deceived the nations and killed God's people (vv. 21–24).

1. *Prelude* (18:1–3)

So magnificent is the event about to be enacted that a dazzling angel of glory bears the divine news. Some interpreters have associated this glory with the shekinah glory that, in Ezekiel's vision, departed from the temple because of the harlotry of the Israelites (Ezek. 11:23) but later returned to the restored temple (Ezek. 43:2).

In words similar to those of the prophets who encouraged the people of God as they faced ancient Babylon, the angel announces that Babylon the Great, mother of all the earthly prostitute cities, has fallen (cf. Isa. 21:9; Jer. 51:8 with Rev. 14:8; 18:2). Again, in words reminiscent of the judgment announced against ancient Babylon that the city would be inhabited only by detestable creatures and evil spirits (Isa. 13:19–22; 34:11; Jer. 50:39), John hears the same fate announced for this mother of prostitutes

(v. 2). "Demons" are associated elsewhere with idolatry (see comments on 9:20 and 16:14). The "haunt" is a watchtower; the evil spirits, watching over fallen Babylon like night birds or harpies waiting for their prey, build their nests in the broken towers that rise from the ashes of the city. She who was a great city has become a wilderness.

The prostitute city will be judged because of her surfeit of fornication (v. 3). Here the same thought as in 17:2 is expanded as we hear echoes of the judgments on ancient Tyre and Babylon (Isa. 23:17; Jer. 51:7; Rev. 14:8). One of the great sins of Babylon was her luxury (cf. comments on 18:7, 9). Because wealth may lead to pride, the prophets and John view surfeit as a manifestation of Babylon (Rev. 18:7; cf. Ezek. 28:4–5, 16–18). The close proximity of fornication to luxury may suggest that there is a fornication with Babylon that not only involves idolatry (cult prostitution) but that may be pride in excessive wealth.

2. A call to separation (18:4–8)

"Come out of her, my people" (v. 4) forms the burden of Jeremiah's refrain concerning Babylon (Jer. 50:8; 51:6–9; cf. Isa. 48:20; 52:11; 2 Cor. 6:17). Even in its Old Testament setting this was no mere warning to leave the actual city of Babylon, much less here in Revelation. John is burdened to exhort the churches to shun the charms and ensnarements of the queen prostitute (v. 7) as her qualities are manifest in the world they live in. Wherever there are idolatry, prostitution, self-glorification, self-sufficiency, pride, complacency, reliance on luxury and wealth, avoidance of suffering, violence against life (v. 24), there is Babylon. Christians are to separate themselves ideologically and, if necessary, physically from all the forms of Babylon. John has already warned the churches of her deceit and snares (chs. 2–3). If they refuse to separate themselves, they will "share in her sins" and also in the divine judgments (NIV, "plagues"). It is not necessary to see this as one last call to repentance addressed to the beast worshipers. Rather, like the warnings in the letters to the churches (chs. 2–3), it is addressed to professing Christians who are being seduced by Satan through the wiles of the queen prostitute to abandon their loyalty to Jesus. If this happens, Christ will be forced by their own decision to blot out their names from the Book of Life and include them in the plagues designed for Babylon when she is judged (cf. 3:5).

God will not forget her crimes, which are multiplied to the height of heaven (v. 5; cf. Gen. 18:20–21; Jer. 51:9). Her punishment will fit her crimes (v. 6; cf. Ps. 137:8; Jer. 50:15, 29; Matt. 7:2). This Old Testament principle of lex talionis is never enjoined on God's people in the New Testament but, as here, is reserved for God alone (Matt. 5:38–42; Rom. 12:17–21). "Mix her a double portion from her own cup" (cf. Exod. 22:4, 7, 9; Isa. 40:2) reflects both the severity of God's judgment on those who persistently refuse to repent and the truth that God's wrath is related to the outworking of sin (cf. Rom. 1:24–32). Verse 7 illustrates the latter point.

In verse 7 Babylon's threefold web of sin is described as satiety ("luxury"), pride ("boasts, . . . sit as a queen"), and avoidance of suffering ("I will never mourn"). The three may be interrelated. Luxury leads to boastful self-sufficiency (Ezek. 28:5), while the desire to avoid suffering may lead to the dishonest pursuit of luxury (Ezek. 28:18). "I sit as a queen" echoes Isaiah's description of judgment on Babylon (Isa. 47:7ff.) and Ezekiel's description of Tyre (Ezek. 27:3). She avoided grief through her satiety and her punishment therefore is grief ("mourning," "sorrow," "misfortune").

Suddenly, "in one day," she will experience what she has avoided by her luxury: "death, mourning and famine" (v. 8). The words "consumed by fire" (cf. 17:16) may refer to the destruction of a city (cf. vv. 9, 18) or to the Old Testament punishment for prostitution if the woman is a priest's daughter (Lev. 21:9). As strong as "Babylon the Great" is, the Lord God is stronger and will judge her.

3. Laments (18:9–19)

Even a quick reading of Ezekiel 27 shows that in these verses Ezekiel's lamentation over the fall of ancient Tyre was in the back of John's mind. Those who entered into fornication with the great mother prostitute wail over her destruction. In terms drawn from the fall of harlot cities in the past, John describes the end of the great reality of evil, Babylon the Great. While allusions to Rome may seem to be present, it is only because Rome, like Tyre, Babylon, or Jerusalem, is herself a prostitute city; and the characteristics of all these cities are found in the queen mother of prostitutes.

a) The kings of the earth lament (18:9–10)

First, the kings of the earth cry out their dirge. There is a connection between their adultery with Babylon and their sharing of her luxury, as if sharing her luxury was part of their adultery (cf. Ezek. 26:16; 27:30–35). So great is the heat and smoke of her burning that they must stand "far off" (v. 10). Though ultimately the kings are all the forces of evil in the heavenly realm that rule in the affairs of earthly kings and kingdoms (see comments on 17:10, 14; cf. 1 Cor. 2:6, 8), in this extended poetic allegory they are the merchant princes who bewail the collapse of the last great city of man under Satan's rule. The lament "Woe, Woe" (cf. 8:13; 9:12; 11:14; 12:12) is repeated three times in the threnody over Babylon and reflects pain at the suddenness of her downfall ("in one hour," cf. vv. 8, 17) and the emptiness of their own existence apart from her.

b) *The businessmen lament* (18:11–17a)

The businessmen have most to lose because Babylon the Great was built on luxury. The lists that follow are inventories of exotic items reminiscent of the Oriental *suks* (marketplaces). In verse 13, the phrase "bodies and souls of men" requires special mention. "Bodies" is a Greek idiom for slaves, while "souls of men" means essentially the same as bodies (slaves). Thus the whole expression means "slaves, that is, human beings."

The refrain (v. 16) also shows the blending of the prostitute image of chapter 17 ("dressed in fine linen," etc.; cf. 17:4) and the city image of chapter 18 ("O great city"). It has been observed that these wares are less representative of Rome than of Asia Minor.

c) *The sea captains lament* (18:17b–19)

Finally, the sea captains and sailors add their lament because they too suffer irreparable loss because of the city's burning (cf. Ezek. 27:28). This language is more suited to Tyre, a great port city, than Rome, which was inland and had the not-too-distant Ostia as its port. In any case, it is not John's intent to describe any one city but the great harlot city, the archetype of the earth's evil cities.

4. *Heaven rejoices* (18:20)

The threefold lament is balanced by a song of heavenly jubilation. Babylon has also persecuted the church of Jesus (saints, apostles, prophets). Except for the mention of false apostles earlier in the book (2:2), this is the only reference to apostles in Revelation (cf. 21:14). If it is correct to see in verse 20 a reference to their being killed (cf. v. 24), perhaps John had in mind Herod's martyring of James (Acts 12:1–2) or Rome's killing of Peter and Paul. The picture of Babylon cannot, however, be confined to the political activity of Rome. Therefore, John attributes the deaths of the martyrs to Babylon the Great. It is she who has killed Jesus (11:7–8) and Stephen by the hands of unbelieving Jews (Acts 7:57–60) and the martyr Antipas by the hands of pagan cultists (2:13; cf. Matt. 23:34–37).

5. *The finale: death* (18:21–24)

The final lament over the fall of Babylon, spoken by an angel, is poignant and beautiful. A mighty angel picks up a huge stone like a giant millstone (four to five feet in diameter, one foot thick, and weighing thousands of pounds) and flings it into the sea. One quick gesture becomes a parable of the whole judgment on Babylon the Great! Suddenly she is gone forever (cf. Jer. 51:64; Ezek. 26:21). The melancholy recollection of the pulsing life that once filled this great city with the joy of life sounds through these verses "like footsteps dying away in the distance in a desolate city which lies in ruins" (Lilje).

All nations were deceived ("led astray") by her "magic spell." John has previously used "magic spell" in conjunction with "murders," "sexual immorality," and "thefts" (see comments on 9:21). With her deceit, Babylon charmed the nations. Compare the similar charge against the harlot city Nineveh for her lies to other nations (Nah. 3:4).

In the final verse, the great sin of Babylon is cited. She has martyred the prophets and followers of Jesus. John has already mentioned this bloodguiltiness (17:6; cf. 19:2). Elsewhere the death of martyrs is attributed to "the inhabitants of the earth" (6:10), the "beast that comes up from the Abyss" (11:7; 13:7), and the "beast, coming out of the earth" (13:15). In the Old Testament, the cities of Jerusalem (Ezek. 24:6, 9; cf. Matt. 23:37) and Babylon (Jer. 51:35) are called cities of bloodshed. In verse 24 "the blood . . . of all who have been killed on the earth" refers to all those who in history have been martyred because of their loyalty to the true God. John's word for "killed" is consistently used for martyrs (5:6, 9, 12; 6:4, 9; 13:8). In John's mind, Babylon the Great (v. 2) is much more comprehensive than ancient Babylon, Nineveh, Jerusalem, or Rome. She encompasses all the persecution against the servants of God until the words of God are fulfilled (cf. 17:17).

E. Thanksgiving for the Destruction of Babylon (19:1–5)

In stark contrast to the laments of Babylon's consorts, the heavenly choirs burst forth in a great liturgy of celebration to God. In these verses (1–5), we hear four shouts of praise for the fall of Babylon. First, there is the sound of a great multitude praising God for His condemnation of the prostitute (19:1–2). Then they shout out in celebration of the city's eternal destruction (v. 3). Following this, we hear in antiphonal response the voices of the twenty-four elders and the four living creatures (v. 4). Finally, a voice from the throne calls on all the servants of God to praise Him (v. 5).

The word "Hallelujah" transliterates the Greek, which in turn transliterates the Hebrew, which means "Praise the Lord!" ("Praise our God" in v. 5 is equivalent to "Hallelujah.") The Hebrew transliteration occurs only in this chapter in the New Testament (vv. 1, 3, 4, 6), but it is a frequent psalm title (Pss. 111:1; 112:1; 113:1, et al.). This phenomenon clearly illustrates the connection of the early church's liturgical worship with the synagogue and temple worship of the first century. These praise psalms formed an important part of the Jewish festival celebrations.

"The Hallel" is the name especially applied to Psalms 113–118. These psalms are also called "The Hallel of Egypt" because of the references in them to the Exodus. They thus have a special role in the Passover Feast.

The Jewish sources also unanimously associate the Hallel with the destruction of the wicked, exactly as this passage in Revelation does.

The Hallel was what Jesus and the disciples sang after the Passover-Eucharist celebration, before going out to the Mount of Olives the night before His death (Matt. 26:30). This close connection between the Hallel, the Passover, and the death of Jesus no doubt explains why all the early church liturgies incorporated the Hallel into the propers for Easter and Easter Week. This Easter liturgy represents the Christian experience of the gospel of redemption from sin, Satan, and death in the victorious triumph of Christ, our Passover. The Paschal liturgy concludes with the celebration of the Eucharist banquet of Christ as He holds intimate communion with His church, giving it light and life. Perhaps the great banquet of verses 7–9 is to be linked to the Eucharist celebration in the early church. One can hardly read this Hallel section of Revelation without thinking of the "Hallelujah Chorus" in Handel's *Messiah*.

The theme of "salvation" has already been sounded in Revelation in connection with victory or divine justice (7:10; 12:10). God has indeed vindicated the injustice visited on His servants by meting out true justice on the great prostitute, Babylon. She deserves the sentence because she corrupted the earth (cf. 11:18; Jer. 51:25) and killed the saints of God (cf. 18:24).

The second Hallel in verse 3 supplements the first one. Babylon's permanent end is celebrated in words reminiscent of ancient Babylon's judgment (Isa. 34:10).

In response to the heavenly Hallels, the twenty-four elders cry out, "Amen, Hallelujah" (v. 4; on "Amen," cf. comments on 1:7; on the elders, cf. comments on 4:4).

The final praise (v. 5) is spoken by a single voice from the throne (cf. 16:17). The voice is probably neither that of God nor that of Christ, because of the words "*our* Lord God Almighty reigns" (v. 6). Here is a clear reference to the great Hallel Psalms 113 and 115. "Praise our God, all you his servants" reflects Psalm 113:1, while "you who fear him, both small and great" reflects Psalm 115:13 (cf. Ps. 135:1, 20). All socio-economic distinctions are transcended in the united worship of the church ("both small and great"; cf. 11:18; 13:16; 19:18; 20:12).

F. The Marriage of the Lamb (19:6–10)

Finally, the cycle of praise is completed with the reverberating sounds of another great multitude (v. 6). If the multitude in verse 1 was angelic, then this one would most certainly be the great redeemed throng (cf. 7:9). They utter the final Hallel in words reminiscent of the great royal psalms (93:1; 97:1; 99:1). The first of these psalms is used in the Sabbath morning and evening services in the synagogue and is the prelude to Psalms 95–99, which are messianic; its theme is the eternal sovereignty of God, who will conquer all His enemies. The Greek verb form translated "reigns" may better be rendered here as "has begun to reign."

There is also rejoicing because the "wedding of the Lamb has come, and his bride has made herself ready" (v. 7). It is John's way of giving a glimmer of the next great vision at the close of the former one (cf. 21:2, 9). Contrast the prostitute and her lovers in the preceding chapters with the Lamb and His chaste bride ("fine linen, bright and clean").

The bride is the heavenly city, the New Jerusalem (21:2, 9), which is the symbol of the church, the bride of Christ, the community of those redeemed by Christ's blood. The wedding imagery, including the wedding supper, was for the Jews a familiar image of the kingdom of God. Jesus used wedding and banquet imagery in His parables of the kingdom (Matt. 22:2ff.; 25:1–13; Luke 14:15–24). The Old Testament used the figure for the bride of Israel (Ezek. 16:1ff.; Hos. 2:19), and New Testament writers have applied it to the church (2 Cor. 11:2; Eph. 5:25ff.). Heaven's rejoicing has signaled the defeat of all the enemies of God. The time of betrothal has ended. Now it is the time for the church, prepared by loyalty and suffering, to enter into her full experience of salvation and glory with her beloved spouse, Christ. The fuller revelation of the realization of this union is described in chapters 21 and 22.

The church's garments are white linen—in marked contrast to the purple and scarlet clothing of the great mother of prostitutes (17:4; 18:16). Linen was an expensive cloth used to make the garments worn by priests and royalty. It has two qualities: brightness and cleanness (cf. 16:6). "Bright" is the color of radiant whiteness that depicts glorification (cf. Matt. 13:43). "Clean" reflects purity, loyalty, and faithfulness, the character of the New Jerusalem (21:18, 21).

An explanatory interjection, probably added by John, states that "fine linen stands for the righteous acts of the saints" (v. 8). In 15:4, "righteous acts" describes the manifest deeds of God that relate to truth and justice. These acts do not imply any kind of meritorious works that would bring salvation. Rather, there is a delicate balance between grace and obedient response to it. The bride is "given" the garments, but she "has made herself ready" for the wedding by faithfulness and loyalty to Christ (cf. 3:4–5, 18). In the parable of the man without a wedding garment, the garment he lacked was probably a clean one supplied by the host that was either refused or soiled through carelessness by the rejected guest. The meaning of the clean garment is probably repentance and obedient response to Christ, both of which the Pharisees lacked (Matt. 22:11f.). Thus John contrasts the faithful disciples of Jesus, who have been true to God, with those who were seduced by the beast and the prostitute. The bride prepared herself, then, by her obedient discipleship (see comments on 12:11).

The beatitude in verse 9 is the fourth of seven in Revelation (1:3; 14:13;

16:15; 20:6; 22:7, 14). In each beatitude there is a subtle contrast to those who are not loyal and faithful followers of the Lamb. The word translated "invited" means "called," which is used in the New Testament of the call to salvation (e.g., Matt. 9:13; Rom. 8:30; 9:24; 1 Cor. 1:9; 2 Thess. 2:14). However, the word may also mean "invited," with no connotation of election (cf. Matt. 22:3, 8; Luke 14:16; John 2:2). The wedding supper began toward evening on the wedding day, lasted for many days, and was a time of great jubilation. Here in Revelation, the wedding is the beginning of the earthly kingdom of God, the bride is the church in all her purity, the invited guests are both the bride and people who have committed themselves to Jesus.

To assure John and his readers of the certainty of both the end of the great prostitute and the announcement of the wedding supper of the Lamb, the angel adds, "These are the true words of God" (cf. 1:2; 17:17; 21:5). A similar sentence later appears to give the same assurance for the whole book (22:6).

John, who was himself a prophet and who had received such a clear revelation about idolatry, now falls prey to this temptation (v. 10). After the final vision, he again slips into idolatry (22:8). Whether John included these references to his own failure because he knew of the tendency toward angel worship in the churches of Asia is not clear. Be that as it may, we need to recognize how easy it is to fall into idolatry. Whenever a Christian gives anyone or anything other than God control of his life, he has broken the first commandment. The "testimony of Jesus" is Jesus' own testimony that He bore in His life and teaching and especially in His death (cf. comments on 1:2, 9; and the same expression in 6:9; 12:11; 14:12; 20:4). Those who hold to or proclaim this testimony are Christian prophets. Thus "the testimony of Jesus is the spirit of prophecy." The words spoken by the Christian prophets come from the Spirit of God, who is the Spirit of the risen Jesus; they are the very words of God.

For Further Study

1. Can you find the "third woe" mentioned in 11:14? Does it seem reasonable to identify the bowl judgments with this third woe? How does this conclusion affect your understanding of the structure of the book?

2. Study the plagues of Egypt (Exod. 7–10) and the bowl judgments for parallels and differences between them. What can you conclude from this?

3. What does Armageddon mean? Will it be a literal battle fought between earth's armies? How is the term used today in a nontheological sense?

4. How should the reality of God's future judgment of the world's evil

affect the attitude and actions of Christians today? Has God abandoned the world? Should we?

5. Do you think Babylon equals Rome in the harlot image? Summarize what can be learned about the deceptive nature of evil from the images of the harlot and the elaborate description of the beast in chapter 17.

6. Using the description and identification of Babylon given in the commentary, can you find modern parallels? How can Christians best heed the command, "come out of her, my people" (18:4)?

7. How would the elaborate description of Babylon's fall (18:1–19:10) encourage Christians in John's day? In what sense do God's people need this message today?

8. Could even the great saint John be guilty of idolatry (19:10)? How can we also fall into this snare?

VISION THREE: *The Return of Christ and the Consummation of the Age*

Chapter 8

The First and Second Last Things: The Rider on the White Horse and the Destruction of the Beast
(Revelation 19:11–21)

This new vision is introduced by the words "I saw heaven standing open." Earlier, John had seen a door standing open in heaven (4:1) and the temple in heaven standing open (11:19), and now, in preparation for a great revelation of God's sovereignty, he sees heaven itself flung wide open to his gaze (cf. Ezek. 1:1). In one sense, this vision (vv. 11–21), which depicts the return of Christ and the final overthrow of the beast, may be viewed as the climax of the previous section (vv. 1–10) or as the first of a final series of seven last things—viz., the return of Christ; the defeat of the beast; the binding of Satan; the Millennium; the release and final end of Satan; the last judgment; and the new heaven, the new earth, and the New Jerusalem.

A. The First Last Thing: The Return of Christ (19:11–16)
Early as well as modern interpretation has for the most part seen in 19:11–16 a description of the second coming of Christ—an event to which the New Testament bears frequent and unified witness. As for the features of this event, they are variously understood by interpreters.

1. *The faithful and true One* (19:11–12)
This great vision reminds us of the first vision of the book (1:12ff.), although its function is entirely different. The whole scene looks alternately to the Old Testament and to the previous references to Christ in Revelation, especially those in the seven letters (chs. 2–3). A white horse with a rider appeared in 6:1. Both white horses represent conquest or victory, but with that the similarity changes to total contrast: The rider here in chapter 19 is "faithful and true" (cf. 1:5; 3:7, 14), in contrast to the forces of Antichrist with their empty promises and lies. Christ will keep His word to the churches. In contrast to those who pervert justice and wage unjust war, John says of Christ, "With justice [righteousness] he judges and makes war," an allusion to the messianic character described

in Isaiah 11:3ff. In only one other place (2:16) is Christ described as making war, and there the reference is to His judgment of the church. Furthermore, the questions in 13:4, "Who is like the beast? Who can make war against him?" anticipate the answer that Christ alone can do this, while in 17:14 the beast and the ten kings wage war against the Lamb.

Although John uses Old Testament language descriptive of a warrior-Messiah, he does not depict Christ as a great *military* warrior battling against earth's sovereigns. John reinterprets this Old Testament imagery while at the same time inseparably linking Christ to its fulfillment. The close proximity in verse 11 of justice and war shows us that the kind of warfare Christ engages in is more the execution of justice than a military conflict. He who is the faithful and true Witness will judge the rebellious nations.

The reference in verse 12 to the blazing eyes definitely connects this vision with that of chapter 1 (cf. 1:14; 2:18). On His head are not just seven crowns (12:3), or ten (13:1), but many crowns of royalty. Perhaps they signify that the royal power to rule the world has now passed to Christ by virtue of the victory of His followers (11:15). All the diadems of their newly won empire meet on His brow (Caird).

So great is Christ's power that His name is known only by Himself. Knowledge of a god's name is in antiquity associated with the power of that god. When a name becomes known, then the power is shared with those to whom the disclosure is made (cf. comments on 2:17). But since two names of Christ are revealed in this vision, "the Word of God" (v. 13) and "KING OF KINGS AND LORD OF LORDS" (v. 16), it may be concluded that the exclusive power of Christ over all creation is now to be shared with His faithful followers (3:21; 5:10; 22:5). On the other hand, the secret name may be one that will not be revealed till Christ's return.

2. *The blood-stained garment* (19:13)

The imagery in this verse has traditionally been related to Isaiah 63:1–6, a passage understood messianically by the Jews and one that John has used in portraying God's wrath in 14:9–11, 17–19. Isaiah pictures a mighty warrior-Messiah who slaughters His enemies. Their life-blood splashes on His clothing as He tramples them down in His anger, as the juice of the grapes splashes on the winetreader in the winepress. But is Christ's blood-dipped robe (v. 13) red with His enemies' blood or with His own blood? There are good reasons for accepting the latter. If the blood is that of His enemies, how is it that Christ comes from heaven with His robe already dipped in blood before any battle is mentioned? Futhermore, the blood that is always mentioned in connection with Christ in the Apocalypse is His own life-blood (1:5; 5:6, 9; 7:14; 12:11). Moreover, the word "dipped" does not fit the imagery of Isaiah 63:2, but it does fit the imagery used in Revelation of believers' garments being washed thoroughly in Christ's blood (7:14; 22:14). Finally, the sword with which Christ strikes down the nations comes from His mouth and is not in His hand (v. 15); and this too is incompatible with battle imagery. In any case, there is sufficient warrant not to press the allusion to Isaiah 63:1–6 too far.

3. *The Word of God* (19:13)

Applying the expression "the Word of God" to Jesus in a personal sense is peculiar to the Johannine writings (John 1:1, 14; cf. 1 John 1:1). In Revelation, "the Word of God" refers to the revelation of God's purpose (1:2; 17:17; 19:9). It is also the message and lifestyle for which the saints suffer oppression and even death (1:9; 6:9; 20:4). The adjectives "true and faithful," which are applied to Christ, are likewise identified with the Word of God (19:9; 21:5; 22:6; cf. 1:5; 3:14; 19:11). Thus Jesus in His earthly life bore reliable and consistent witness in all His words and actions to the purposes of God and was completely obedient in doing this. In Him the will of God finds full expression. The Word of God and the person of Christ are one.

4. *A peculiar warrior* (19:14–16)

Verse 14 seems somewhat parenthetical because it does not refer directly to Christ's person or His actions. The armies of heaven mounted on white horses are understood by most to be angelic hosts, since some passages in the Old Testament and New Testament speak of the armies or soldiers of heaven as angels (Pss. 103:21; 148:2; Luke 2:13; Acts 7:42). Moreover, elsewhere in the New Testament the coming of Christ is associated with angels (e.g., Matt. 13:41; 16:27; 24:30–31). Yet this may not be John's meaning. These soldiers, like their leader, are riding white horses of victory—something hardly true of angels. Their clothing of bright and clean linen is identical to the bride's attire (cf. v. 8). Thus it is probably the victors who accompany Christ, either all of them (resurrected and raptured; 1 Thess. 4:16–17) or the company of the martyrs. Revelation 17:14 confirms this: "They [the beast and the ten kings] will make war against the Lamb, but the Lamb will overcome them because he is Lord of lords and King of kings—*and with him will be his called, chosen and faithful followers*" (italics added; cf. 15:1–2).

In verse 15 there are three Old Testament allusions to the warrior-Messiah: He strikes down the nations (Isa. 11:3ff.); He rules them with an iron rod (Ps. 2:9); He tramples out the winepress of God's wrath (Isa. 63:1–6; see comments on v. 13.) In the first Old Testament allusion, John makes significant changes in the imagery. In Revelation, the Lamb-Messiah does not wield a sword in His hand, but His sword comes from His mouth (cf. comments on 1:16 and 2:16). This has no exact Old Testament parallel and cannot be accidental, since John emphasizes it so much in Revelation (1:16; 2:12, 16; 19:15, 21). Christ conquers by the power of His *word*. Yet it is not necessary to see the sword coming from Christ's mouth as pointing to the expansion of Christianity and the conquest of the nations by their conversion to Christ: the scene here is the eschatological return of Christ and His judgment of the nations, not the church age. Besides, Christ's words are the instruments of His judgment as well as of His salvation (Matt. 12:37; John 12:48). On "the rod of iron" and the relationship between "rule" and "shepherd," see comments on 2:27. For the winepress image, see 14:17ff.

The third name of Christ, "KING OF KINGS AND LORD OF LORDS" (v. 16), which all can read, is displayed on that most exposed part of His cloak, the part that covers the thigh, where it cannot escape notice. The name has already appeared as that of the Lamb (17:14). He is the absolute Lord and King, full of the divine power and authority.

B. The Second Last Thing: The Defeat of the Beast (19:17–21)

1. *The great supper of God's judgment* (19:17–18)

This section brings us to the second last thing (cf. introduction to 19:11–21): the anticipated great confrontation between the beast and his soldiers and the Lamb (vv. 17–21; cf. 16:12–16; 17:14). First, there is the summons to the vultures to come to God's great supper and gorge themselves on the slain corpses of the battlefield—a horrible picture of human carnage. The language is borrowed from Ezekiel 39:17ff., which describes the eschatological overthrow of Gog. It may be unnecessary to press the literalness of the description; this battlefield language is designed to indicate that a great victory is about to occur.

2. *The beast and his armies destroyed* (19:19–21)

The contrast between the assembling of the beast's might with his kings and their soldiers and the ease with which he is overthrown and captured highlight the beast's powerlessness before his mighty conqueror. The "kings of the earth" are the ten horns (kings) of the beast, which is another way of describing the beast's power (see comments on 17:12–14). Both the beast and the false prophet (13:1ff.) are simply seized and thrown into the lake of fire (v. 20). Their followers fall before the sword (word) of Christ (v. 21). No battle is actually fought. Only the assembling of the foes and the defeat of the beast are described. Is this accidental? Does John indicate that the battle has already been fought and that this is simply the final realization of that previous victory? In chapter 5 the Lamb had overcome (won the victory) by His death (5:5, 9). Furthermore, we are told that there was a battle in heaven, and Satan was cast out and defeated by the blood of the Lamb and the word of His followers' testimony (12:7–9, 11). There seems to be only one actual battle described in Revelation. Thus these further scenes may be understood as more judicial in character than as literal battlefield descriptions. Because of John's christological reinterpretation, no great eschatological military battle, such as that envisaged in the Qumran War Scroll, will actually be fought. The decisive battle has already been won at the Cross. These armies and the beast are the destroyers of the earth (11:18), who ultimately are the satanic principalities of the world who ally themselves with the human puppets for their idolatrous ends. These have been positionally defeated at the Cross (Col. 2:15), but they will finally be stripped of all power at Christ's return. Certainly John would not have denied that Satan and his evil powers are active in the world and that they use historical persons, such as a Nero or a Hitler, and oppose and harass Christians today.

Although Satan has been dealt a death blow at the Cross (cf. John 12:31; 16:11), he nevertheless continues to promulgate evil and deception during this present age (cf. Eph. 2:2; 1 Thess. 3:5; 1 Peter 5:8–9; Rev. 2:10). Yet he is a deposed ruler who is now under the sovereign authority of Christ, but who for a "little time" is allowed to continue his evil until God's purposes are finished. In this scene of the overthrow of the beast and his kings and their armies, John shows us the ultimate and swift destruction of these evil powers by the King of Kings and Lord of Lords. They have met their Master in this final and utterly real confrontation. (On the "lake of fire," see comments on 20:14.)

For Further Study

1. Do you feel that 19:11–21 refers to the second coming of Christ? Cite evidence from the text of Revelation to support this view.

2. What is the sword that comes out of the Lord's mouth? How does this affect our understanding of the kind of Messiah Jesus is?

3. Study Isaiah 63:1–6. Explain the two main views of the blood on Jesus' garment. How does your view affect the way in which you see John's christology affect his interpretation of the Old Testament?

4. How should this vision of Christ's return affect Christian living now?

5. Is any actual battle fought when the beast is defeated? Explain.

Chapter 9

The Third and Fourth Last Things: The Binding of Satan and the Millennium
(Revelation 20:1–6)

A. Introduction

This passage has been described as a constant source of insurmountable difficulty for the exegete. The Millennium has been called one of the most controversial and intriguing questions of eschatology. Certainly one's view of Revelation 20 is internally connected with the rest of one's eschatology. While the Old Testament and later Jewish literature point forward to a time when the kingdom of God will be manifest in the world, nowhere in Jewish literature is the time of the reign of the Messiah stated to be a thousand years.

The exegesis of the passage leads me to a *premillennial* interpretation (see discussion below). It should be recognized, however, that there are problems with this view of Revelation 20:1–6, just as there are problems with other views of this difficult portion of the book, and that responsible Christian scholars vary in its interpretation according to their convictions and presuppositions.

For the moment the question of the duration of the reign of Christ (which is equal to the duration of the binding of Satan) may be delayed. The main problem is whether the reference to a Millennium (from the Latin *mille*, thousand; *annus* or *ennus*, year) indicates an earthly historical reign of peace that will manifest itself at the close of this present age, or whether the whole passage is symbolic of some present experience of Christians or some future nonhistorical reality.

1. History of interpretation[1]

In the first place, we may note that the ancient church down to the time of Augustine (354–430) with minor exceptions unquestionably held to the teaching of an earthly, historical reign of peace that was to follow the

---

[1]For an interesting modern discussion, see G.R. Beasley-Murray, Herschel Hobbs, and Ray F. Robbins, *Revelation: Three Viewpoints* (Nashville: Broadman, 1977).

defeat of Antichrist and the physical resurrection of the saints but to precede both the judgment and the new creation. To be sure, in the ancient church there were various positions as to the material nature of the Millennium (see comments on v. 4), but the generally accepted conception of the thousand years was a balance between the worldly aspects of the kingdom and its spiritual aspects as a reign with Christ.

a) *Amillennial Views*

Tyconius and Augustine. It is well known that the break with this earlier position came with the views of the late fourth-century interpreter Tyconius, an African Donatist, who, partly dependent on the Alexandrian allegorizing approach of Origen, developed a view of the Millennium based on a recapitulation method of interpretation. In applying this principle, Tyconius viewed Revelation as containing a number of different visions that repeated basic themes throughout the book. Although Tyconius's original work is not available, his exegesis of the Apocalypse can be largely reconstructed through his prime benefactor, Augustine, and Tyconius's many Roman Catholic followers. When he came to chapter 20, he interpreted the thousand years in nonliteral terms and understood the period as referring to the church age, the time between the first and second advents of Christ. Tyconius interpreted the first resurrection as the resurrection of the soul from spiritual death to the new life, while the second resurrection was the resurrection of the body at the end of history. The binding of Satan had already taken place in that the devil cannot seduce the church during the present age. Moreover, the reign of the saints and their "thrones of judgment" (v. 4) had already begun in the church on its rulers. Augustine, following Tyconius, cast the die against the expectation of a millennial kingdom for centuries to come. The recapitulation method adopted by Augustine continued to find adherents through the centuries and has its modern exponents in both the Protestant and Roman Catholic branches of the church; it is the first main option in modern nonmillennial (or amillennial) interpretations of Revelation 20.

Joachim of Floris. Augustine's approach, however, was not to remain unchallenged. Joachim of Floris (c. 1135–1202) saw in the Apocalypse a prophecy of the events of Western history from the time of Christ until the end. He thought the Millennium was still future in his time but soon to begin. The Franciscans, who followed Joachim, identified Babylon with ecclesiastical Rome and the Antichrist with the papacy. The Reformers followed suit. In modern times, the conservative New Testament scholar Henry Alford (1810–71) adopted this view.

Ribera. During Reformation times, still another type of interpretation developed, expounded by a Jesuit scholar named Ribera (1537–91). He held that almost all the events described in the Apocalypse are future and apply to the end times rather than to the history of the world or contemporary Rome and the papacy. He still, however, held to Augustine's view of the Millennium as the period between the first and second advents of Christ. But on one important point he changed Augustine's view: instead of the Millennium taking place on earth between the advents, Ribera saw it as taking place in *heaven*. It is a reward for faithfulness. When the saints at any time in history are martyred, they do not perish but live and reign with Christ in heaven in the intermediate state before the final resurrection. This is the second main option today for nonmillennialists. John's basic message in Revelation 20 is, according to this viewpoint, pastoral. If Christians face the prospect of suffering death for Jesus, they should be encouraged, because if they are killed they will go to reign with Him in heaven. This seems to be the drift of the conclusions of the Dutch reformed scholar G.C. Berkouwer and of the earlier Princeton conservative scholar B.B. Warfield.

The Augustinian view of Revelation 20 and its variant espoused by Joachim, though widely held, cannot, in my opinion, be harmonized with a serious exegesis of Revelation 20 on two important counts. In the first place, it founders on the statements concerning the binding of Satan (vv. 1–3); and second, it must handle in an absurd fashion the statements about the coming to life of the martyrs, which cannot be exegetically understood as anything other than *physical* resurrection without seriously tampering with the sense of the words (cf. comments on 20:1–4). While it is popular among certain nonmillennialists to view 20:1–6 as a symbolic description of the reward to be granted the martyrs on their entrance into heaven, this variation of the Augustinian exegesis, while removing the criticism that the passage refers to the present rule of Christ in the church age, fails to deal seriously with the binding of Satan and other details of the text.

b) *The postmillennial view*

A variation of Augustine's view known as postmillennialism or evolutionary chiliasm teaches that the forces of Antichrist will gradually be put down in this age and the gospel will permeate and transform the world into an interim reign of peace *before* the return of Christ. This view has many similarities to the amillennial positions described above. However, it differs from these views in its advocacy of a future, earthly reign of peace, which will precede the actual return of Christ, who will then inaugurate the new heavens and earth. A chief objection is the inability of postmillennialism's advocates to defend themselves adequately on any serious scriptural basis. This may account for the paucity of interpreters who hold this position. The remarks on verses 1–6 will attempt to address the weaknesses of this view.

c) The premillennial view

There is yet another view that, though not free of problems, does more justice to the Book of Revelation as a whole and to the exegesis of chapter 20 in particular. This view rejects both the Augustinian interpretation that the Millennium is the rule of Christ during this dispensation and the variant of Joachim that locates the resurrection and the reign of the martyrs in heaven for an interim period before their bodily resurrection and the return of Christ. This view is the premillennial option. Though the earliest view in the church, a number of varieties of this position have flourished since the nineteenth century, especially in North America.

The view espoused in this commentary argues that the Millennium will be in history and on the earth as an eschatological reality. Much in the same manner as the kingdom of God was eschatologically present in the life and ministry of Jesus—present, yet still future—so the Millennium is at once the final historical event of this age and the beginning of the eschatological kingdom of Christ in eternity. One of the principal advocates of this view states:

> The millennium is future and is, so to speak, the very last part of Christ's lordship, which at the same time extends into the new aeon. Consequently, the thousand-year kingdom should be identified neither with the whole chronological extent of Christ's lordship nor with the present Church. That lordship is the larger concept; it has already begun and continues in the aeon for an undefined length of time. The thousand-year reign, on the other hand, belongs temporally to the final act of Christ's lordship, the act which begins with his return and thus already invades the new aeon (Oscar Cullmann).

This variety of the premillennial view is called the "end-historical" view. It follows the same chronological sequence as the early church's premillennial position, i.e., Parousia (return of Christ)—defeat of Antichrist—binding of Satan—resurrection—Millennium—release of Satan—final judgment—new heavens and earth. It differs slightly from earlier chiliasm in viewing the Millennium as an end-historical event that at the same time is the beginning of the eternal reign of Christ and the saints.

While the viewpoint of this commentary falls within the sphere of historic premillennialism, it is hoped that there might be mutual tolerance and respect among adherents of the various opinions in this area of doctrine where the church has traditionally not had unanimity.

2. The sequence question

The problem as to the limits of the description of the Millennium in Revelation 20–22 is more difficult. A group of expositors of varying theological persuasions believe that 21:9–22:5, 14–15 belong with 20:1–10 as a further description of the millennial reign, whereas 21:1–5 refers to the eternal state, which follows the final judgment of the dead.

This approach is an attempt to harmonize a more literal understanding of certain statements in 21:9ff. with the assumed conditions during the eternal state. For example, according to some the references to nations and kings seem to describe an earthly kingdom better than they describe the eternal condition (21:24, 26); the reference to leaves "healing" the nations (22:2) seems to describe an imperfect condition better than the perfected eternal state; and finally, the blessing pronounced on those who come and eat of the tree of life while a curse rests on all those outside the city (22:14–15) seems to relate better to the thousand years than to the eternal state when the wicked are in the lake of fire.

Admittedly, this is a possible solution that has the advantage of giving more descriptive content to the millennial reign. This approach, however, suffers from two serious criticisms. First, though it rightly assigns 21: 1–5 to the postmillennial New Jerusalem in the context of the new heaven and earth, it arbitrarily assigns 21:9ff. to the millennial New Jerusalem without the slightest hint from the text that this is a recapitulation of 20:1–10. Thus, there is an eternal-state New Jerusalem followed immediately by a millennial New Jerusalem, both bearing the same title. This is hardly plausible. Second, this view strongly argues for historical progression in 19:11–21:5 (Parousia—defeat of Antichrist—binding of Satan—first resurrection—Millennium—release of Satan—last judgment—new heavens and earth) and then argues for recapitulation in 21:9ff.

It therefore seems best, despite some problems, to regard the sequence that begins in 19:11 as running chronologically through 22:6, thus placing all the material in 21:1ff. after the Millennium. At this point, a suggestion might be offered for further study. If the Millennium is a true eschatological, historical event like the person, ministry, and resurrection of Jesus, may not 21:1ff. be viewed as the full manifestation of the kingdom of God, a partial manifestation of which will be realized in the thousand-year reign of Christ and the saints, during which Christ will defeat all His enemies, including death (1 Cor. 15:23–28)? Some of the same conditions described in 21:1ff. would then, at least in part, characterize the Millennium.

3. Why a Millennium?

There are at least four answers to this question:

1. During the Millennium, Christ will openly manifest His kingdom in world history; the Millennium will provide an actual demonstration of the truthfulness of the divine witness borne by Christ and His followers during their life on earth. It will be a time of the fulfillment of all God's covenant promises to His people.

2. The Millennium will reveal that man's rebellion against God lies deep in man's own heart, not in the devil's deception. Even when Satan is

bound and righteousness prevails in the world, some people will still rebel against God. The final release of Satan will draw this hidden evil out into the open.

3. The release of Satan after the Millennium shows the invulnerability of the city of God and the extent of the authority of Christ, since the Devil is immediately defeated and cast into the lake of fire forever.

4. The Millennium will serve as a long period required to do the general "housecleaning" needed after the preceding ages during which sin was prevalent.

B. The Third Last Thing: The Binding of Satan (20:1–3)

Verses 1–3 are integrally related to 19:20–21. After the destruction of the beast and his followers and of the false prophet, Satan (the dragon, the ancient serpent) is dealt with. He is thrown into the Abyss to be imprisoned there for a thousand years, which is the third last thing (see introduction to 19:11–21). The Abyss is the demonic abode (see comments on 9:1; cf. 11:7). The angel's mission is to restrain Satan from deceiving the nations—hence the key, the chain, and the violent casting into the Abyss. That this whole action is not a recapitulation of earlier descriptions of Satan is evident from a number of points. In 12:9 (where the same titles are mentioned), Satan is "hurled" out of heaven "to the earth," where he goes forth with great fury to work his deception and persecute God's people (13:14; 18:23c). But in 20:1–3, the situation is completely different. Here Satan is cast *out of the earth* into a place where he is kept from "deceiving the nations." The former period of Satan's restriction to earth is described as a "short time" (12:9, 12), while here in 20:1–3 the time of his binding is a thousand years. In the earlier references to Satan, he is very active on the earth (2:10, 13; 12:17; 16:13, cf. 1 Peter 5:8); here he is tightly sealed in "prison" (v. 7). The binding of Satan removes his deceptive activity from among "the nations," a term never used to describe the redeemed community until ch. 21 (after Satan's permanent end).

From at least the time of Victorinus (d. ca. 303), some have interpreted the binding of Satan as the work of Christ in the lives of believers. Thus Satan is "bound" for believers since he no longer deceives them, but he is still "loose" for unbelievers who are deceived. This explanation, however, does not take seriously the language of the Abyss and the prison in which Satan is confined, nor does it account for the releasing of Satan after the thousand years. The binding of spirits or angels is mentioned in Isaiah 24:21–23 and Jude 6. In these references there is no question of the spirits being bound in some respects and not in others; it signifies a complete removal as to a prison, usually in the depths of the underworld. A recent observation is well taken: "The elaborate measures taken to insure his custody are most easily understood as implying the complete

cessation of his influence on earth (rather than a curbing of his activities)"
(Mounce).

Only one New Testament reference seems to imply a limited binding of
Satan. In the parable in Mark 3:27, Jesus refers to the strong man's being
bound before his goods can be plundered. The reference is to Satan's
being bound by Christ and specifically relates to the temptation of Jesus,
or to Jesus' exorcisms mentioned in the immediate context. In any case,
the binding of Satan by the ministry of Jesus did not totally immobilize
the devil but struck him a vital blow. But does the reference in Mark
provide a true analogy to the binding of Satan in 20:1–3, as Augustine
claimed? A careful examination of Mark 3:27 and Revelation 20:1–3 leads
to the conclusion that the two passages are not teaching the same truth.
There is a sense in which, according to the gospel account, Satan is in the
process of being bound by the activity of Christ and the kingdom of God;
but this is clearly an event different from the total consigning of Satan to
the Abyss as taught in Revelation 20:1–3.

Finally, it may be noted that the thousand-year binding of Satan is
concurrent with and inseparable from the thousand-year reign of the
resurrected martyrs. For a thousand years on this earth, within history,
the activity of Satan leading mankind into false worship and active rebellion against God and His people will be totally curbed under the authority
of Christ in His kingdom. If that reign is yet future, the binding is future.
If the binding refers to an earthly situation, which it clearly does, the
thousand-year reign most naturally also refers to an earthly situation.

C. The Fourth Last Thing: The Thousand-Year Reign of Christ (20:4–6)

a) *The throne* (20:4)

The fourth last thing (see introduction to 19:11–21) is the thousand-
year reign of Christ on the earth. John does not give us a picture of life in
the Millennium in these verses: he only states who will participate in it.
He sees thrones, and judges sitting on them. The scene is usually connected with Daniel's vision of the Son of Man (Dan. 7:9, 22, 27). In
Daniel, justice was done for the saints by the Ancient of Days, after which
they began their kingdom reign. The thought may be similar here; if so,
those who sit on the thrones are the angelic court. However, those on the
thrones may be the resurrected martyrs who exercise judgmental and
ruling functions during the Millennium. This possible reinterpretation of
Daniel seems preferable in the light of other New Testament teaching as
well as of Revelation itself (cf. Luke 22:30; 1 Cor. 6:2; Rev. 2:26). They
who were once judged by earth's courts to be worthy of death are now the
judges of the earth under Christ.

Who will participate? A more difficult question concerns the identity of
those who will rule with Christ. They are the "beheaded" martyrs who

have previously occupied John's attention. The cause of their death is attributed to their faithful witness to Jesus and the word of God (concerning these terms, see comments on 1:9; cf. 6:9; 12:11). The reference to "souls" immediately recalls 6:9, where the same expression is used of the slain witnesses under the altar. The word describes those who have lost their bodily life but are nevertheless still alive in God's sight. This term prepares us for their coming to (bodily) life again in the first resurrection. It is a mistake to take "souls" to imply a later spiritual resurrection or rebirth of the soul as did Augustine and many since.

These martyrs are also those who did not worship the beast or his image or receive his mark on them (cf. 13:1ff.; 15:2); in a word, they are the followers of the Lamb. At his point, the NIV omits a very important term. Between the description of those beheaded and the description concerning the worship of the beast in verse 4 are the two words "and who." This construction is capable of bearing two different meanings. It could simply introduce a phrase further qualifying the identification of the martyrs (so NIV, TEV). But it may also be understood to introduce a second group. There are then (1) those who were beheaded for their witness and (2) "also those who" did not worship the beast (see JV, BV: "and of these also"; NASB: "and those who"). This immediately alleviates the thorny problem why only the martyrs should live and reign with Christ. Usually in Revelation the relative pronoun "who" simply refers to the preceding group and adds some further detail (2:24; 9:4; 17:12); but in one other reference, which alone has the identical introductory terms, the phrase so introduced singles out a special class or group from the more general group in the preceding statement (1:7). Thus the "and who" clause introduces a special class of the beheaded, i.e., those who were so beheaded because they did not worship the beast, etc. In any case, it seems that John has only the beheaded in mind (cf. 14:13).

But this presents a problem, because John has elsewhere indicated that the kingdom reign will be shared by every believer who overcomes (2:26–28; 3:12, 21) and is purchased by Christ's blood (5:10). Also, in 1 Corinthians 6:2–3 Paul clearly speaks of all believers—not just martyrs—exercising judgment in the future. Revelation 5:10 indicates that the kingdom will be a "reign on the earth." Unless only those beheaded by the beast will reign in the Millennium, another explanation is demanded. The pastoral approach would explain John's reference to only the martyrs as a piece of special encouragement to them, while not implying that others would be left out.

I feel somewhat more comfortable with the view expressed earlier (see comments on 6:9)—viz., that the martyrs represent the whole church that is faithful to Jesus, whether or not they have actually been killed. They constitute a group that can in truth be described as those who "did not love their lives so much as to shrink from death" (12:11). As such, the term is a synonym for "overcomers" (chs. 2–3). Thus John could count himself in this group, though he may never have suffered death by the axe of the beast. In 2:11, those who during persecution are faithful to Christ even to the point of death are promised escape from the second death, which in 20:6 is promised to those who share in the first resurrection, i.e., the beheaded (v. 4). In fact, a number of the other promises to overcomers in the letters to the seven churches also find their fulfillment in chapter 20 (cf. 2:11 with 20:6; 2:26–27 with 20:4; 3:5 with 20:12, 15; 3:21 with 20:4).

The meaning of "come to life." The martyrs "came to life." The interpretation of these words is crucial to the whole passage. Since Augustine, the majority of interpreters have taken the words to refer to a spiritual resurrection, or new birth, or to the triumph of the church. Some, for example, see the parallel with Christ's resurrection (2:8) but seem to spiritualize Jesus' resurrection and conclude that resurrection for the martyrs "means that they have been let loose into the world" (Caird). This substitutes a symbolic sense for the historical event of physical resurrection. Others, rightly chastened by a more serious exegesis of the text, hold that the language teaches bodily resurrection, but that the whole section (20:1–10) is apocalyptic language, figurative of the consolation and reward promised to the martyrs, and should not be taken as predicting events within history. A typical nonmillennialist explains what the passage means:

> We may not tamper with the real, graphic nature of the vision of Revelation 20, nor may we spiritualize the first resurrection. But one question is still decisive: does this vision intend to sketch for us a particular phase of *history*? If one does interpret it this way, it seems to me that he must include the first (bodily) resurrection in his concept of a future millennium. . . . This vision is not a narrative account of a future earthly reign at all, but is the apocalyptic unveiling of the reality of salvation in Christ as a backdrop to the reality of the suffering and martyrdom that still continue as long as the dominion of Christ remains hidden (italics his) (Berkouwer).

While alleviating the criticism of a spiritual resurrection, Berkouwer fails to take seriously the language of the thousand-year reign, which is everywhere in the Apocalypse a reign on the *earth* within *history*.

The verb "came to life" is used in verse 4 of the martyrs and in verse 5 of the "rest of the dead" who did not come to life until the thousand years were completed. When the context is that of bodily death, the verb is used in the New Testament to connote *physical* resurrection (John 11:25; Acts 1:3; 9:41), though the normal word is "raise up." More importantly, Revelation clearly uses "to live" for the resurrection of Christ (1:18; 2:8) and also, curiously, for the sea beast (13:14). John 5:25 is sometimes cited as evidence that the word refers to spiritual life, not physical resurrection. But a careful reading of the context clearly shows that, while John 5:25 does indeed use the verb in the sense of spiritual life (as do other New

Testament passages), John 5:29 definitely refers to physical resurrection and uses the phrase "rise to live." John plainly says in Revelation 20:5 that "this is the first resurrection." The word "resurrection," which occurs over forty times in the New Testament, is used almost exclusively of physical resurrection (Luke 2:34 is the only exception). There is no indication that John has departed from this usage in these verses.

b) *The first resurrection and the second death* (20:5–6)

Why does John call this the "first" resurrection? The term "first" clearly implies the first in a series of two or more. John does not refer directly to a second resurrection; it is, however, correctly inferred both from the use of "first" and from the expression "the rest of the dead did not come to life until the thousand years were ended" (v. 5). Irenaeus (c. 140–c. 202) clearly connects John's first resurrection with the "resurrection of the just" (Luke 14:14). Likewise, Justin Martyr held to a physical resurrection before the Millennium and a general physical resurrection after the thousand years, though he does not explain whether believers will also participate in the latter. From at least the time of Augustine, the first resurrection was understood as a regeneration of the soul and the second resurrection as the general physical, bodily resurrection of just and unjust. It must be insisted, however that it is exegetically weak to make the first resurrection spiritual and the second one physical, unless the text itself clearly indicates this change, which it does not.

Another response would be to understand "the rest of the dead" (v. 5), who did not live until the close of the thousand years, to be all the faithful except the martyrs, plus the entire body of believers. This view, in our opinion, runs aground on the fact that John clearly seems to relate exclusion from the second death to those who are part of the first resurrection, thus strongly implying that those who participate in the second resurrection are destined for the second death.

Therefore, following the lead of the earlier exegesis of Irenaeus, we may understand the first resurrection to be the raising to physical life of all the dead in Christ (cf. 1 Cor. 15:12ff.; 1 Thess. 4:13ff.); this is the resurrection to life of John 5:29 (NIV: "rise to live"). As to those who participate in this resurrection, "the second death [the lake of fire; 20:14] has no power over them" (v. 6). Therefore, they are "blessed and holy" (the fifth beatitude in Revelation; see comments on 1:3) and shall be priests of God and Christ for the thousand years. On the other hand, those over whom the second death will have power must be "the rest of the dead" (v. 5), who will be participants in the second resurrection, the "rise to be condemned" of John 5:29 (cf. Acts 24:15).

In the only place other than Revelation 2:11 and 20:6 where the second death is mentioned, it refers to exclusion from physical resurrection (v. 14). Likewise, in the Palestinian Targum on Deuteronomy 33:6, the

Old Testament *locus theologicus* in rabbinic Judaism for proving the resurrection from the dead, the Targum reads: "Let Reuben live in this world and not die in the second death in which death the wicked die in the world to come." In the Targum the second death means exclusion from the Resurrection. Not to die the second death, then, means to rise again to eternal life.

What now may be said as to the length of the kingdom reign?[2] In the first place, the number symbolisms of John in Revelation should not be used to argue against an earthly kingdom. It might be said that the number is symbolic of a perfect period of time of whatever length. The essence of premillennialism lies in its insistence that the reign will be on earth, not in heaven, for a period of time before the final judgment and the new heavens and earth and *after* Christ's return. For example, we may rightly understand the 1,260 days (forty-two months) of earlier chapters as a symbolic number, but it still refers to an actual historical period of whatever length during which the beast will destroy the saints. If we look at the time of suffering of the Smyrna Christians, it is "ten days" (2:10), a relatively short time in comparison to a thousand years of victorious reign with Christ. In any case, it is not of primary importance whether the thousand years are actual 365-day years or symbolic of a shorter or longer period of bliss enjoyed by believers as they reign with Christ on earth (cf. 5:10 with 11:15; 22:5).

For Further Study

1. Look up the terms amillennialism, postmillennialism, and premillennialism in a good Bible dictionary. Which views have ancient roots and which are more recent?

2. Does the binding of Satan seem to be a partial limiting of his power through the gospel in the present age or a total cessation of his influence?

3. Does the millennium seem to be a completely symbolic figure for the reward of the saints in heaven or does it seem to refer to some period of Christ's rule with the saints on earth? Why? Are only martyrs involved?

4. What purpose would a transitional age of a thousand years fulfill?

5. How important do you think the millennial question is to Christian doctrine and living?

---

[2]For a detailed discussion of the possible origins of the thousand-year length and its meaning, see Johnson, EBC, 12, p. 585.

Chapter 10

The Fifth Last Thing: The Release and Final End of Satan
(Revelation 20:7–10)

The fifth last thing (see introduction to 19:11–21) is the defeat of Satan. In verse 3 the release of Satan after the Millennium was anticipated: "He must be set free for a short time" (cf. 12:12). He *must* once again be released so that he can "deceive the nations" throughout the world and lead them into conflict against "God's people." But why should God allow this? Certainly, if man alone were prophetically writing the history of the world, he would not bring the archdeceiver back after the glorious reign of Christ (20:4–6). But God's thoughts and ways are not man's (Isa. 55:8). Ezekiel's vision of Gog brought out of the land of Magog seems to be clearly in John's mind (Ezek. 38–39). Ezekiel also saw an attack on God's people, who had been restored for some time ("after many days," Ezek. 38: 8)—i.e., after the commencement of the kingdom age.

In Ezekiel 38–39, Gog refers to the prince of a host of pagan invaders from the North, especially the Scythian hordes from the distant land of Magog. In Revelation, however, the names are symbolic of the final enemies of Christ duped by Satan into attacking the community of the saints. The change in meaning has occurred historically through the frequent use in rabbinic circles of the expression "Gog and Magog" to symbolically refer to the "nations" of Psalm 2 who are in rebellion against God and His Messiah.

If the beast and his armies are already destroyed (19:19ff.), who are these rebellious nations? It may be that the beast and his armies in the earlier context are the demonic powers and those in 20:7ff. human nations in rebellion—not an unlikely solution (see comments on 19:19ff.)—or it may be that not all the people in the world will participate in the beast's armies; those mentioned here in v. 8 then are other people who during the millennial reign defected in their hearts from the Messiah. In any case, this section shows something of the deep, complex nature of evil. The source of rebellion against God does not lie in man's environment or fundamentally with the Devil but deep within man's own heart. The return of Satan will demonstrate this in the most dramatic manner once for all. The temporal reign of Christ will not be fulfilled until this final challenge to His kingdom occurs and He demonstrates the power of His victory at the Cross and puts down all His enemies (1 Cor. 15:25). His kingdom is invulnerable. He is truly Lord of Lords and King of Kings.

The gathered army, which is extensive and world-wide, advances and in siege fashion encircles the "camp of God's people, the city he loves." Most commentators take the expressions "camp" and "city" as different metaphors for God's people. The word "camp" in the New Testament refers to either a military camp or the camp of Israel (Acts 21:34, 37; 22:24; Heb. 11:34; 13:11, 13). It is a word that reminds us of the pilgrim character of the people of God even at the end of the Millennium, as long as evil is active in God's creation.

The "city he loves" presents more difficulty. According to standard Jewish eschatology, this should refer to the restored and spiritually renewed city of Jerusalem in Palestine (Pss. 78:6–8; 87:2). A number of modern commentators of various theological schools have taken this Jewish identification as a clue and have so understood the passage.

On the other hand, John may have intended to refer merely to the community of the redeemed without any specific geographical location in mind. This would be in harmony with his previous references to the city elsewhere in the book (cf. comments on 3:12; 11:2, 8). There are only two cities or kingdoms in the Apocalypse—the city of Satan, where the beast and harlot are central, and the kingdom of God, where God and the Lamb are central, The city, then, is the kingdom of God in its millennial manifestation; it is the same city that appears in its final, most glorious form in the last two chapters. Wherever God dwells among His people, there the city of God is (21:2–3). Following this understanding of the beloved city in no way weakens the validity of an earthly reign of Christ and the saints.

The swiftness and finality of the divine judgment (v. 9) emphasize the reality of the victory of Christ at the Cross. The fire imagery may reflect Ezekiel's vision of the destruction of Gog (Ezek. 38:22; 39:6). Note that here, in contrast to the Qumran and Jewish apocalyptic literature, it is God, not the saints, who destroys the enemy (cf. comments on 19:19). The devil is now dealt the long-awaited final and fatal blow (Gen. 3:15; John 12:31). The "lake of fire" imagery is probably related to the teaching of Jesus about hell (Matt. 5:22; 7:19; 10:28; 13:49–50; Mark 9:48, et al.). The "lake" may be related to certain Jewish descriptions of eternal judgment (cf. 2 Enoch 10:2: "a gloomy fire is always burning, and a fiery river goes forth"). The figure may intensify the idea of the permanency of the judgment (cf. comments on 14:11; also 19:20; 20:14–15; 21:8). That the beast and false prophet are already there does not argue for their individuality, since later in the chapter "death" and "Hades," nonpersonal entities that for the sake of the imagery are personified, are cast into the same lake of fire (20:14).

For Further Study

1. Why is Satan released after the thousand years? How does he deceive the nations today?

2. Which do you think is more probable, that the "city he loves" refers to the earthly Jerusalem in Palestine or to the church? Why?

3. How will the banishment forever of Satan affect human life on the earth?

Chapter 11

The Sixth Last Thing: The Great White Throne Judgment
(Revelation 20:11-15)

John describes in vivid pictures the sixth last thing (see introduction to 19:11-21), the final judgment of mankind. Unlike many of the vivid, imaginative paintings based on this vision, John describes here a strange, unearthly scene. Heaven and earth flee from the unidentified figure who sits on the majestic white throne. The language of poetic imagery captures the fading character of everything that is of the world (1 John 2:17). Now the only reality is God seated on the throne of judgment, before whom all must appear (Heb. 9:27). His verdict alone is holy and righteous (expressed symbolically by the "white" throne). It is possible that in Revelation the earth and sky refer more to the religio-political than to the cosmological order (Caird). Since 20:11-12 makes use of the theophany of Daniel 7:9-10, the One seated on the throne is presumably God Himself; but since 22:1, 3 mention the throne of God *and of the Lamb*, it may well be that here Jesus shares in the judgment (John 5:27). God has kept the last judgment in His own hands. This vision declares that even though it may have seemed that the course of earth's history ran contrary to His holy will, no single day or hour in the world's drama has ever detracted from the absolute sovereignty of God (Lilje).

But who are the dead (vv. 12-13)? Earlier in the chapter, John has mentioned the "rest of the dead" who are not resurrected till the thousand years are completed (v. 5). It has been noted that "if the first resurrection is limited to actual martyrs, then the judgment of verses 11-15 involves both believer and impenitent. If the second resurrection is of the wicked only, then the judgment is of those who will in fact be consigned to the lake of fire" (Mounce). While no resurrection is mentioned in verses 11-15, the dead may well be those who did not participate in the first resurrection. Since the second death has no power over those who were raised in the first resurrection (v. 6), it may be argued that only those who are the enemies of God—i.e., the wicked dead—stand before this throne (John 5:24). This is by no means a necessary inference, though it is the most satisfactory exegesis.

A moment of tension arrives—the books are opened. It is sobering to ponder that in God's sight nothing is forgotten; all will give an account of their actions (v. 13). Judgment always proceeds on the basis of works (Matt. 25:41ff.; Rom. 2:6; 2 Cor. 5:10; Heb. 4:12–13). The "books" are the records of human deeds (v. 12). While in Jewish thought there are references to books of good and evil deeds being kept before God, John is probably alluding to Daniel 7:10: "The court was seated, and the books were opened." We are not told whether these books contain both good and evil works or only the latter.

John is more concerned about another book, the book of life, which alone seems to be decisive (vv. 12, 15; cf. comments on 3:5; also 13:8; 17:8; 21:27). How can these two pictures be harmonized? In reality there is no conflict. Works are unmistakable evidence of the loyalty of the heart; they express either belief or unbelief, faithfulness or unfaithfulness. The judgment will reveal through the records whether or not the loyalties were with God and the Lamb or with God's enemies. John's theology of faith and its inseparable relation to works is the same as Jesus' and Paul's (John 5:29; Rom. 2:6ff.). This judgment is not a "balancing of the books," a weighing of good works and bad works. Those who have their names in the Lamb's book of life will also have records of righteous deeds. The opposite will be true as well. The imagery reflects the delicate balance between grace and obedience (cf. comments on 19:6–8).

Three places are mentioned as containing the dead: the sea, death, and Hades (v. 13). The sea represents the place of unburied bodies, while death and Hades represent the reality of dying and the condition entered into at death (cf. 1:18; 6:8). The imagery suggests release of the bodies and persons from places where they were confined after death: i.e., it portrays resurrection. They rise to receive sentence (John 5:29b). Death and Hades are personified (cf. 6:8) and, in a vivid image, are cast into the lake of fire to be permanently destroyed (cf. 19:20; 20:10). This not only fulfills Paul's cry concerning the last enemy, death, which will be defeated by the victorious kingdom of Christ (1 Cor. 15:16), but also signals the earth's new condition: "There will be no more death" (21:4).

The final scene in this dark and fearful passage is in verse 15. From the English rendering it might be inferred that John is doubtful whether anyone will be thrown into the lake of fire. The Greek, however, is not so indefinite. John uses a construction that assumes the reality of the first clause and shows the consequences in the second clause. Thus we might paraphrase the verse: "If anyone's name was not found written in the book of life, and I assume there were such, he was thrown into the lake of fire." When taken seriously, this final note evaporates all theories of universalism. God's mercy is vast beyond comprehension, but His mercy is not limitless. He will never reject any who come to Him for mercy, nor will He force Himself on any who choose to live without Him.

For Further Study

1. Why is judgment in the New Testament based on works rather than faith?

2. Do you believe that the redeemed will be present at this judgment? Why?

3. Explain the second death in chapter 20 (vv. 6, 14; cf. 2:11; 21:8).

4. How does the absence of a belief in future judgment affect people's behavior in our society today?

VISION FOUR: *The New Heaven and the New Earth*

Chapter 12

The Seventh Last Thing: The New Heaven and the New Earth and the New Jerusalem
(Revelation 21:1–22:5)

The seventh last thing (see introduction to 19:11–21) is the vision of the new heaven, the new earth, and the New Jerusalem. A striking remark, which captures something of the freshness of this moment, is worth remembering at the outset of the exposition of this incredibly beautiful finale:

> From the smoke and pain and heat of the preceding scenes it is a relief to pass into the clear, clean atmosphere of the eternal morning where the breath of heaven is sweet and the vast city of God sparkles like a diamond in the radiance of his presence (J.B. Moffatt).

Countless works of art and music have through the ages been inspired by this vision. Cathedral architecture has been influenced by its imagery. John discloses a theology in stone and gold as pure as glass and color. Archetypal images abound. The church is called the bride (21:2). God gives the thirsty "to drink without cost from the spring of the water of life" (21:6). Completeness is implied in the number twelve and its multiples (21:12–14, 16–17, 21) and fullness in the cubical shape of the city (21:16). Colorful jewels abound, as do references to light and the glory of God (21:11, 18–21, 23, 25; 22:5). There is the "river of the water of life" (22:1) and the "tree of life" (22:2). The "sea" is gone (21:1).

Allusions to the Old Testament abound. Most of John's imagery in this chapter reflects Isaiah 60 and 65 and Ezekiel 40–48. John weaves Isaiah's vision of the New Jerusalem together with Ezekiel's vision of the new temple. The multiple Old Testament promises converging in John's mind seem to indicate that he viewed the New Jerusalem as the fulfillment of all these strands of prophecy. There are also allusions to Genesis 1–3: the absence of death and suffering, the dwelling of God with men as in Eden, the tree of life, the removal of the curse, etc. Creation is restored to its pristine character.

The connection of this vision with the promises to the overcomers in the letters to the seven churches (chs. 2–3) is significant. For example, to the overcomers at Ephesus was granted the right to the tree of life (2:7; cf. 22:2); at Thyatira, the right to rule the nations (2:26; cf. 22:5); at Philadelphia, the name of the city of my God, the New Jerusalem (3:12 and 21:2, 9ff.). In a sense, a strand from every major section of the Apocalypse appears in chapters 21–22. Moreover, almost every major theme and image found in these chapters can be duplicated from Jewish literature. But there is in the totality of John's vision a dimension that is clearly lacking in the Jewish parallels. Furthermore, his theology of the Lamb's centrality in the city and the absence of a temple in the New Jerusalem is unique.

In other New Testament passages, the vision of the heavenly city is described as having the character of eschatological promise. The kingdom reality of the age to come has already appeared in history in the life of Jesus and also in the presence of the Holy Spirit in the church. But the reality is now present only in a promissory way. Therefore, while the Jerusalem that is from above has present implications for believers (Gal. 4:25–31), they are nevertheless, like Abraham, "looking forward to the city with foundations" (Heb. 11:10; 13:14). In this sense, the medieval synthesis that made the church on earth and the kingdom synonymous and built its cathedrals to depict that notion was misdirected. John's vision in chapters 21–22 is one of eschatological promise, future in its realization, totally dependent on God's power to create it, yet having present implications for the life of the church in this age.

Outlines of the chapters are necessarily arbitrary because of the familiar Semitic style of doubling back and elaborating on previous subjects. Perhaps 21:1–8 may be seen as a preface or introduction to the vision of the New Jerusalem (21:9–22:6), and 22:7–21 as a conclusion following the vision.

A. Preface: A Brief Glimpse of the City (21:1–8)

1. *The new heaven and the new earth* (21:1)

The new heaven and earth were foreseen by Isaiah (65:17) as part of his vision of the renewed Jerusalem. It is remarkable that John's picture of the final age to come focuses not on a platonic ideal or distant paradise but on the reality of a new earth and heaven. God originally created the earth to be man's permanent home. But sin and death entered the world and transformed the earth into a place of rebellion and alienation; it became enemy-occupied territory. But God has been working in salvation history to effect a total reversal of this consequence of evil and to liberate earth and heaven from bondage to sin and corruption (Rom. 8:21). The first heaven and earth encompasses the whole order of life in the world, an order tainted by sin, death, suffering, and idolatry (cf. v. 4: "the old order of things [death, mourning, crying, pain] has passed away"). John's emphasis on heaven and earth is not primarily cosmological but moral and spiritual. So Peter also speaks of the new heaven and earth, "the home of righteousness" (2 Peter 3:13).

The word for "new" means "new in quality, fresh," rather than "recent or new in time." What makes the new heaven and earth "new" is above all else the reality that now "the dwelling of God is with men, . . . They will be his people, and God himself will be with them and be their God" (v. 3). The heaven and earth are new because of the presence of a new community of people who are loyal to God and the Lamb, in contrast to the former earth in which a community of idolaters lived.

The sea—the source of the satanic beast (13:1) and the place of the dead (20:13)—will be gone. Again, the emphasis is not geological but moral and spiritual. The sea serves as an archetype with connotations of evil (cf. comments on 13:1). Therefore, no trace of evil in any form will be present in the new creation.

2. *The Holy City, the New Jerusalem* (21:2-4)

The Holy City, the New Jerusalem, occupies John's vision for the remainder of the book. Here heaven is depicted as a city, with life, activity, interest, and people, as opposed to e.g., the Hindu ideal of heaven as a sea into which human life returns like a raindrop to the ocean. First, John sees the city "coming down out of heaven from God"—a phrase he uses three times (3:12; 21:2, 10) in an apparent spatial reference. But the city never seems to come down; it is always seen as a "descending-from-heaven kind of city" (Caird). Therefore, the expression stresses the idea that the city is a gift of God, forever bearing the marks of His creative activity.

Second, John calls the city a "bride" (cf. 21:9; 22:17). Earlier he referred to the bride of the Lamb (19:7-8). The multiple imagery is needed to portray the tremendous reality of the city. A bride-city captures something of God's personal relationship to His people (the bride) as well as of their life in communion with Him and one another (the city, with its social connotations). The purity and devotedness of the bride are reflected in her attire.

The name of the Holy City, "the new Jerusalem," raises a question. The "old" Jerusalem was also called the "holy city" and a "bride" (Isa. 52:1; 61:10). Since the Jerusalem from above is the "new" Jerusalem, we may suppose that it is connected in some manner with the old one, so that the new is the old one renewed. The old Jerusalem was marred by sin and disobedience. In it was the blood of prophets and apostles. Still worse, it became a manifestation of Babylon the Great when it crucified the Lord of glory (11:8). The old Jerusalem always involved more than merely its inhabitants and their daily lives: it represented the covenant community of God's people, the hope for the kingdom of God on earth. Thus the Old Testament looked forward to a renewed Jerusalem, rebuilt and transformed into a glorious habitation of God and His people. But the prophets also saw something else. They saw a new heaven and a new earth and a Jerusalem connected with this reality. Thus it is not altogether clear precisely what the relationship is between the old and the new, the earthly, restored Jerusalem of the prophets and the Jerusalem associated with the new heaven and earth, the Jerusalem called a "heavenly Jerusalem" in later Jewish thought (cf. Gal. 4:25–31; Heb. 11:10; 12:22; 13:14). But any exegesis that completely rejects any connection with the old city cannot take seriously the name "new" Jerusalem, which presupposes the old. To speak of the heavenly Jerusalem is not to deny an earthly city, as some suggest, but to stress its superiority to the older Jewish hope and to affirm the eschatological nature of that hope—a hope that could not be fulfilled by the earthly Jerusalem, a hope John now sees realized in the Holy City of the future. This city is the church in its future glorified existence—it is the final realization of the kingdom of God.

God's "dwelling" among His people (v. 3) is a fulfillment of Leviticus 26: 11–13, a promise given to the old Jerusalem but forfeited because of apostasy. As a backdrop for the scene, consider Genesis 3, where man lost his fellowship with God (cf. Exod. 25:8; Ezek. 37:26–27). Thus the Holy Jerusalem is not only mankind's eternal home but the city where God will place His own name forever. God's presence will blot out the things of the former creation. In a touching metaphor of motherly love, John says that God "will wipe away every tear from their eyes" (v. 4; cf. 7:17; Isa. 25:8). These tears have come from sin's distortion of God's purposes for man. They are produced by death or mourning for the dead, by crying or pain. An enemy has done this to the old order. Now God has defeated the enemy and liberated His people and His creation.

3. God's own word of attestation and invitation (21:5–6)

Now, for the second time in the book, God Himself is the speaker (cf. 1:8). From His throne comes the assurance that the One who created the first heaven and earth will indeed make all things new (v. 5). This is a strong confirmation that God's power will be revealed and His redemptive purposes fulfilled. Since these words are in truth God's words (cf. 19:9; 22:6), it is of utmost importance that this vision of the new heaven and the New Jerusalem be proclaimed to the churches.

With the same word that declared the judgment of the world to be finished, God proclaims that He has completed His new creation: "It is done" (v. 6; cf. 16:17). The names of God, "the Alpha and the Omega, the Beginning and the End," emphasize His absolute control over the world as well as His creatorship of everything (cf. comments on 1:8; cf. also 22:13).

To those who thirst for Him, God offers the water of life without cost (cf. 7:17; 22:1, 17; John 7:37–39; Rom. 3:24). In verse 6, salvation is beautifully depicted by the image of drinking at the spring of life. Twice in these last two chapters of Revelation God offers an invitation to those who sense their need and are drawn toward Him. John knows that the visions of God's glory among His people, which he proclaims as the Word of God, will create a thirst to participate in the reality of this glory. Nothing is required except to come and drink.

Those who come and drink and remain loyal to Christ as overcomers (see comments on 2:7, 11, et al.) will inherit all the new things of the city of God (v. 7). They will be God's children, and He will be their Father. This is the essence of salvation—intimate, personal relationship with God Himself, age upon age unending (cf. John 17:3). For John this is really what the heavenly city is all about.

4. The cardinal choice and its consequences (21:7–8)

Before John shows us the city, however, he must first confront us with a choice. This choice must be made because there are two cities: the city of God and the city of Babylon. Each has its inhabitants and its destiny. Those who drink from salvation's springs supplied by God Himself are true followers of Christ. The "cowardly" ("fearful") are those who fear the persecution that arises from faith in Christ. Not having steadfast endurance, they are devoid of faith (Matt. 8:26; Mark 4:40; cf. Matt. 13:20–21). Thus they are linked by John to the "unbelieving" and "vile" (the latter word is from a verb meaning "to detest" "abhor," which is used of idolatry; Rom. 2:22). They are called "murderers" because they are guilty of the death of the saints (17:6; 18:24). The "sexually immoral" (fornicators), practitioners of "magic arts, the idolaters and all liars" are those associated with idolatrous practices (cf. 9:21; 18:23; 21:27; 22:15; contrast 14:5). By their own choice, Babylon, not the New Jerusalem, is their eternal home (Caird). Thus this passage is not a picture of universal salvation in spite of man's recalcitrance, though it contains a universal invitation for all who thirst to drink the water of life. None will be turned away who come and drink.

B. The Description of the City of God (21:9–21)

In this and the next section (21:9–22:5), the vision of the New Jerusalem introduced in verses 1–8 is fully described. (For reasons why this section does not describe the millennial kingdom of ch. 20, see introduction to ch. 20). Verses 9–14 focus on the description of the gates and the walls of the city. This is followed by the action of the angel who measures the city and John's precise listing of the precious stones in the twelve foundations (vv. 15-21). Finally, John describes various aspects of the life of the city (21:22-22:5).

1. *The true identity and character of the city* (21:9-14)

The bride of Christ (vv. 9-10). Here the parallelism with 17:1 is clearly deliberate. The bride, the wife of the Lamb, contrasts with the great prostitute. As the prostitute was found to be John's archetypal image for the great system of satanic evil, so the bride is the true counterpart. She is pure and faithful to God and the Lamb, whereas the prostitute is a mockery. To see the prostitute, John was taken to the desert; but now he is elevated by the Spirit to the highest pinnacle of the earth to witness the exalted New Jerusalem (cf. comments on 1:10; 4:2; 17:3). As his vision will be a reinterpretation of Ezekiel's temple prophecy (Ezek. 40-48), John, like the prophet, is taken to a high mountain (Ezek. 40:2). For the moment, the author drops the bridal metaphor and in magnificent imagery describes the church in glory as a city with a lofty wall, splendid gates, and jeweled foundations. There is no warrant for thinking of the city as descending like a space platform to the mountain or hovering over the earth as some suggest (see comments on v. 2).

The effulgence of God's glory (v. 11). In John's description of the city, precious stones, brilliant colors, and the effulgence of light abound. The problem of the literalness of the city has received much attention. If the city is the bride and the bride the glorified community of God's people in their eternal life, there is little question that John's descriptions are primarily symbolic of that glorified life. This in no way diminishes the reality behind the imagery. In the most suitable language available to John, much of it drawn from the Old Testament, he shows us something of the reality of the eschatological kingdom of God in its glorified existence.

Its appearance is all-glorious, "with the glory of God" (v. 11; cf. Ezek. 43:4). The city has a "brilliance" ("light-bearer"), given it by God's presence, that appears as crystal-clear jasper (Isa. 60:1-2, 19; Rev. 21:23). Jasper is mentioned three times in chapter 21 (vv. 11, 18-19); earlier in Revelation it refers to the appearance of God (4:3). It is an opaque quartz mineral and occurs in various colors: commonly red, brown, green, or yellow, rarely blue or black, and seldom white. Some suggest it is an opal; others believe it to be a diamond, which is, of course, not quartz but a crystalline carbon. Still others think the rare and valuable white jasper is referred to here. Actually, there is no basis for certainty on this point.

The old and new covenant people (vv. 12-14). The *wall* is very high (about 200 ft.), its height symbolizing the greatness of this city as well as its impregnability against those described in 21:8, 27. The twelve *gates* (vv. 12-13) are distributed three on each of the four sides of the wall

(v. 13). These may be like the triple gates that can now be seen in the excavated wall of the old Jerusalem. Later John describes the gates as twelve single pearls (v. 21). What impresses him at this point about the gates is their angelic guards and the inscribed names of the twelve tribes of Israel. The presence of angels proclaims that this is God's city, while the twelve tribes emphasize the complete election of God (cf. comments on 7:4). Here there seems to be a deliberate allusion to Ezekiel's eschatological Jerusalem, on whose gates the names of the twelve tribes appear (Ezek. 48:30–34). Ezekiel 48:35 says, "The name of the city from that time on will be: THE LORD IS THERE" (cf. Rev. 21:3; 22:3–4).

Like the gates, the twelve *foundations* of the wall have twelve names written on them—in this case the names of the twelve apostles of the Lamb. Foundations of ancient cities usually consisted of vertical extensions of the rows of huge stones that made up the wall, down to the bedrock. Jerusalem's first-century walls and foundation stones have recently been excavated; huge stones, some of which are about five feet wide, four feet high, and thirty feet long, weighing eighty to one hundred tons each and going down some fourteen to nineteen layers below the present ground level, have been found.

In verses 19–21, John turns to the precious stones that make up the foundations. In verse 14, however, he stresses the names of the twelve apostles. Theologically, it is significant that he brings together the twelve tribes and the twelve apostles of the Lamb and yet differentiates them. This is not unlike what Matthew and Luke tell us Jesus said (Matt. 19:28; Luke 22:30). The earlier symbolic use of "twelve" (see comments on 7:4), representing in Revelation completeness, implies that it is unnecessary for us to know precisely which twelve will be there. Judas fell and was replaced by Matthias (Acts 1:21–26), but Paul also was a prominent apostle. Furthermore, the number "twelve" is sometimes used to refer to the elect *group* when all twelve apostles are not in view (John 20:24 has ten; 1 Cor. 15:5 eleven; cf. Luke 9:12). The group of apostles represents the church, the elect community built on the foundation of the gospel of Jesus Christ, the slain Lamb. The dual election here depicted admittedly entails some difficulty for those who identify the twelve tribes in 7:4ff. with the church, as this writer and other commentators have done (see comments on 7:1ff.). Some commentators have therefore insisted that the "twelve tribes" refers to an eschatological purpose for the elect Jewish people.

2. Further descriptions of the city (21:15–21)

The measurements (vv. 15–17). The angel measures the city with a golden measuring rod. (Concerning the significance of measuring, see comments on 11:1.) The act of measuring signifies securing something for

blessing, to preserve it from spiritual harm or defilement. Ezekiel's elaborate description of the future temple and its measuring was to show the
glory and holiness of God in Israel's midst (Ezek. 43:12). The measuring
reveals the perfection, fulfillment, or completion of all God's purposes for
His elect bride. Thus the city is revealed as a perfect *cube* of twelve
thousand stadia (12 x 1000; about 1,400 miles). The wall is 144 cubits (12 x
12; about 200 ft.) thick. These dimensions should not be interpreted as
providing architectural information about the city. Rather, we should
think of them as theologically symbolic of the fulfillment of all God's
promises. The New Jerusalem symbolizes the paradox of the completeness of infinity in God. The cube reminds us of the dimensions of the
Most Holy Place in the tabernacle (10 x 10 x 10 cubits [15 x 15 x 15 ft.])
and in the temple (20 x 20 x 20 cubits [30 x 30 x 30 ft.]). John adds that the
measurement was both human and angelic (divine): "by man's measurement, which the angel was using" (v. 17). This statement is not unimportant; it shows that both the human and the divine will intersect in the
Holy City. Others take verse 17 to be John's way of making the reader
realize the "disparity" between the city and the size of the wall, thus
forcing us to seek a deeper meaning in the angel's measurements (Kiddle).

The materials (vv. 18–21). In verses 18–21, John describes in more
detail the priceless materials of which the city, with its foundations and
gates, is made (cf. Isa. 54:11–15). The symbolism is not meant to give the
impression of wealth and luxury but to point to the glory and holiness of
God. The *wall* of jasper points to the glory of God (4:2–3; see comments
on 21:11), while the material of the city is pure gold—as clear as glass
(v. 21). Such imagery portrays the purity of the bride and her splendor in
mirroring the glory of God (cf. Eph. 5:27).

The *foundation stones* are decorated with twelve precious stones. Here
the imagery may reflect three possible sources: (1) the high priest's
breastplate (Exod. 28:17–20); (2) the jewels on the dress of the king of
Tyre (Ezek. 28:13); or (3) the signs of the zodiac. The second one, though
referring to only nine stones, suggests the splendor of ancient royalty and
might be appropriate as a symbol for the glorious kingdom reign in the
Holy City. But there is something inappropriate about taking this pagan
king as symbolic of the future kingdom. Some prefer the first option—
that of the high priest's breastplate. But while the twelve stones are
perhaps the same, the order of their mention is different. This leaves the
third option. According to Philo and Josephus, Israel associated these
same stones with the signs of the zodiac, and their tribal standards each
bore a sign of the zodiac. If we begin with Judah, the tribe of Christ (7:5),
the sign is Aries, the Ram, which has jasper as its stone. So the first
zodiacal sign agrees with the twelfth foundation stone and the last zodiacal
sign with the first foundation. In fact, the whole list agrees with John's,

but in reverse order. This may be a significant device to show John's disapproval of pagan cults. But these matters are uncertain.[1]

The *gates* are twelve great pearls. Though pearls are not mentioned in the Old Testament, some rabbinic texts refer to gates for Jerusalem hewn out of jewels about forty-five feet square. As for the one main street of the Holy City, it is, like the city itself, of pure gold, clear as glass (see comments on 21:18).

C. Life in the City (21:22–22:5)

John turns from this beautiful description of the city to the life within it (v. 22). In antiquity, every notable city had at least one central temple. The New Jerusalem differs in this respect not only from the ancient cities but also from all Jewish speculation about the age to come. Illuminated by the overflowing radiance of the presence of the glory of God, the Holy City no longer needs a temple. Yet paradoxically it has a temple, for the Lord God Almighty and the Lamb are its temple (v. 22). And in a sense, the whole city is a temple, since it is patterned after the Most Holy Place (v. 16). Jewish expectation was centered on a rebuilt temple and the restoration of the ark of the covenant. In his glorious vision, John sees the fulfillment of these hopes in the total presence of God with His purified people, while the Lamb, the sign of the new covenant, is the fulfillment of the restoration of the ark of the covenant (see comments on 11:19; cf. John 4:21, 23). As long as there is uncleanness in the world, there is need for a temple were God's presence and truth are in contrast to the uncleanness. But in the new city no such symbol is needed any longer.

In fulfillment of Isaiah 60:19–20, there will be no further need, as in ancient temples, for any natural or artificial lighting, because the glory of God will dim the most powerful earthly light into paleness (v. 23; cf. Zech. 14:7). In the earthly tabernacle and temple, there was, to be sure, artificial lighting (the seven-branched lampstand); but the Most Holy Place had no such lighting because of the shekinah, the light of God's own presence.

Verses 24–26 present a remarkable picture of "the nations" and "the

---

[1]The most recent study on this whole question casts serious doubt on the connection between the jewels and the tribes of Israel (in any order) or zodiac signs. Instead, the author argues that the gems and their order are unique to John and symbolize the presence of God, the divine origin of the city, and the new people of God (the twelve tribes are associated not with the foundation stones but explicitly with the gates of pearl in Rev. 21:12!). They form a contrast to the jewels of the whore of Babylon (17:4; 18:12). "The end-time city is diametrically opposed to the lascivious ruling city of this present world." See William W. Reader, "The Twelve Jewels of Revelation," *Journal of Biblical Literature*, 100/3 (1981), pp. 433–57.

kings of the earth" entering the city and bringing their splendor ("glory," "honor," "magnificence") into it. John sees a vision of social life, bustling with activity. Elsewhere in Revelation, the "nations" are the pagan, rebellious peoples of the world who trample the Holy City (cf. comments on 11:2; 11:18), who have become drunk with the wine of Babylon, the mother of prostitutes (18:3, 23), and who will be destroyed by the second coming of Christ (19:15). The same applies to the "kings of the earth." But there is another use of these terms in Revelation. They stand for the peoples of the earth who are the servants of Christ, the redeemed nations who follow the Lamb and have resisted the beast and Babylon (1:5; 15:3; 19:16; 2:26; 5:9; 7:9; 12:5). It is this latter group that John describes figuratively as having part in the activity in the Holy City, the kingdom of God. What this may involve regarding the relation of this life to the future kingdom is not stated.

Life in the age to come will certainly involve continuing activities and relationships that will contribute to the glory of the Holy City throughout eternity. Instead of the nations bringing their precious possessions to Babylon, the harlot city, the redeemed nations will bring these offerings to the throne of God (cf. Isa. 60:3ff.).

So certain is its perpetual light and security that the gates will never be shut for fear of evil by night (v. 25; cf. Isa. 60:11). This imagery should not, however, be allegorized as indicating some sort of perpetual invitation to salvation.

One thing is absolutely certain: nothing impure ("common," "profane") will ever enter the city's gates (v. 27). By this John means ceremonial impurity (cf. 21:8; 22:15). No idolatrous person may enter. Only those can enter whose names are in "the Lamb's book of life" and who thus belong to Him through redemption (cf. 3:5; 20:12, 15). This should not be taken as implying that there will still be unsaved roaming around outside the New Jerusalem who may now and then enter it by repenting. Instead, the exhortation warns present readers that the only way to participate in the future city is to turn one's total loyalties to the Lamb now (cf. 21:7).

D. The River of Life and the Tree of Life (22:1–5)

This section continues the description of the Holy City begun in 21:9, but now with the emphasis on its inner life. John returns to his archetypal images from Genesis 1–3 and Ezekiel 40ff. The paradisiacal quality of the future age is briefly but beautifully described. Here Paradise is regained.

As in the Old Testament imagery of the age to come, metaphors of water and light abound (cf. Isa. 12:3; Zech. 14:7–8).

1. *The waters of salvation* (22:1)

The river of the water of life recalls Ezekiel 47:1ff. (cf. Joel 3:18) and the pastoral scene of Revelation 7:17 (q.v.). In both Testaments, water is frequently associated with the salvation of God and the life-imparting and cleansing ministry of the Holy Spirit (Isa. 44:3; cf. John 3:5; 4:13–14; 7:37–39; 13:10; 19:34; Titus 3:5). In the new city of God the pure water does not issue from the temple as in Ezekiel but comes from the throne of God, since this whole city is a Most Holy Place with God at its center. Life from God streams unceasingly through the new world.

2. *The tree of life* (22:2)

The tree of life spreads all along the great street of the city. What was once forfeited by our forebears in Eden and denied to their posterity is now fully restored (cf. Gen. 3:22–24). In Ezekiel's vision there are multiple trees on each side of the river that bear fruit monthly, whose leaves are for healing (Ezek. 47:12); therefore, the tree John speaks of may be a collective word for Ezekiel's trees. So abundant is its vitality that it bears a crop of fruit each month! Its leaves produce healing for the nations. The imagery of abundant fruit and medicinal leaves should be understood as symbolic of the far-reaching effects of the death of Christ in the redeemed community, the Holy City. So powerful is the salvation of God that the effects of sin are completely overcome. The eternal life God gives the redeemed community will be perpetually available, will sustain, and will cure eternally every former sin.

3. *Eden's curse removed* (22:3)

Thus the curse pronounced in Eden will be removed (cf. Gen. 3:17). This may mean that no one who is cursed because of idolatry will be in the city (v. 15). Instead of Babylon and its servants occupying the earth, the throne of God will be central and His servants will serve Him (cf. 2:13). Wherever the throne is in sight, the priestly service of the saints will be perpetual (cf. 1:6). Here our true liturgy is fulfilled (cf. Rom. 12:1). Observe John's emphasis on God and the Lamb (21:22–23; 22:1, 3). They share the same glory and the same throne, and they are the temple. The christology of John's vision is everywhere evident even though stated in functional terms.

4. *The beatific vision realized* (vv. 4-5)

With no restrictions such as those that pertain to Moses (Exod. 33:20, 23) or the high priests (Heb. 9:7), the redeemed community will be in Christ's presence, beholding perpetually His glory (cf. Ps. 17:15; Matt. 5:8; 1 Cor. 13:12; 2 Cor. 3:18; 1 John 3:2). Eternal life is perfect communion, worship, the vision of God, light, and victory. Since God and the Lamb are always viewed together, there is no point in saying that the redeemed will see Jesus but not the Father. (Concerning the name on their foreheads, see comments on 14:1.)

A final burst of light engulfs the whole scene, and an announcement that the saints will reign for ever and ever fulfills the first promise of the book (1:6; cf. 5:10; 20:4-6; and esp. 11:15). The logical sequence as well as the inner relationship of the words "his servants will serve" (v. 3) and "they will reign" (v. 5) have deep implications for the whole nature of God's kingdom in contrast to that of the satanic Babylon. Surely it is fitting for such a book of prophecy as Revelation to close around the throne, with God's servants both worshiping and ruling.

For Further Study

1. What is the significance of the kingdom of God being described as a bride-city?

2. Make a list of the chief details mentioned in the Holy City (e.g., wall, foundations, etc.) and indicate the probable sense of these symbols.

3. What is the significance of the fact that the New Jerusalem is shaped like a cube? Are the 12,000 stadia and 144 cubits related to the 24 elders and the 144,000 sealed (12,000 from each tribe)?

4. How do you understand that the nations and kings of earth will be involved in the New Jerusalem?

5. Construct as many parallels between Genesis 1-3 and Revelation 21-22 as you can, e.g., creation—recreation; curse—removeal of curse; death enters—death exits; etc.

6. What does the river of life symbolize? The leaves of the tree of life that are for the healing of the nations?

7. Explain how seeing the face of Christ and God is the ultimate goal of salvation. How should this hope shape our present Christian lives?

John's Conclusion

Chapter 13

John's Conclusion
(Revelation 22:6-21)

The pageant is over, and the final curtain has been drawn (Summers). With consummate artistry, the notes of the introit (1:1-8) are sounded again in the conclusion: the book ends with the voices of the angel, Jesus, the Spirit, the bride, and, finally, John (v. 20). The book is a seamless garment. While this section almost defies outlining, we can identify three major emphases in the conclusion: (1) confirmation of the genuineness of the prophecy (vv. 6-7, 16, 18-19); (2) the imminence of Jesus' coming (vv. 7, 12, 20); (3) the warning against idolatry and the invitation to enter the city (vv. 11-12, 15, 17-19). ·

A. The First Words of Confirmation (22:6)

A word of assurance similar to those in 19:9 and 21:5 provides the transition from the glorious vision of the Holy City to the final words of the book. An angel declares that it is "the Lord, the God of the spirits of the prophets," the One from whom the prophets like John receive their message, who assures the readers of the speedy fulfillment of all that has been revealed (cf. 1:1; 10:6-7). John has been the recipient of divine prophecy that will have its immediate consequences (cf. v. 10).

B. The First Announcement of the Imminent Return of Jesus (22:7)

This first declaration of the imminent coming of Jesus is Jesus' own response to the yearnings of the church (cf. comments on 1:7; 2:25; and esp. 3:11). It is the sixth beatitude in Revelation; and, like the first one (1:3), it is directed toward those who keep (obey) the words of the prophecy (cf. vv. 18-19).

C. The Warning Against Idolatry (22:8-9)

The "I, John" is reminiscent of 1:4, 9. His confession that he "heard and saw these things" and the repetition of the prohibition against John's worshiping the angel (cf. 19:10) serve a purpose. No believer, not even one of great spiritual stature like John, is beyond the subtle temptation to worship what is good in itself in place of God who alone is to be worshiped.

D. The Necessity for Immediate Choices (22:10–11)

These verses stand in contrast to the command given to Daniel to seal up his book (8:26; 12:4, 9–10) and in contrast to Jewish apocalypses in general. John's message cannot be concealed because the contents of the vision are needed immediately by the churches. (On the sealing metaphor, see comments on 7:3.) Verse 11 appears at first glance to be fatalistic, but on further reflection stresses the imminency of the return of Jesus and the necessity for immediate choices. It echoes the aphorism "As now, so always." Far from being an encouragement to remain apathetic, it is evangelistic in spirit. It may also allude to the great ordeal John viewed as imminent. To the unfaithful and wicked, this appeal would be a deep confirmation of their choice, while it would alert the faithful to the necessity of guarding themselves against apostasy (cf. Jude 20–21). There is no reason to take this passage as teaching the irreversibility of human choices. Repentance is always a live option as long as a person is living. After death, however, there remains only judgment, not repentance (Heb. 9:27).

E. The Second Announcement of the Imminent Return of Jesus (22:12–13)

This second of three announcements of the imminent return of Jesus in this chapter (cf. vv. 7, 20) is associated with the truth of rewards and judgments based on deeds (cf. comments on 20:12; also 11:18). (On the terms "Alpha and Omega," etc., see comments on 1:8, 17.)

F. An Invitation to Enter the City of God (22:14–15)

The seventh and last beatitude in Revelation is evangelistic in emphasis (cf. 21:6; 22:11, 17). Strands of the earlier imagery are blended in it. In 7:14, the washing of the robes indicates willing identification with Jesus in his death and also carries the thought of martyrdom during the great ordeal for the saints (cf. 6:11). Thus it symbolizes a salvation that involves obedience and discipleship, since it is integrally related to the tree of life (cf. comments on 22:2) and the gates of the city (cf. 21:25).

John has already made it clear that no idolaters can ever enter the city but only those whose names are in the Lamb's book of life (cf. comments on 21:8, 27). Such are "the dogs" (those who practice magic arts, etc.)—i.e., those who rebel against the rule of God (cf. Deut. 23:18, where a "dog" signifies a male prostitute; Matt. 15:26, where "dogs" refers to Gentiles; Phil. 3:2–3, where it refers to the Judaizers). There is no doubt that such people will not be admitted through the gates of the Holy City. They will be in the lake of fire (20:15). But the problem involves what appears to be their present exclusion from the city at the time of John's writing. Are they "outside" now? As has been previously argued in this commentary, the city is future and is not to be identified with the present historical church (see introduction to ch. 21 and comments on 21:2). Only in an eschatological sense can it be maintained that the new city exists in the present.

On the other hand, it is not necessary to place the time of verse 15 in the present. There is no verb in the Greek text of the verse; the time of the action is therefore determined by the context. Since the fulfillment of verse 14 lies in the future, the time of verse 15 is also most naturally future. The word "outside" is simply a figure that agrees with the whole imagery of the Holy City: it means exclusion. To be outside the city means to be in the lake of fire. Thus it is not necessary either to place the Holy City in the present or to place it in a millennial Jerusalem. The Holy City, as we have previously argued, is a symbol for the future realization of the corporate community of God's people (i.e., the eschatological kingdom of God), and as such it does not have a geographical location other than that it is on the new earth.

G. The Second Words of Confirmation (22:16)

As in 1:8, 17–20, in this verse Christ addresses John and the churches directly. The "you" is plural in the Greek text. Here Christ's words authenticate the whole Book of Revelation ("this testimony") as being a message to the churches. Therefore, any method of interpreting Revelation that blunts the application of this message in its entirety to the present church must disregard these words of Christ. He is the Messiah of Israel, "the Root and the Offspring of David" (cf. Isa. 11:1; see comments on Rev. 5:5) and the fulfillment of the promise to the overcomers at Thyatira (see comments on 2:28).

H. The Final Invitation to Salvation (22:17)

The first two sentences in this verse are not an evangelistic appeal but express the yearning of the Holy Spirit and the "bride" (the whole church, cf. 21:9) for the return of Christ. In verse 20 John gives us the Lord Jesus' answer: "Yes, I am coming soon." Those who hear—the members of the local congregations in John's time—join in the invitation for Christ to return. Then, any in the congregations who are not yet followers of Jesus are invited to come and take the water of life as a free gift ("freely," cf. Rom. 3:24; Rev. 21:6). (On the water of life, cf. 21:6; 22:1; also, for liturgical and eucharistic use of this verse, see comments on v. 20.)

I. The Final Warning Against False Prophets (22:18–19)

These verses should not be taken as a warning against adding anything to the Bible. Early interpreters understood them as a warning to false prophets not to alter the sense of John's prophecy, i.e., Revelation. The force of these words has been likened to the curses pronounced on disobedience in the covenant law codes of the Old Testament (cf. Deut. 4:2; 12:32). Verses 18–19 are a strong warning against any who would tamper with the contents of "this book" (Revelation), either textually or in its moral and theological teaching (cf. 1 Cor. 16:22). So severe is the danger he warns against that John says that those who teach contrary to the message of Revelation will not only forfeit any right to salvation in the Holy City but will have visited on them the divine judgments (plagues) inflicted on the beast worshipers.

J. The Final Announcement of the Imminent Return of Jesus (22:20)

This is the third affirmation (in ch. 22) of Jesus' imminent return and perhaps the response to the longing cry in verse 17. John responds to the Lord Jesus' declaration by saying, "Amen. Come, Lord Jesus." These fervent words are part of the liturgy of the early church; they were a prayer used at the close of the meal in the eucharistic liturgy. These words may be the earliest expression of the recognition that the Lord's Day (Sunday) is the day of the Resurrection. As Jesus appeared to His disciples alive on the first day of the week, so He was expected to be present in the Spirit at every first-day Eucharist celebration and to appear again at the end, which is often represented by the picture of a messianic meal (Oscar Cullmann). The expression "Come, Lord Jesus" is equivalent to the Aramaic *marana tha* (cf. 1 Cor. 16:22, "Come, O Lord," NIV). So in closing Revelation, John alludes to chapter 1, with its reference to the Lord's Day (1:10).

K. The Benediction and Congregational Amen (22:21)

A conclusion such as this, which would not be suited to a Jewish apocalypse, is wholly appropriate for this prophetic message addressed to the ancient church and, indeed, to the whole body of Christ. The benediction is reminiscent of Paul's usual practice (cf. the final verses of Romans, 1 Thessalonians, Colosians, et al.). Whether we should accept the textual reading "with all" or "with all the saints" cannot be completely settled. We may, however, agree that nothing less than God's grace is required for us to be overcomers and triumphantly enter the Holy City of God, where we shall reign with Him for ever and ever. AMEN!

For Further Study

1. Find all the evangelistic appeals to become believers in chapters 21–22. What images are used? What does this indicate about John's concern? Ours?

2. Is there a sense in which we who believe have already entered the city? (22:14–15).

3. Can you see the relationship between the invitation to Jesus to come back in verse 17, His own response, and the congregational response in verse 20? Can we hasten His coming by our yearning for it?

BIBLIOGRAPHY

Commentaries on Revelation

Space allows the mention of only representative books. Some defy exact categories and it may be unfair to classify them. We have used the interpretation of the beast (ch. 13) and Babylon (ch. 17) as the chief indicators of the nature of the books listed.

A. *Futurist*

1. *Dispensational*

Smith, J.B. *A Revelation of Jesus Christ.* Scottdale, Pa.: Herald, 1961.
Tenney, Merrill C. *Interpreting Revelation.* Grand Rapids: Eerdmans, 1957.
Walvoord, John F. *The Revelation of Jesus Christ.* Chicago: Moody, 1966.

2. *Purely Eschatological*

Eller, Vernard. *The Most Revealing Book of the Bible: Making Sense Out of Revelation.* Grand Rapids: Eerdmans, 1974.
Lilje, Hanns. *The Last Book of the Bible: The Meaning of the Revelation of St. John.* Philadelphia: Muhlenberg, 1955.

3. *Preterist-Futurist*

Beasley-Murray, G.R. "The Revelation." In *The New Bible Commentary*, rev. ed. Edited by D. Guthrie, et al. Grand Rapids: Eerdmans, 1970.

_____ . *The New Century Bible Commentary: Revelation*, rev.
ed. Grand Rapids: Eerdmans, 1981.

Beckwith, Isbon T. *The Apocalypse of John*. New York: Macmillan, 1922.

Bruce, F.F. "The Revelation to John." In *A New Testament Commentary*.
Edited by G.C.D. Howley, F.F. Bruce, and H.L. Ellison. Grand
Rapids: Zondervan, 1969.

Ladd, George E. *A Commentary on the Revelation of John*. Grand
Rapids: Eerdmans, 1972.

Morris, Leon. *The Revelation of St. John*. Grand Rapids: Eerdmans,
1969.

Mounce, Robert H. *The Book of Revelation. New International Commentary*. Grand Rapids: Eerdmans, 1977.

B. *Historicist*

Alford, Henry. "The Revelation." In *The Greek Testament*. London:
Rivington's, 1884.

Elliot, E.B. *Horae Apocalypticae*. 4 vols. Eng. tr. 3d ed. London: Seeley,
Burnside, and Seeley, 1828.

C. *Preterist*

Barclay, William. *The Revelation of John*. 2 vols. The Daily Study Bible
Series. Philadelphia: Westminster, 1959.

Boer, Harry R. *The Book of Revelation*. Grand Rapids: Eerdmans, 1979.

Caird, G.B. *The Revelation of St. John the Divine. Harper's New Testament Commentaries*. New York: Harper, 1966.

Charles, R.H. *A Critical and Exegetical Commentary on the Revelation
of St. John*. 2 vols. *International Critical Commentary*. Edinburgh:
T. & T. Clark, 1920.

Ellul, Jacques. *Apocalypse*. New York: Seabury, 1977.

Ford, J. Massyngberde. *Revelation. The Anchor Bible*. New York:
Doubleday, 1975.

Glasson, T.F. *The Revelation of John. The Cambridge Bible Commentary
on the New English Bible*. New York: Cambridge at the University
Press, 1965.

Hailey, Homer. *Revelation*. Grand Rapids: Baker, 1979.

Harrington, Wilfred J. *The Apocalypse of St. John: A Commentary*. London: Geoffrey Chapman, 1969.

Heidt, William G. *The Book of the Apocalypse. New Testament Reading
Guide*. Collegeville, Minn.: Liturgical, 1962.

Pieters, Albertus. *Studies in the Revelation of St. John*. Grand Rapids:
Eerdmans, 1954.

Summers, Ray. *Worthy is the Lamb*. Nashville: Broadman, 1951.

Sweet, J.P.M. *Revelation*. Philadelphia: Westminster, 1979.

Swete, Henry Barclay. *The Apocalypse of St. John*. New York: Macmillan, 1906.

D. *Idealist*

Calkins, Raymond. *The Social Message of the Book of Revelation*. New York: Woman's, 1920.

Carrington, Philip. *The Meaning of the Revelation*. New York: Macmillan, 1931.

Hendriksen, W. *More Than Conquerors*. Grand Rapids: Baker, 1940.

Kiddle, Martin. *The Revelation of St. John. Moffat New Testament Commentary*. New York: Harper, 1940.

Milligan, William. *The Book of Revelation. The Expositor's Bible*. Hodder& Stoughton, 1909.

Minear, Paul S. *I Saw a New Earth: An Introduction to the Visions of the Apocalypse*. Cleveland: Corpus Books, 1968.

Rissi, Mathias. *Time and History*. Richmond: John Knox, 1966.